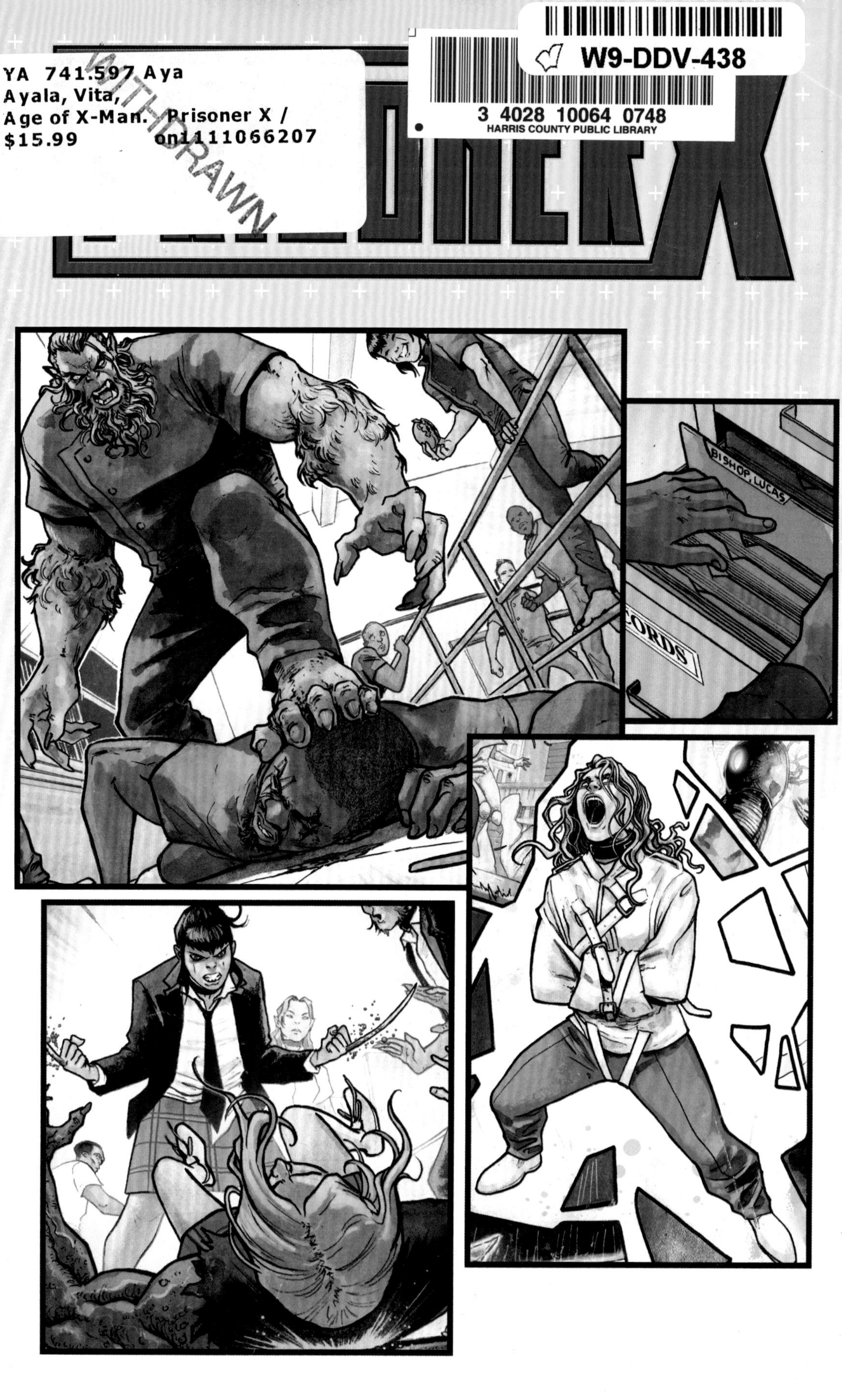
BISHOP, LUCAS
CORDS

Welcome to a perfect world.
Everyone is a mutant — special, powerful, individual.
No more strife, oppression or dependence.
The Age of X-Man: a dream made real.
A dream that must be protected...at any cost.

The Danger Room Prison Complex houses mutants
who have disturbed the status quo multiple times
and continue to make the same mistakes; they are
sentenced to re-evaluation, where they will relearn to be
a harmonious part of society.

WRITER **VITA AYALA**

ARTISTS **GERMÁN PERALTA** (#1-4)
WITH **MATT HORAK** (#5)

COLOR ARTIST **MIKE SPICER**

LETTERER **VC's JOE SABINO**

COVER ART **PATCH ZIRCHER** &
BRIAN REBER

ASSISTANT EDITORS **DANNY KHAZEM**
& **LAUREN AMARO**

EDITOR **DARREN SHAN**

X-MEN SENIOR EDITOR **JORDAN D. WHITE**

COLLECTION EDITOR **JENNIFER GRÜNWALD**   **CAITLIN O'CONNELL** ASSISTANT EDITOR
ASSOCIATE MANAGING EDITOR **KATERI WOODY**   **MARK D. BEAZLEY** EDITOR, SPECIAL PROJECTS
VP PRODUCTION & SPECIAL PROJECTS **JEFF YOUNGQUIST**   **SALENA MAHINA** WITH **JAY BOWEN** BOOK DESIGNERS

SVP PRINT, SALES & MARKETING **DAVID GABRIEL**   **SVEN LARSEN** DIRECTOR, LICENSED PUBLISHING
EDITOR IN CHIEF **C.B. CEBULSKI**   **JOE QUESADA** CHIEF CREATIVE OFFICER
PRESIDENT **DAN BUCKLEY**   **ALAN FINE** EXECUTIVE PRODUCER

AGE OF X-MAN: PRISONER X. Contains material originally published in magazine form as AGE OF X-MAN: PRISONER X #1-5. First printing 2019. ISBN 978-1-302-91579-7. Published by MARVEL WORLDWIDE, INC., a subsidiary of MARVEL ENTERTAINMENT, LLC. OFFICE OF PUBLICATION: 135 West 50th Street, New York, NY 10020. © 2019 MARVEL No similarity between any of the names, characters, persons, and/or institutions in this magazine with those of any living or dead person or institution is intended, and any such similarity which may exist is purely coincidental. **Printed in Canada.** DAN BUCKLEY, President, Marvel Entertainment; JOHN NEE, Publisher; JOE QUESADA, Chief Creative Officer; TOM BREVOORT, SVP of Publishing; DAVID BOGART, Associate Publisher & SVP of Talent Affairs; DAVID GABRIEL, SVP of Sales & Marketing, Publishing; JEFF YOUNGQUIST, VP of Production & Special Projects; DAN CARR, Executive Director of Publishing Technology; ALEX MORALES, Director of Publishing Operations; DAN EDINGTON, Managing Editor; SUSAN CRESPI, Production Manager; STAN LEE, Chairman Emeritus. For information regarding advertising in Marvel Comics or on Marvel.com, please contact Vit DeBellis, Custom Solutions & Integrated Advertising Manager, at vdebellis@marvel.com. For Marvel subscription inquiries, please call 888-511-5480. **Manufactured between 7/12/2019 and 8/13/2019 by SOLISCO PRINTERS, SCOTT, QC, CANADA.**
10 9 8 7 6 5 4 3 2 1

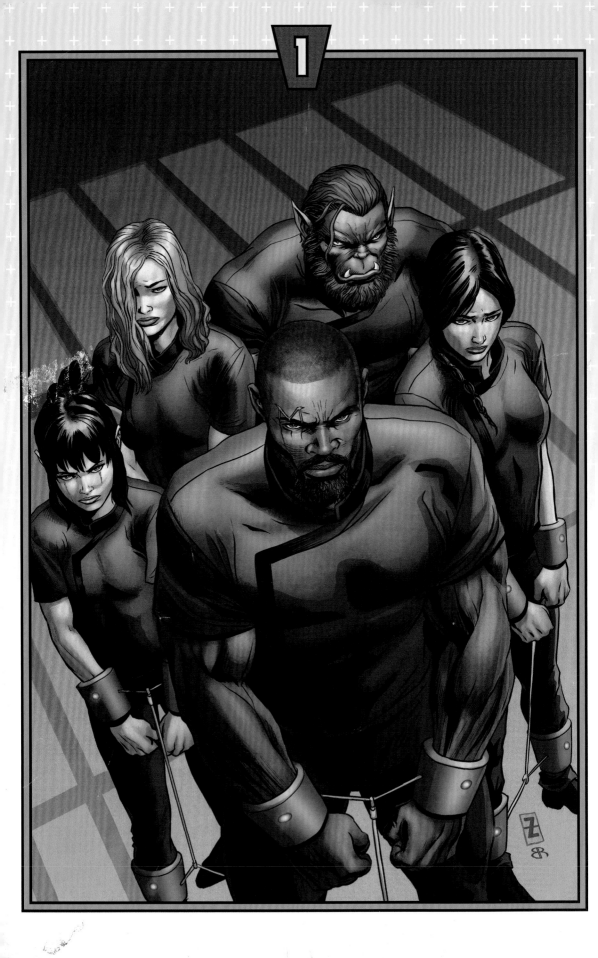

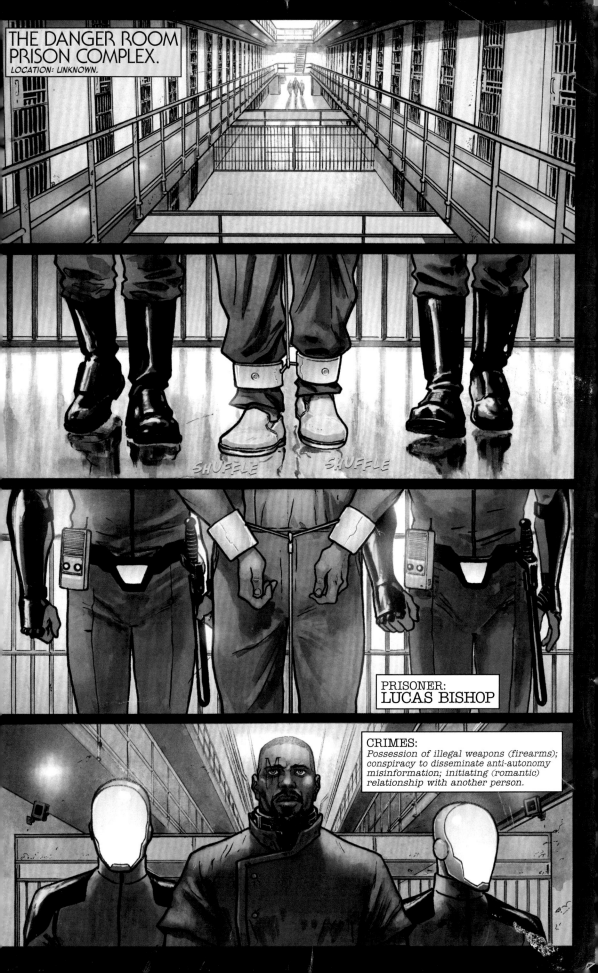

THE DANGER ROOM
PRISON COMPLEX.
LOCATION: UNKNOWN.

SHUFFLE   SHUFFLE

PRISONER:
LUCAS BISHOP

CRIMES:
Possession of illegal weapons (firearms);
conspiracy to disseminate anti-autonomy
misinformation; initiating (romantic)
relationship with another person.

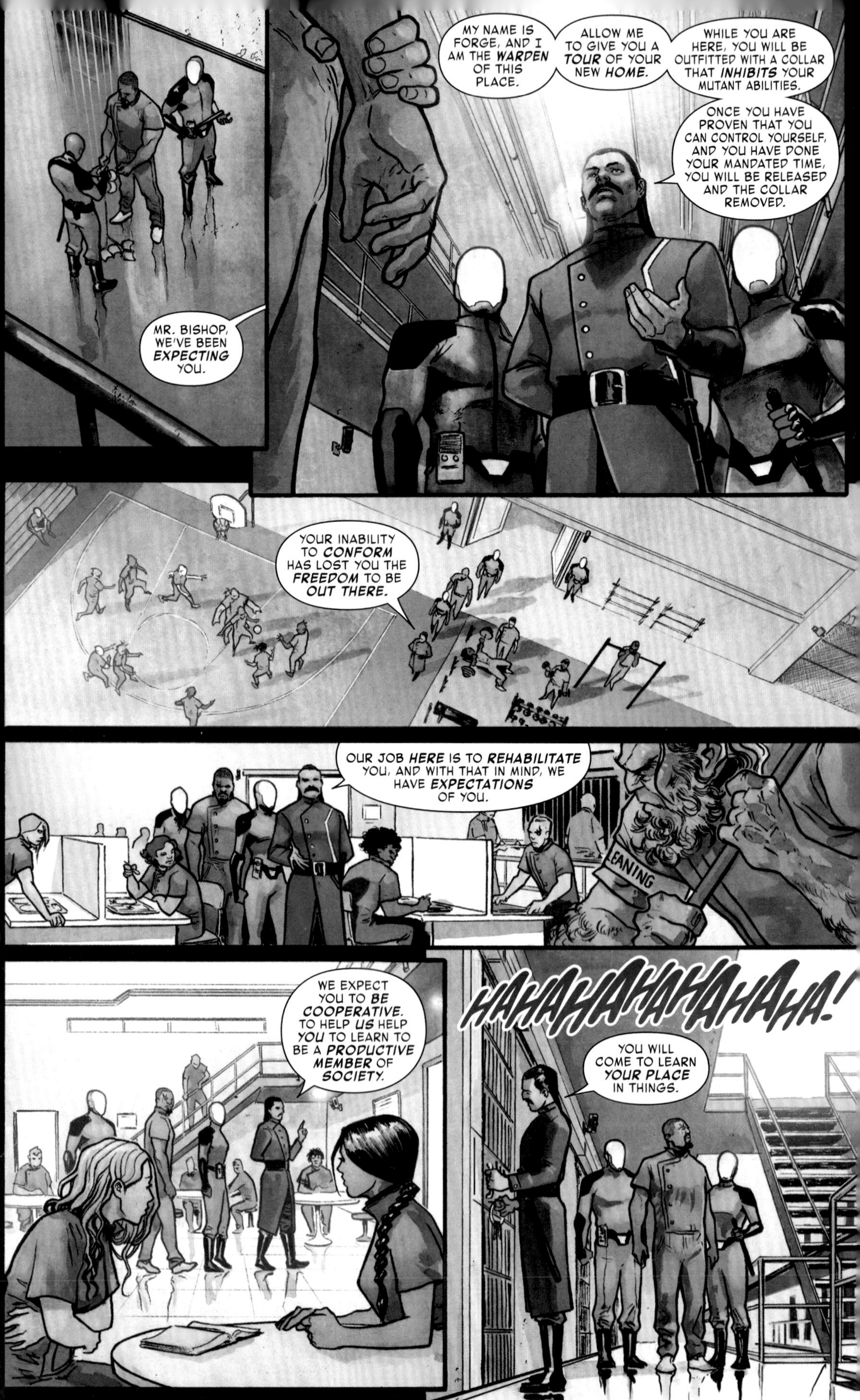
MR. BISHOP, WE'VE BEEN EXPECTING YOU.
MY NAME IS FORGE, AND I AM THE WARDEN OF THIS PLACE.
ALLOW ME TO GIVE YOU A TOUR OF YOUR NEW HOME.
WHILE YOU ARE HERE, YOU WILL BE OUTFITTED WITH A COLLAR THAT INHIBITS YOUR MUTANT ABILITIES.
ONCE YOU HAVE PROVEN THAT YOU CAN CONTROL YOURSELF, AND YOU HAVE DONE YOUR MANDATED TIME, YOU WILL BE RELEASED AND THE COLLAR REMOVED.
YOUR INABILITY TO CONFORM HAS LOST YOU THE FREEDOM TO BE OUT THERE.
OUR JOB HERE IS TO REHABILITATE YOU, AND WITH THAT IN MIND, WE HAVE EXPECTATIONS OF YOU.
EANING
WE EXPECT YOU TO BE COOPERATIVE. TO HELP US HELP YOU TO LEARN TO BE A PRODUCTIVE MEMBER OF SOCIETY.
HAHAHAHAHAHAHAHA!
YOU WILL COME TO LEARN YOUR PLACE IN THINGS.

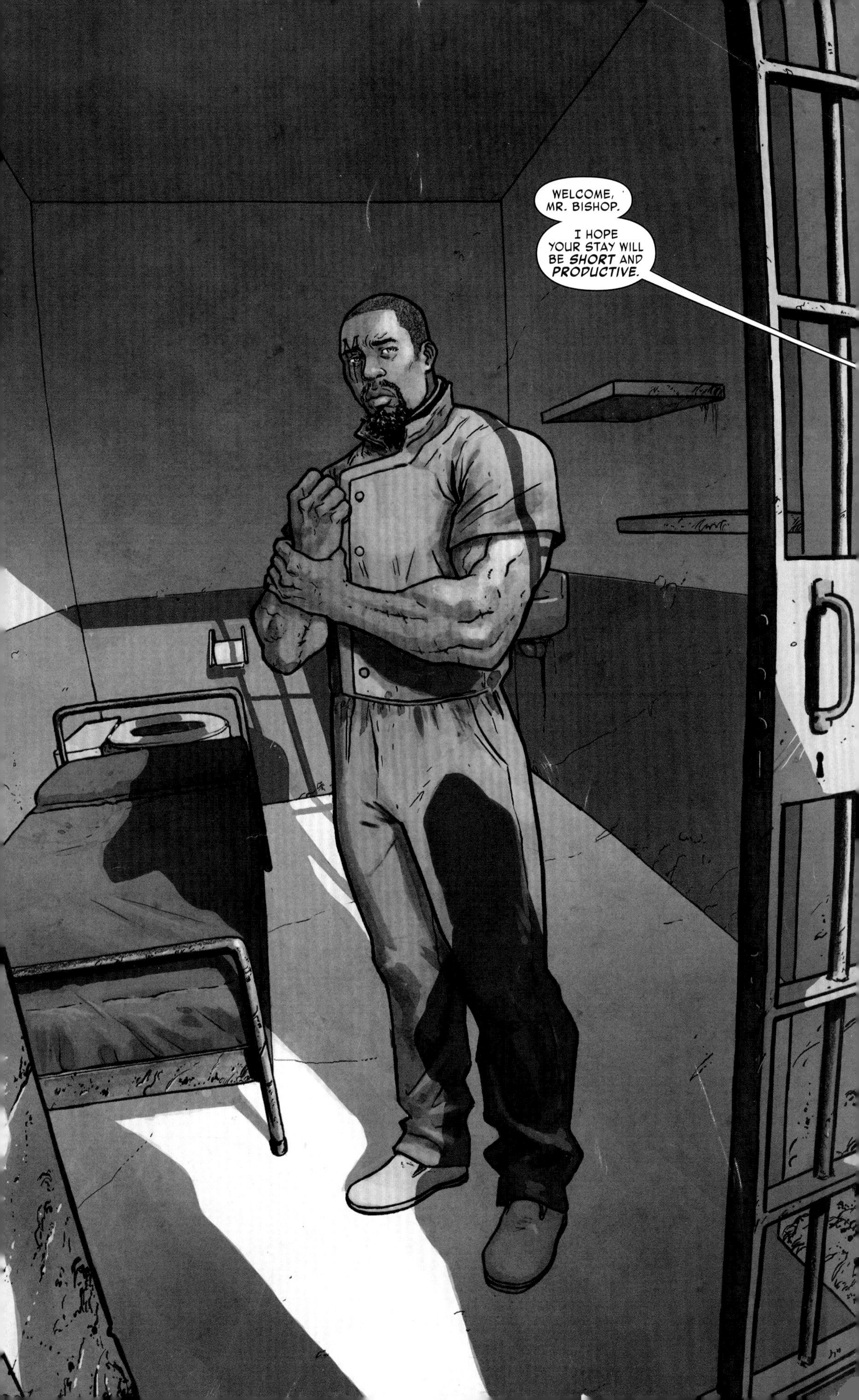
WELCOME, MR. BISHOP.
I HOPE YOUR STAY WILL BE SHORT AND PRODUCTIVE.

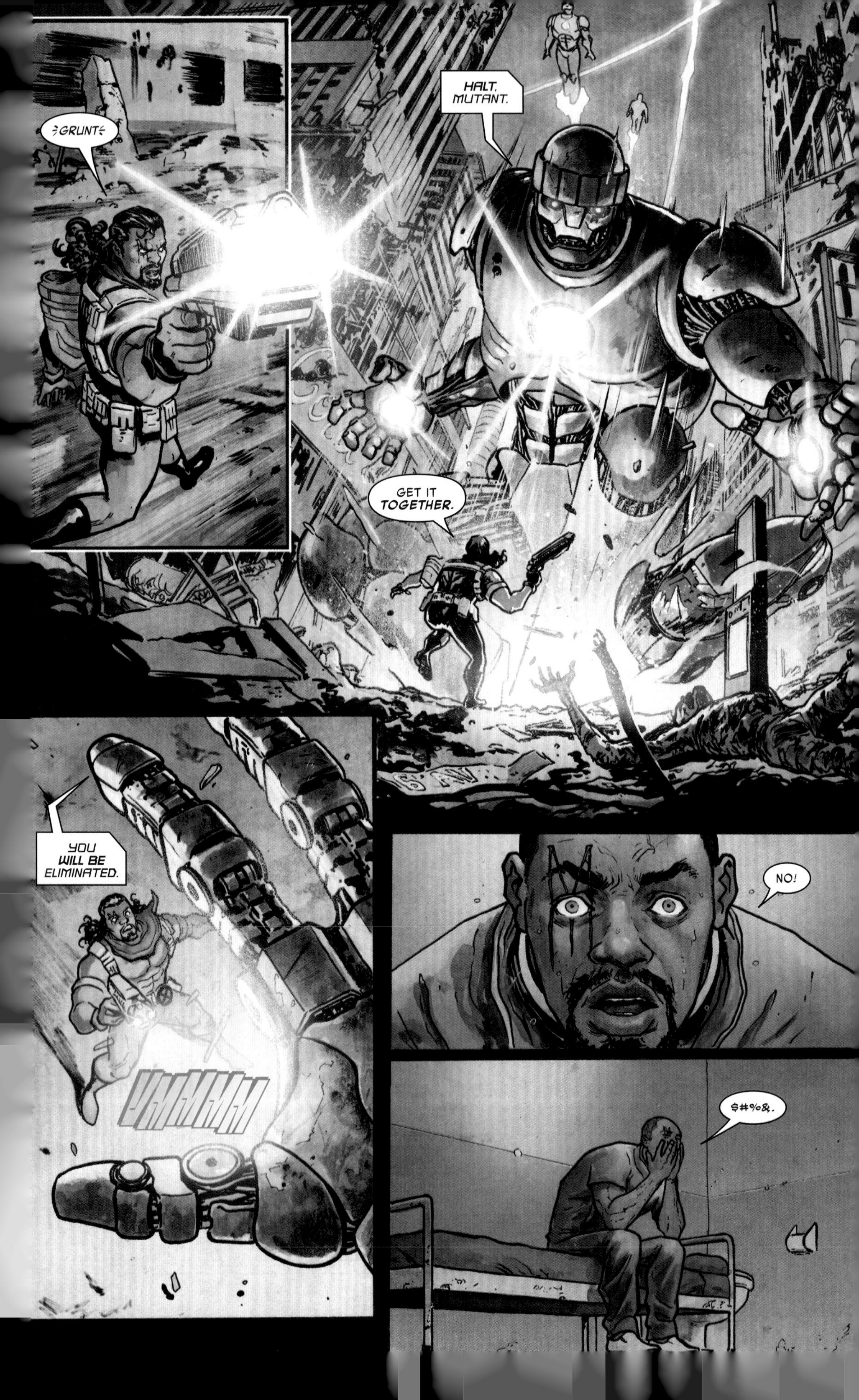

GRUNT
HALT, MUTANT.
GET IT TOGETHER.
YOU WILL BE ELIMINATED.
VMMMMM
NO!
$#%&.

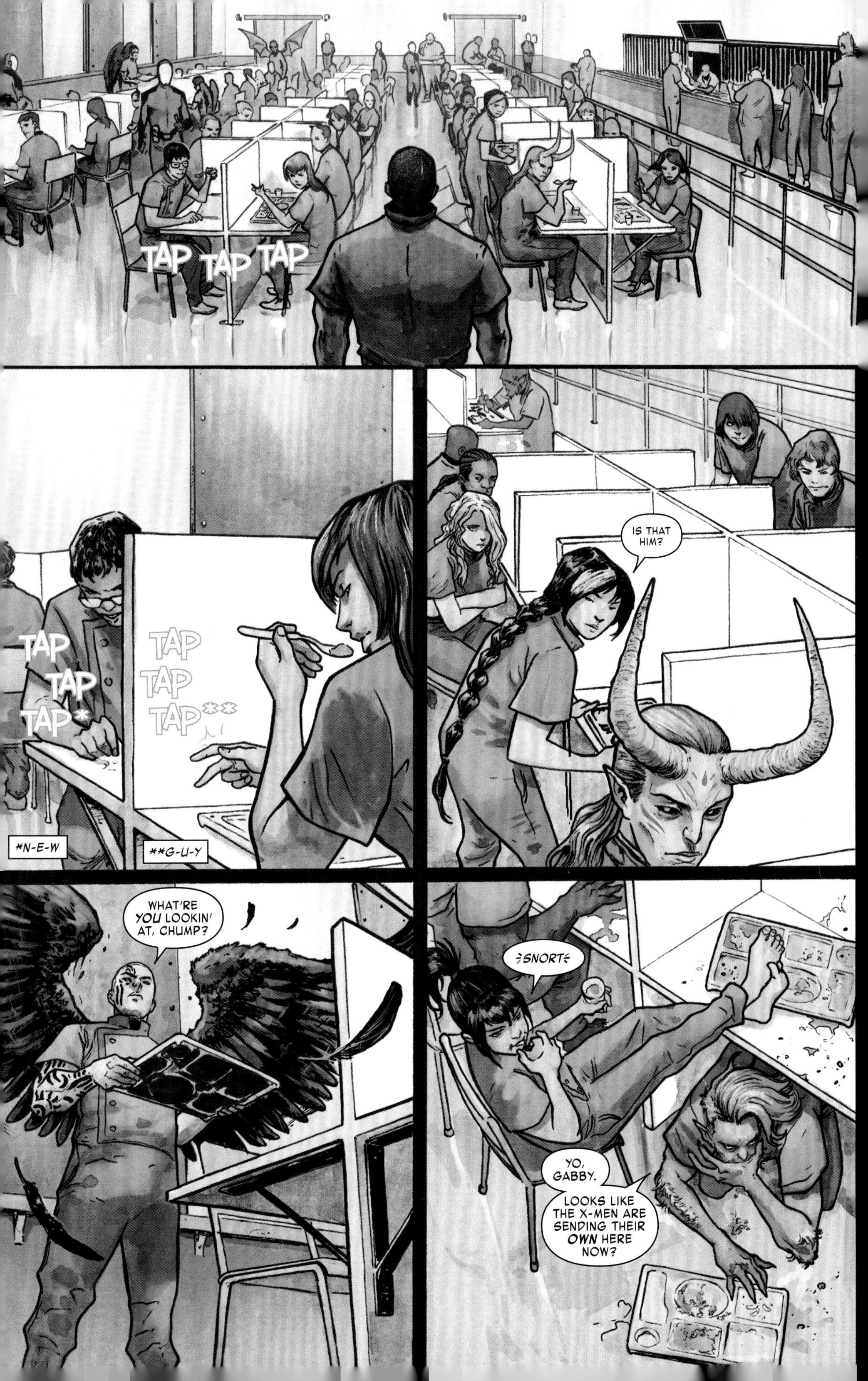
TAP TAP TAP
TAP
TAP
TAP*
TAP
TAP
TAP**
*N-E-W
**G-U-Y
IS THAT HIM?
WHAT'RE *YOU* LOOKIN' AT, CHUMP?
SNORT
YO, GABBY.
LOOKS LIKE THE X-MEN ARE SENDING THEIR *OWN* HERE NOW?

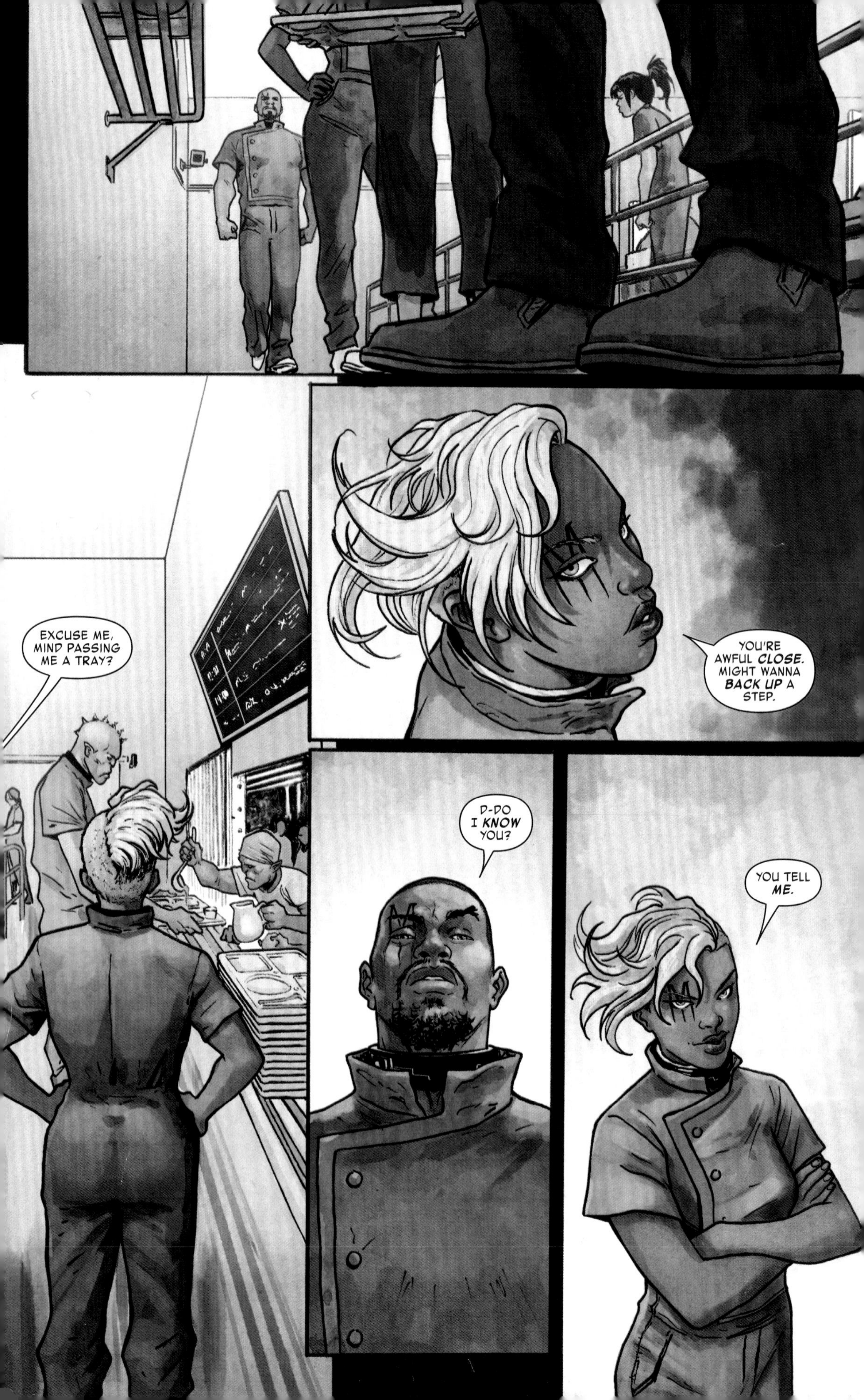
EXCUSE ME, MIND PASSING ME A TRAY?
YOU'RE AWFUL CLOSE. MIGHT WANNA BACK UP A STEP.
D-DO I KNOW YOU?
YOU TELL ME.

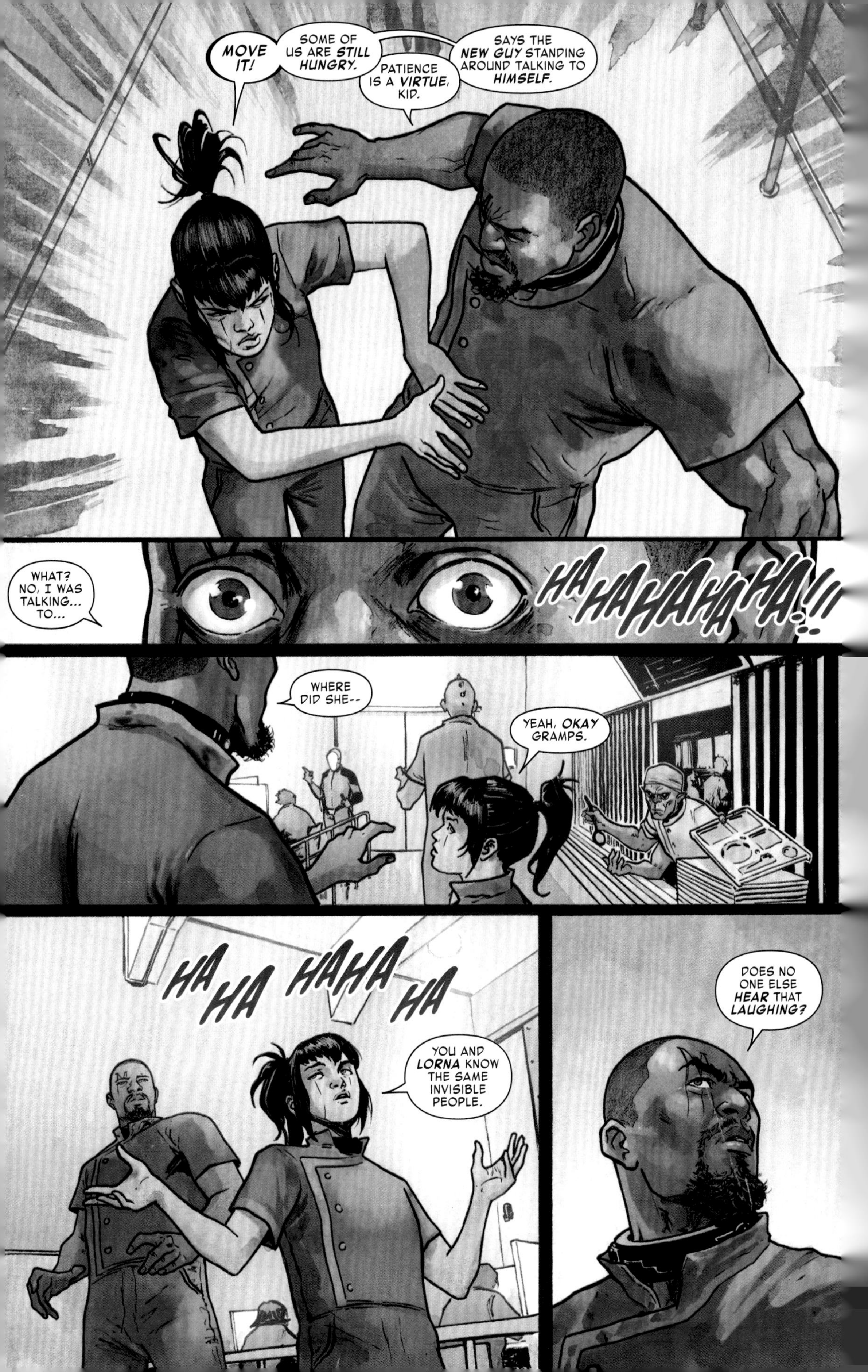
MOVE IT!
SOME OF US ARE STILL HUNGRY.
PATIENCE IS A VIRTUE, KID.
SAYS THE NEW GUY STANDING AROUND TALKING TO HIMSELF.
WHAT? NO, I WAS TALKING... TO...
HA HA HA HA HA HA!!!
WHERE DID SHE--
YEAH, OKAY GRAMPS.
HA HA HAHAHA HA
YOU AND LORNA KNOW THE SAME INVISIBLE PEOPLE.
DOES NO ONE ELSE HEAR THAT LAUGHING?

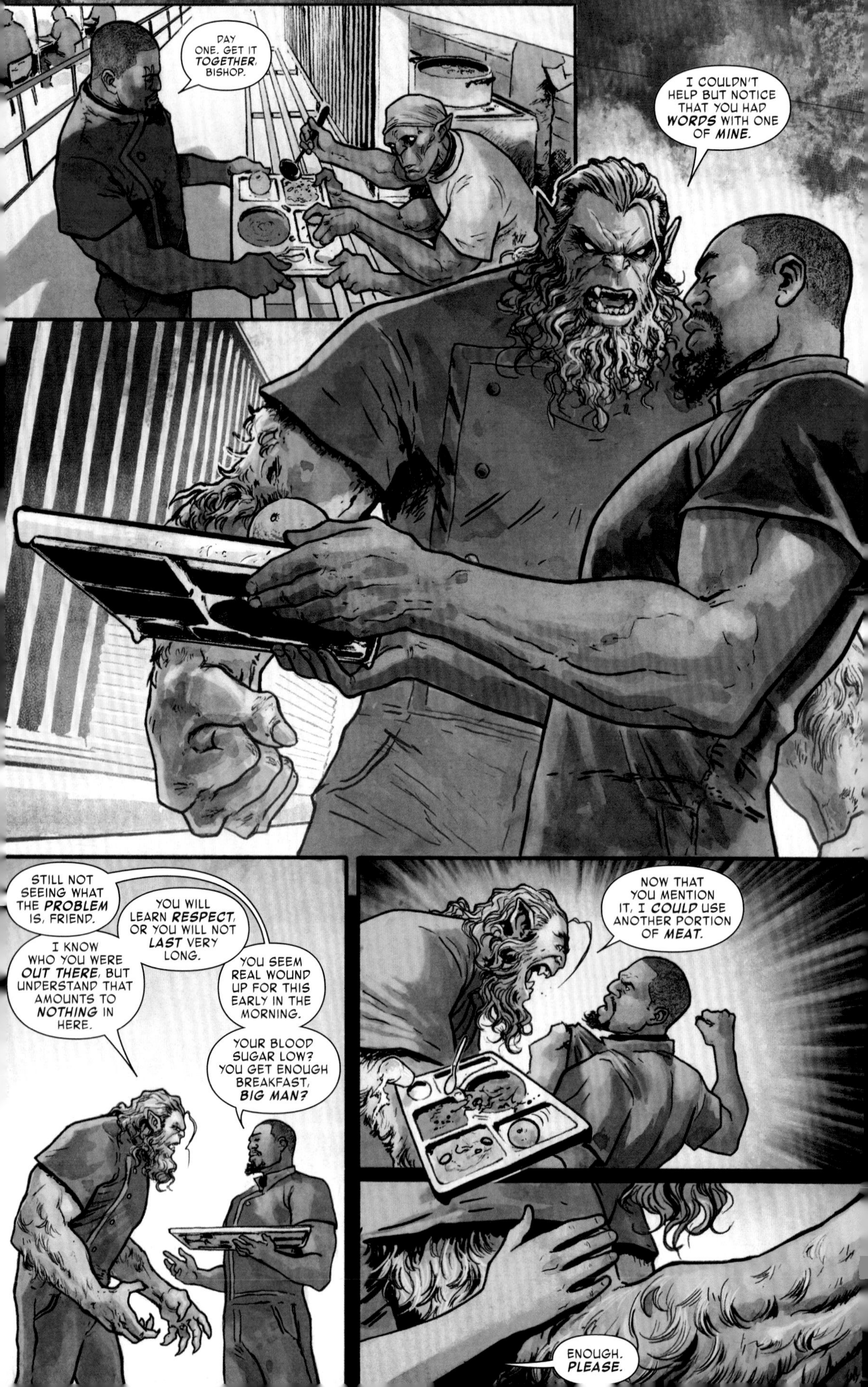
DAY ONE. GET IT TOGETHER, BISHOP.
I COULDN'T HELP BUT NOTICE THAT YOU HAD WORDS WITH ONE OF MINE.
STILL NOT SEEING WHAT THE PROBLEM IS, FRIEND.
YOU WILL LEARN RESPECT, OR YOU WILL NOT LAST VERY LONG.
I KNOW WHO YOU WERE OUT THERE, BUT UNDERSTAND THAT AMOUNTS TO NOTHING IN HERE.
YOU SEEM REAL WOUND UP FOR THIS EARLY IN THE MORNING.
YOUR BLOOD SUGAR LOW? YOU GET ENOUGH BREAKFAST, BIG MAN?
NOW THAT YOU MENTION IT, I COULD USE ANOTHER PORTION OF MEAT.
ENOUGH. PLEASE.

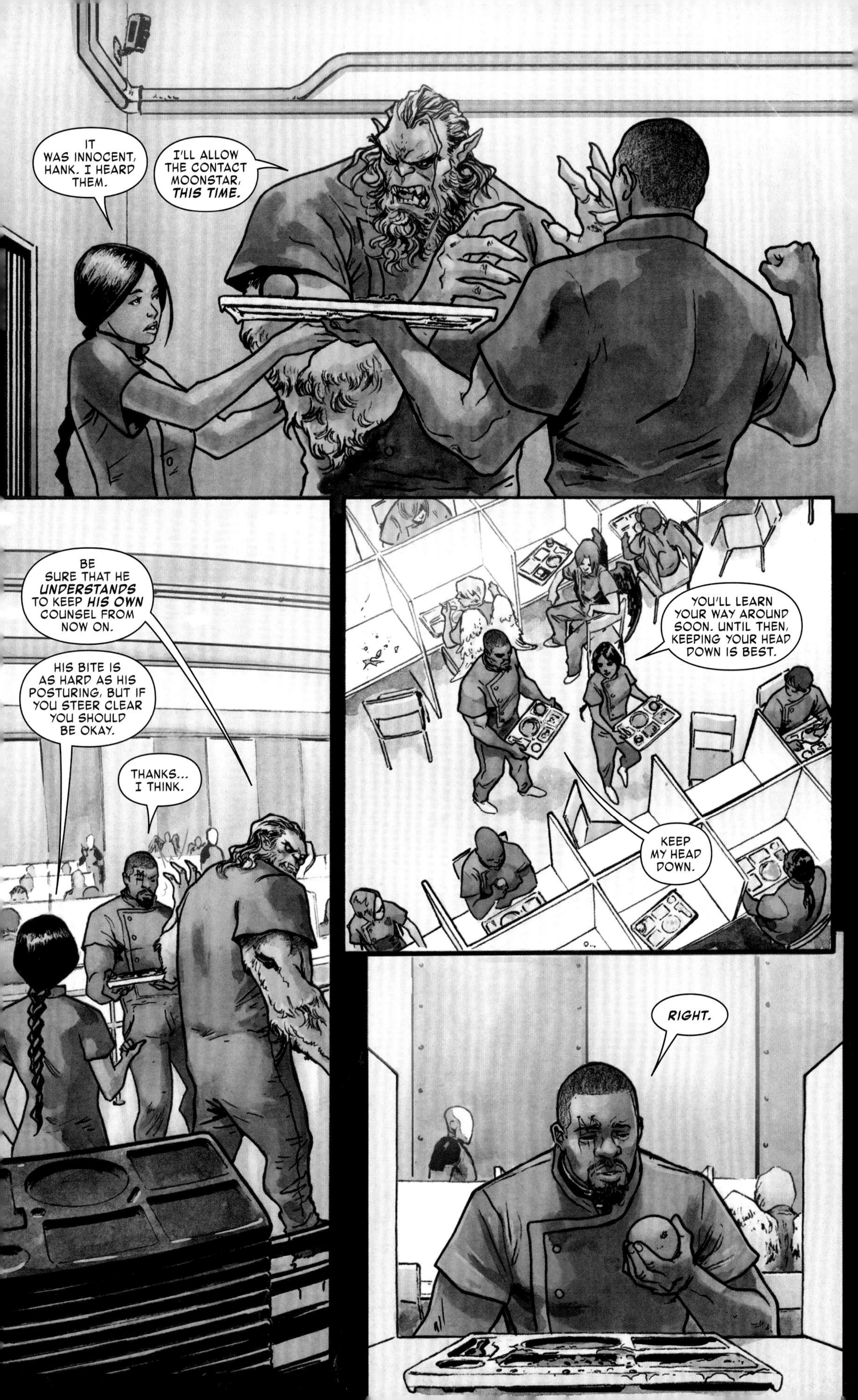
IT WAS INNOCENT, HANK. I HEARD THEM.
I'LL ALLOW THE CONTACT MOONSTAR, THIS TIME.
BE SURE THAT HE UNDERSTANDS TO KEEP HIS OWN COUNSEL FROM NOW ON.
HIS BITE IS AS HARD AS HIS POSTURING, BUT IF YOU STEER CLEAR YOU SHOULD BE OKAY.
THANKS... I THINK.
YOU'LL LEARN YOUR WAY AROUND SOON. UNTIL THEN, KEEPING YOUR HEAD DOWN IS BEST.
KEEP MY HEAD DOWN.
RIGHT.

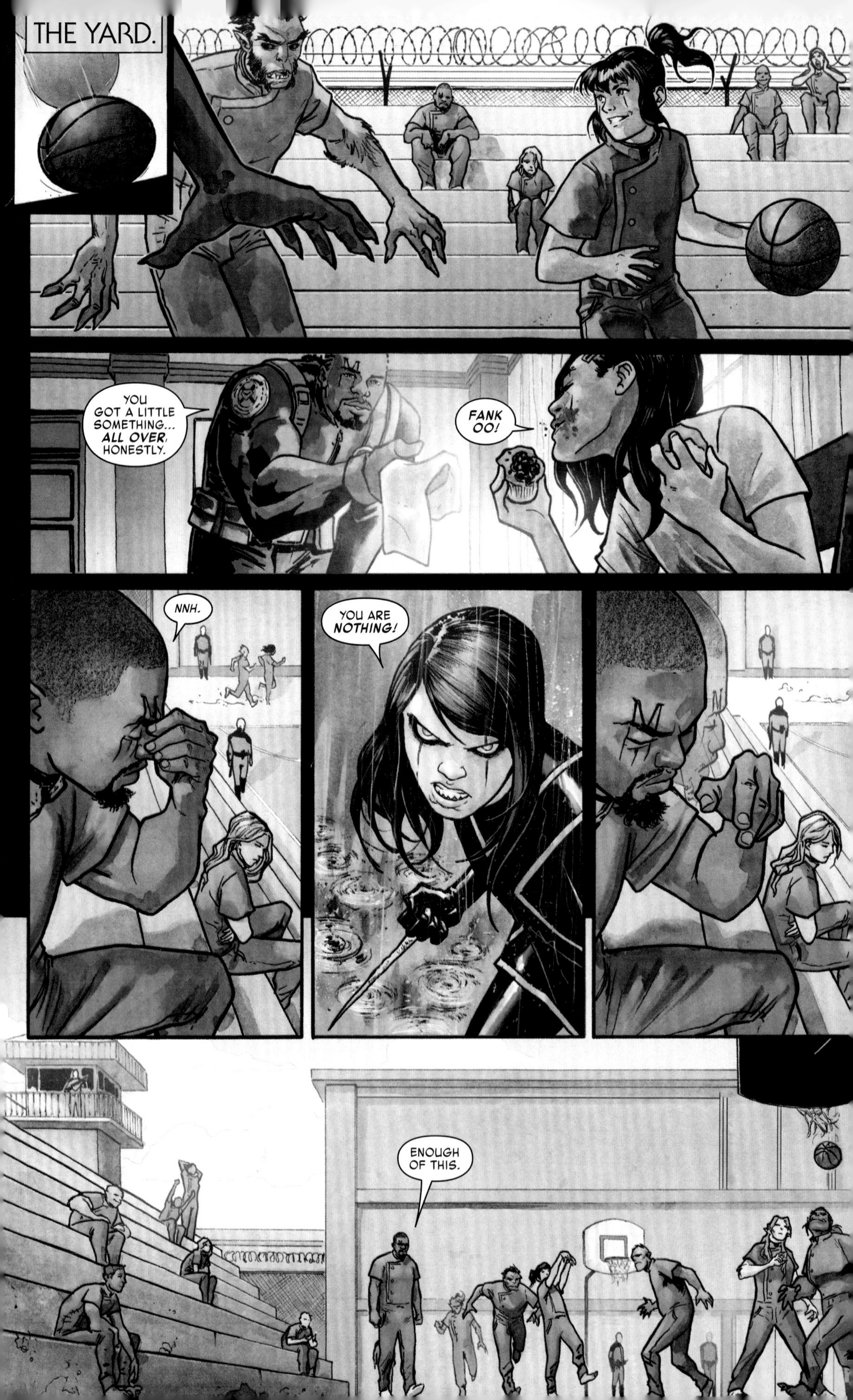
THE YARD.
YOU GOT A LITTLE SOMETHING... ALL OVER, HONESTLY.
FANK OO!
NNH.
YOU ARE NOTHING!
ENOUGH OF THIS.

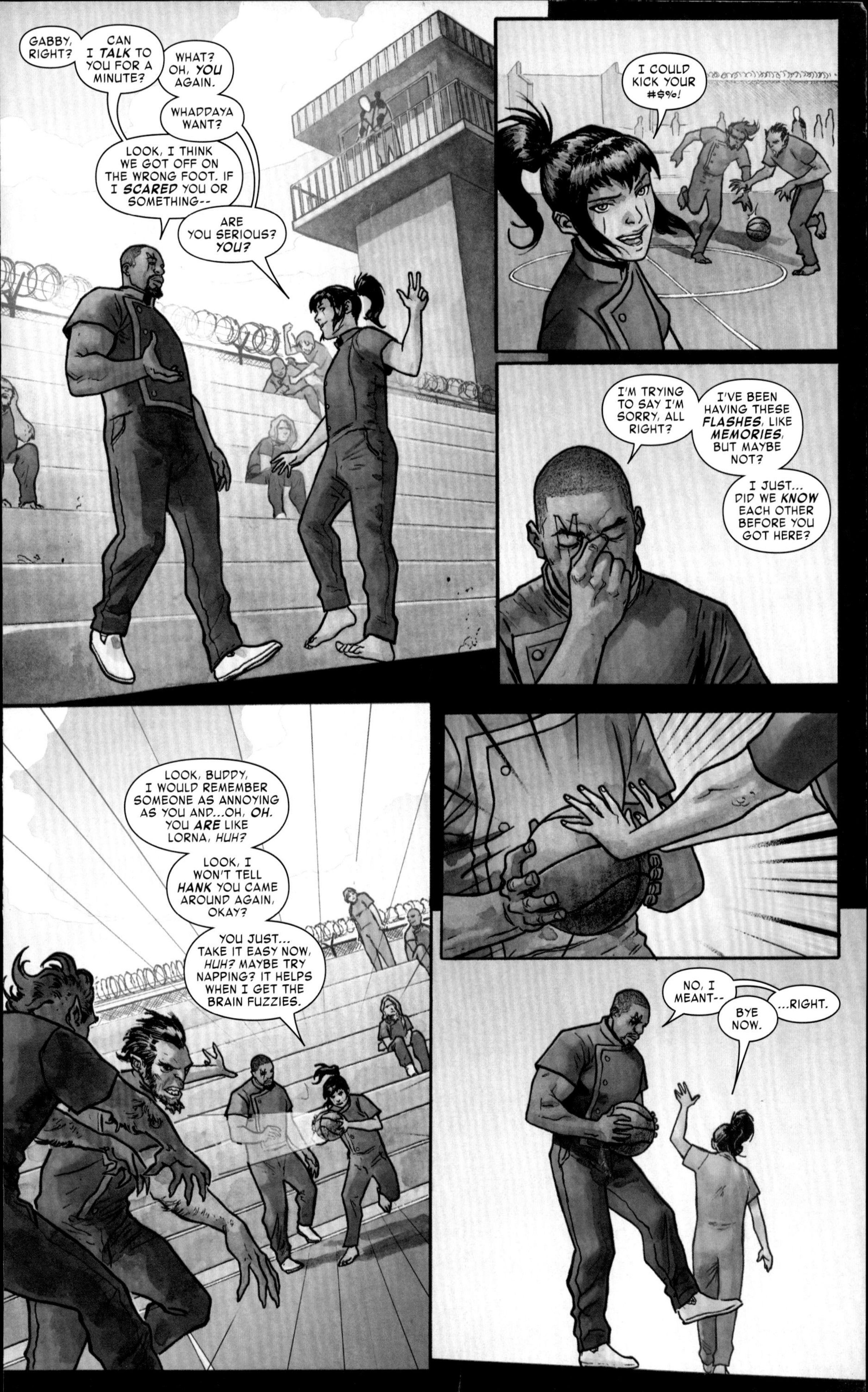
GABBY, RIGHT?
CAN I TALK TO YOU FOR A MINUTE?
WHAT? OH, YOU AGAIN.
WHADDAYA WANT?
LOOK, I THINK WE GOT OFF ON THE WRONG FOOT. IF I SCARED YOU OR SOMETHING--
ARE YOU SERIOUS? YOU?
I COULD KICK YOUR #$%!
I'M TRYING TO SAY I'M SORRY, ALL RIGHT?
I'VE BEEN HAVING THESE FLASHES, LIKE MEMORIES, BUT MAYBE NOT?
I JUST... DID WE KNOW EACH OTHER BEFORE YOU GOT HERE?
LOOK, BUDDY, I WOULD REMEMBER SOMEONE AS ANNOYING AS YOU AND...OH, OH. YOU ARE LIKE LORNA, HUH?
LOOK, I WON'T TELL HANK YOU CAME AROUND AGAIN, OKAY?
YOU JUST... TAKE IT EASY NOW, HUH? MAYBE TRY NAPPING? IT HELPS WHEN I GET THE BRAIN FUZZIES.
NO, I MEANT--
BYE NOW.
...RIGHT.

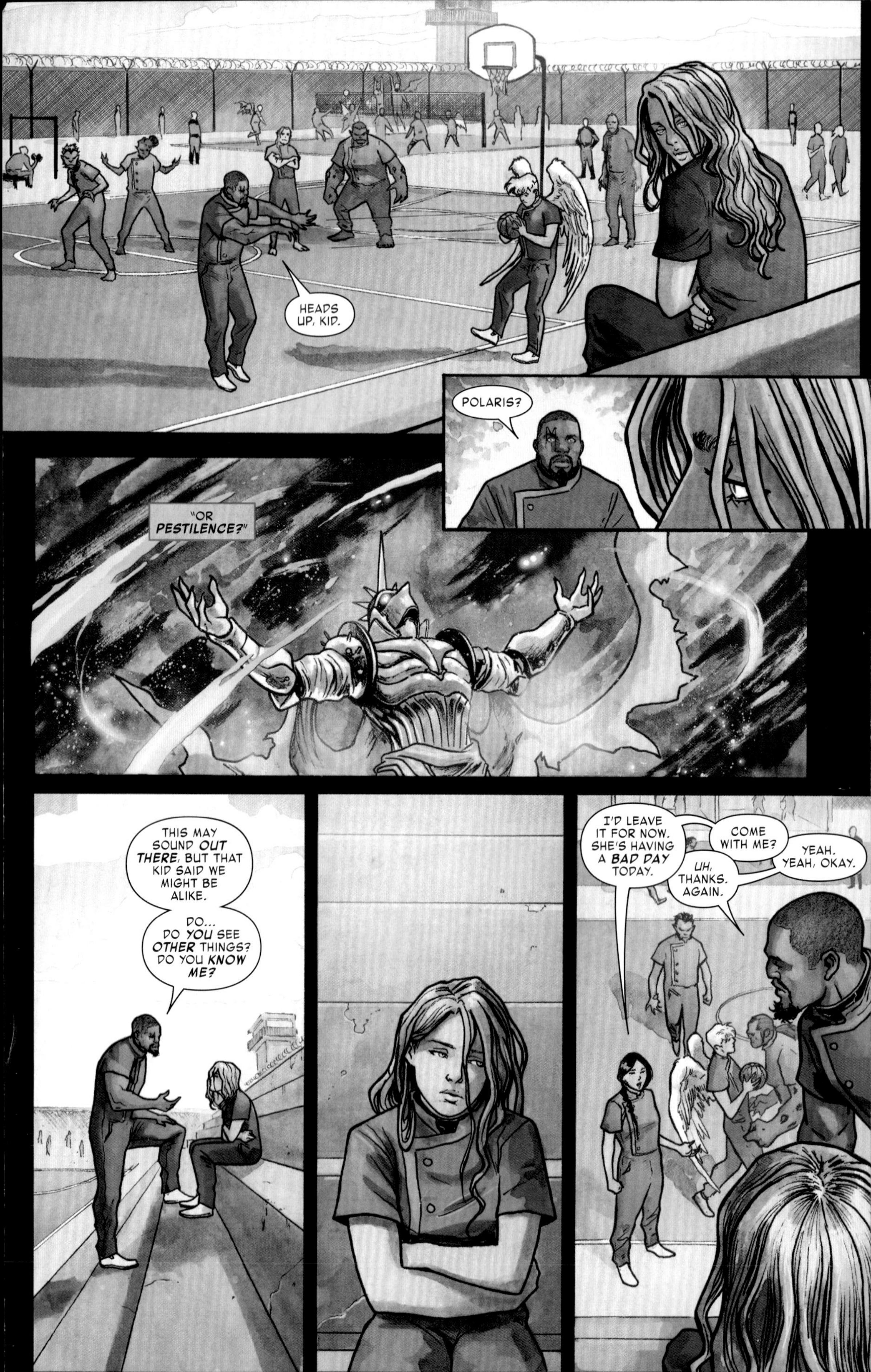

HEADS UP, KID.
POLARIS?
"OR PESTILENCE?"
THIS MAY SOUND OUT THERE, BUT THAT KID SAID WE MIGHT BE ALIKE.
DO... DO YOU SEE OTHER THINGS? DO YOU KNOW ME?
I'D LEAVE IT FOR NOW. SHE'S HAVING A BAD DAY TODAY.
COME WITH ME?
UH, THANKS. AGAIN.
YEAH. YEAH, OKAY.

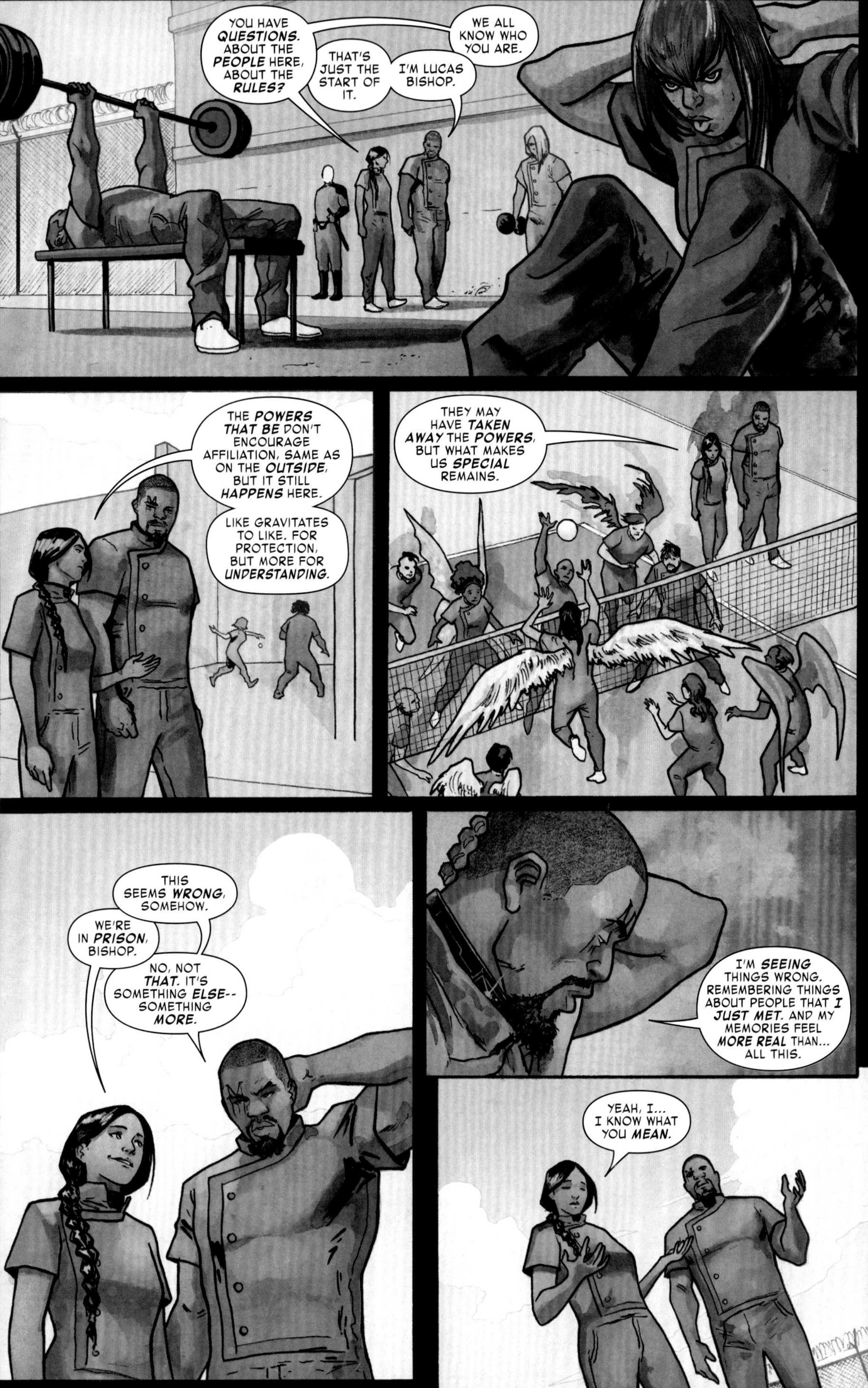
YOU HAVE QUESTIONS. ABOUT THE PEOPLE HERE, ABOUT THE RULES?
THAT'S JUST THE START OF IT.
I'M LUCAS BISHOP.
WE ALL KNOW WHO YOU ARE.
THE POWERS THAT BE DON'T ENCOURAGE AFFILIATION, SAME AS ON THE OUTSIDE, BUT IT STILL HAPPENS HERE.
LIKE GRAVITATES TO LIKE. FOR PROTECTION, BUT MORE FOR UNDERSTANDING.
THEY MAY HAVE TAKEN AWAY THE POWERS, BUT WHAT MAKES US SPECIAL REMAINS.
THIS SEEMS WRONG, SOMEHOW.
WE'RE IN PRISON, BISHOP.
NO, NOT THAT. IT'S SOMETHING ELSE-- SOMETHING MORE.
I'M SEEING THINGS WRONG. REMEMBERING THINGS ABOUT PEOPLE THAT I JUST MET. AND MY MEMORIES FEEL MORE REAL THAN... ALL THIS.
YEAH, I... I KNOW WHAT YOU MEAN.

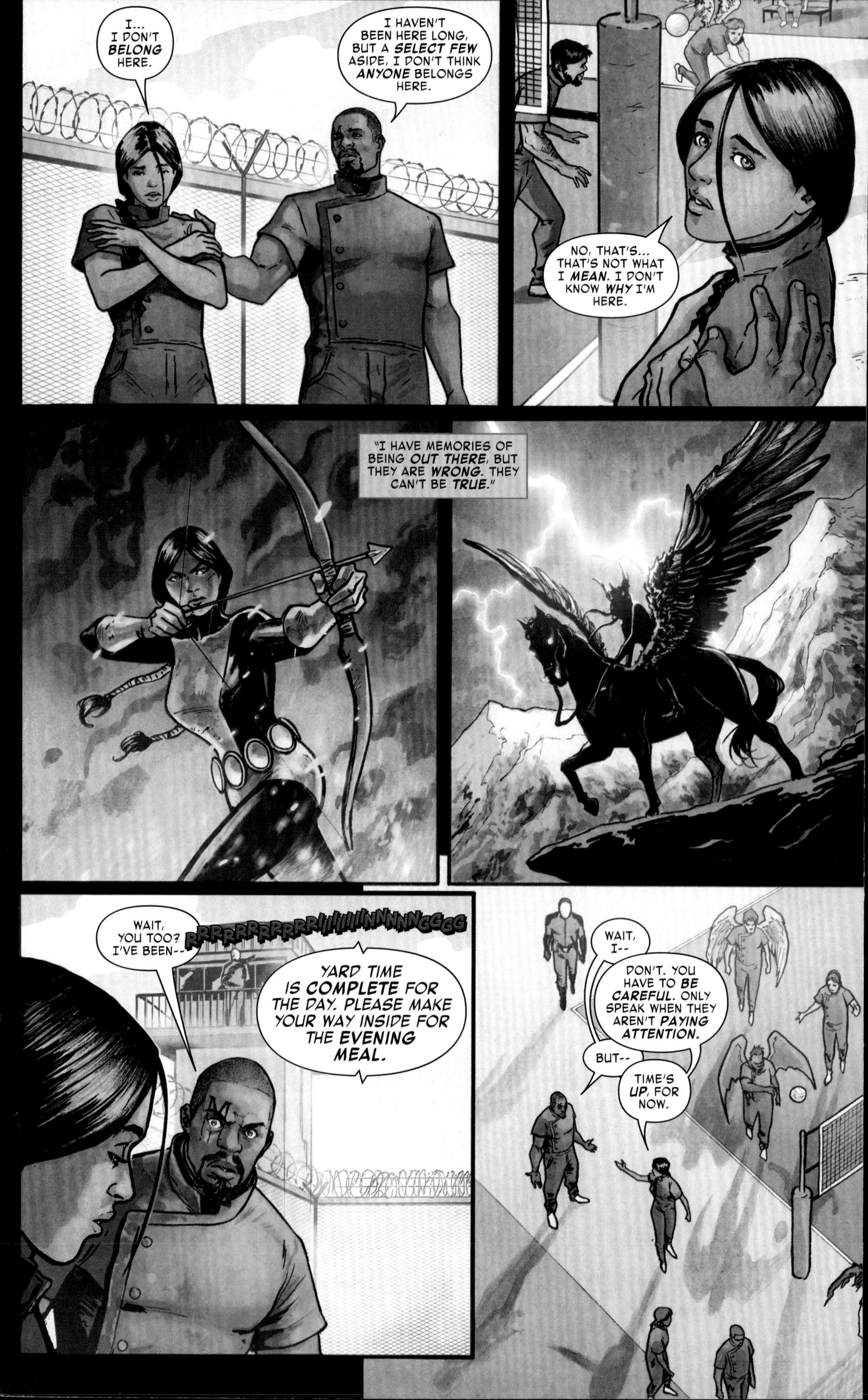
I... I DON'T BELONG HERE.
I HAVEN'T BEEN HERE LONG, BUT A SELECT FEW ASIDE, I DON'T THINK ANYONE BELONGS HERE.
NO, THAT'S... THAT'S NOT WHAT I MEAN. I DON'T KNOW WHY I'M HERE.
"I HAVE MEMORIES OF BEING OUT THERE, BUT THEY ARE WRONG. THEY CAN'T BE TRUE."
WAIT, YOU TOO? I'VE BEEN--
RRRRRRRRRRRRIIIIIIIIIINNNNNNGGGG
YARD TIME IS COMPLETE FOR THE DAY. PLEASE MAKE YOUR WAY INSIDE FOR THE EVENING MEAL.
WAIT, I--
DON'T. YOU HAVE TO BE CAREFUL. ONLY SPEAK WHEN THEY AREN'T PAYING ATTENTION.
BUT--
TIME'S UP, FOR NOW.

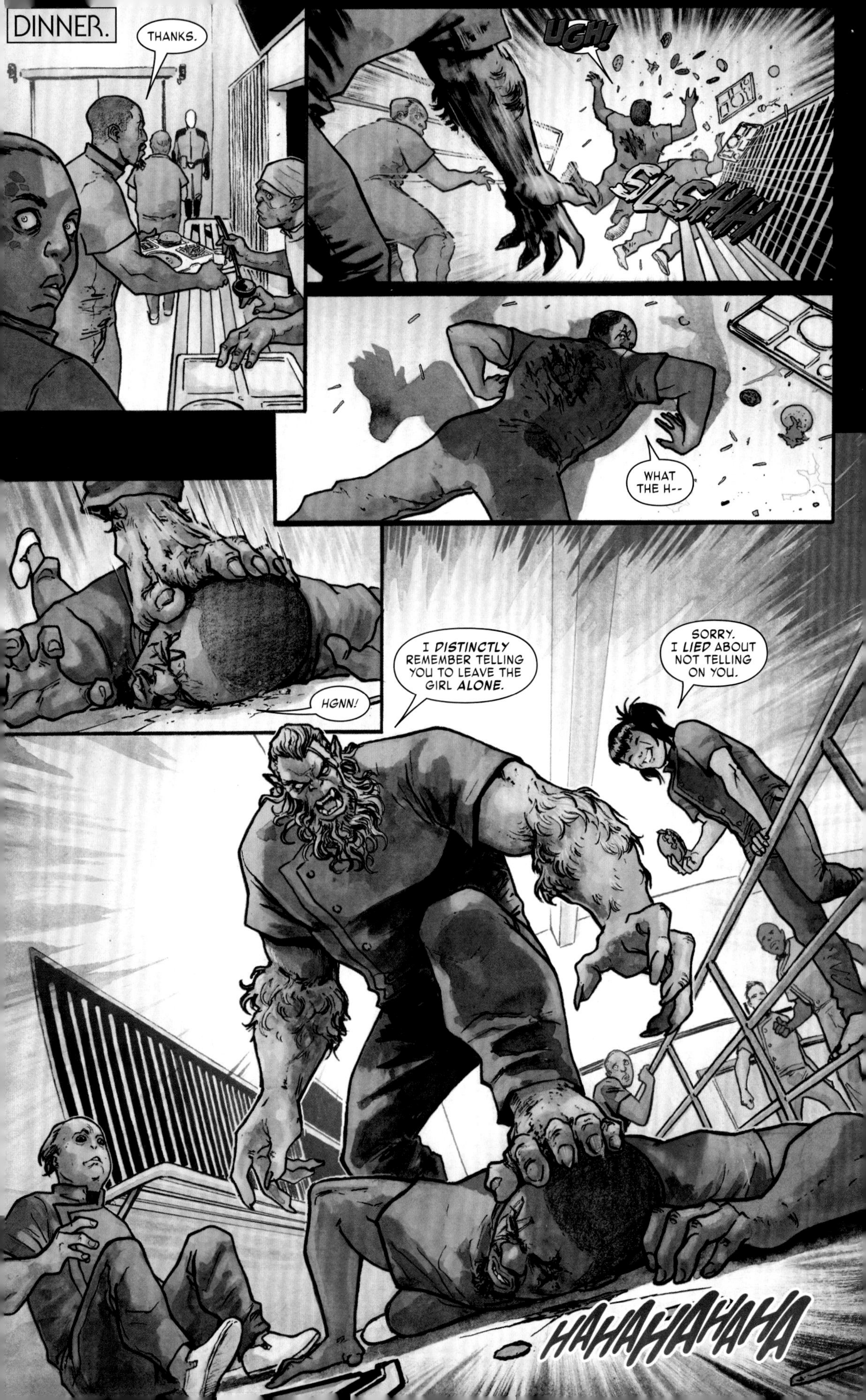
DINNER.
THANKS.
UGH!
SLSHHH
WHAT THE H--
HGNN!
I DISTINCTLY REMEMBER TELLING YOU TO LEAVE THE GIRL ALONE.
SORRY. I LIED ABOUT NOT TELLING ON YOU.
HAHAHAHAHAHA

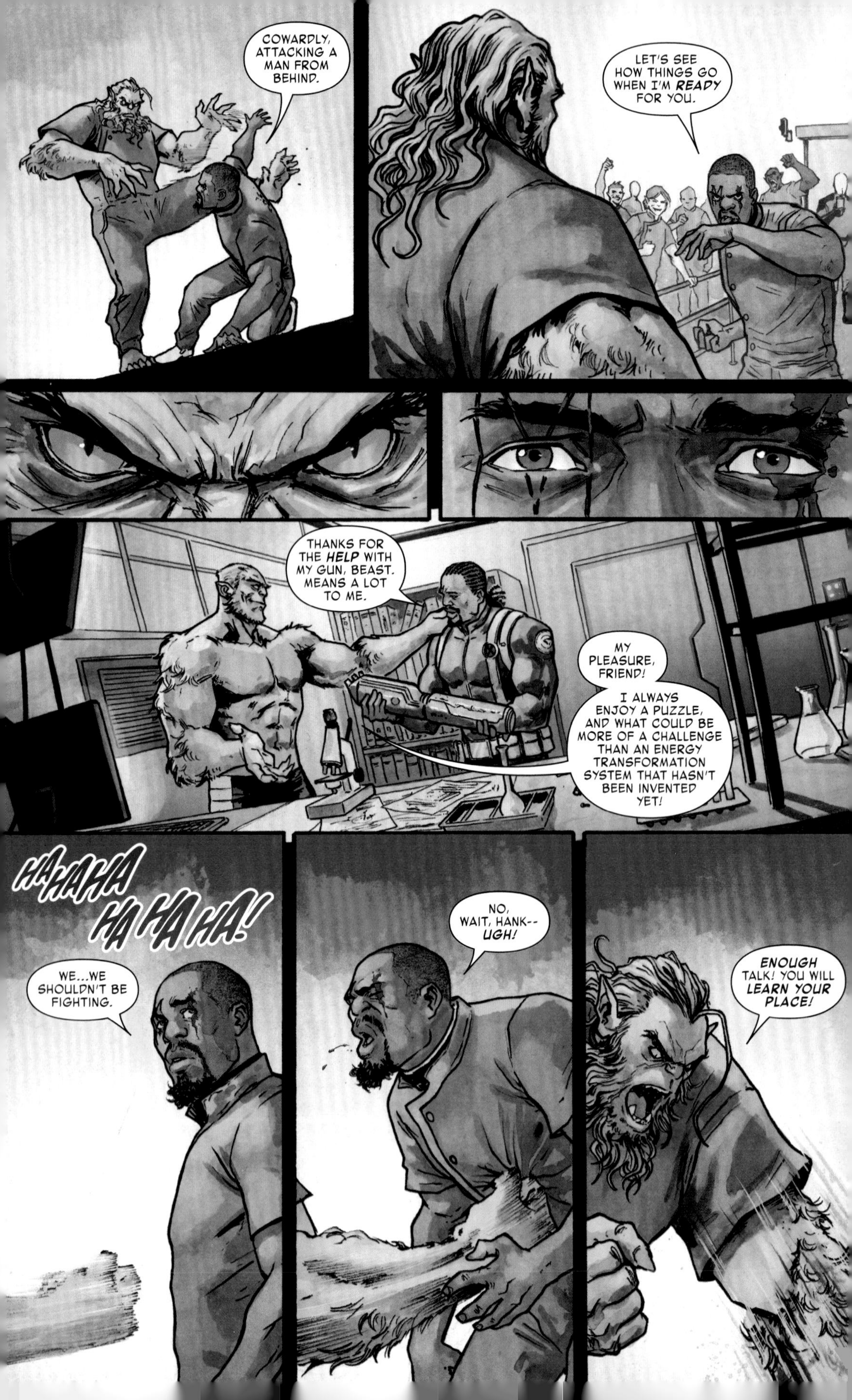

COWARDLY, ATTACKING A MAN FROM BEHIND.
LET'S SEE HOW THINGS GO WHEN I'M *READY* FOR YOU.
THANKS FOR THE *HELP* WITH MY GUN, BEAST. MEANS A LOT TO ME.
MY PLEASURE, FRIEND!
I ALWAYS ENJOY A PUZZLE, AND WHAT COULD BE MORE OF A CHALLENGE THAN AN ENERGY TRANSFORMATION SYSTEM THAT HASN'T BEEN INVENTED YET!
HA HA HA HA HA HA HA!
WE...WE SHOULDN'T BE FIGHTING.
NO, WAIT, HANK-- *UGH!*
ENOUGH TALK! YOU WILL *LEARN YOUR PLACE!*

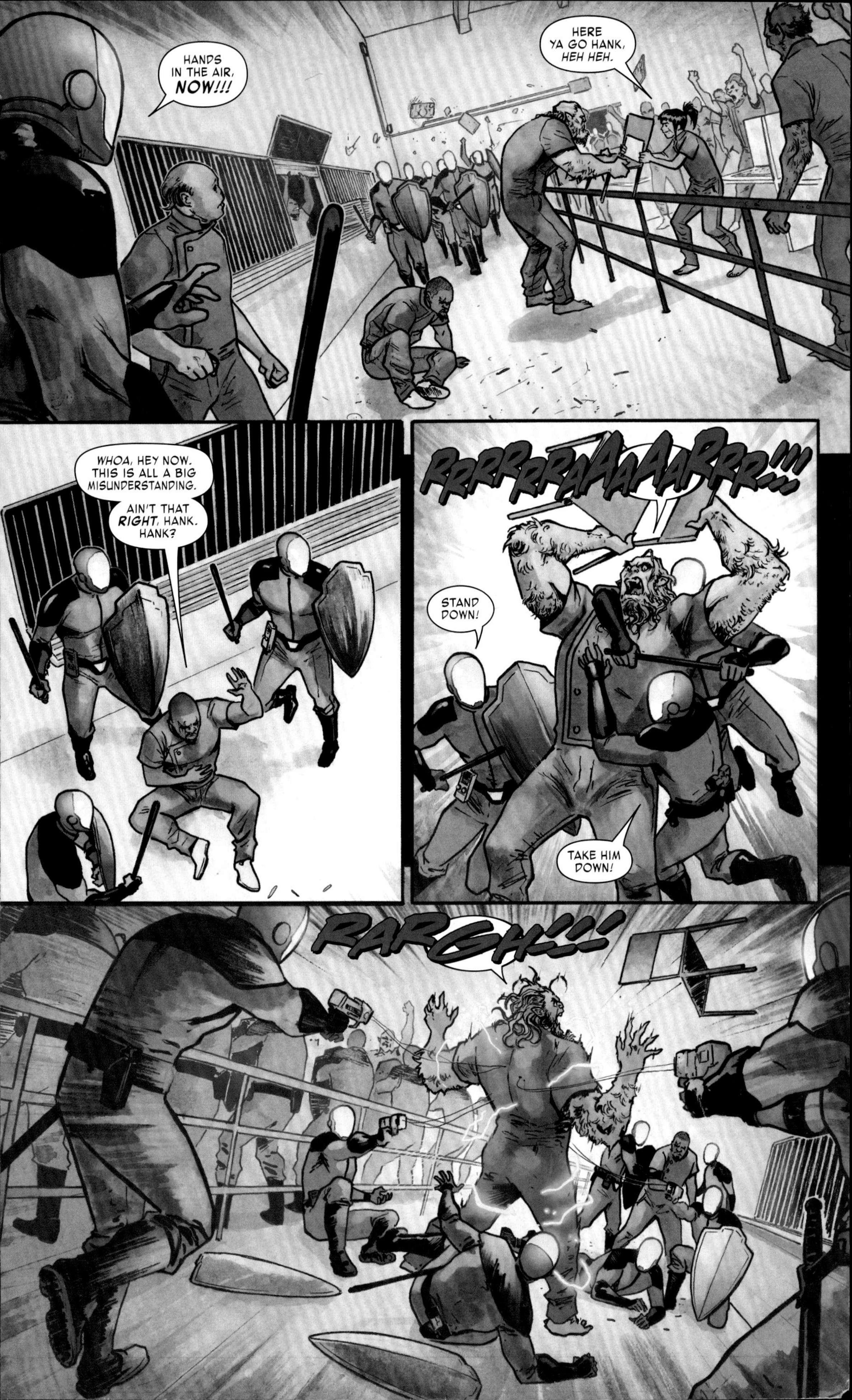
HANDS IN THE AIR, NOW!!!
HERE YA GO HANK, HEH HEH.
WHOA, HEY NOW. THIS IS ALL A BIG MISUNDERSTANDING.
AIN'T THAT RIGHT, HANK. HANK?
RRRRRRAAAAAARRR!!!
STAND DOWN!
TAKE HIM DOWN!
RARGH!!!

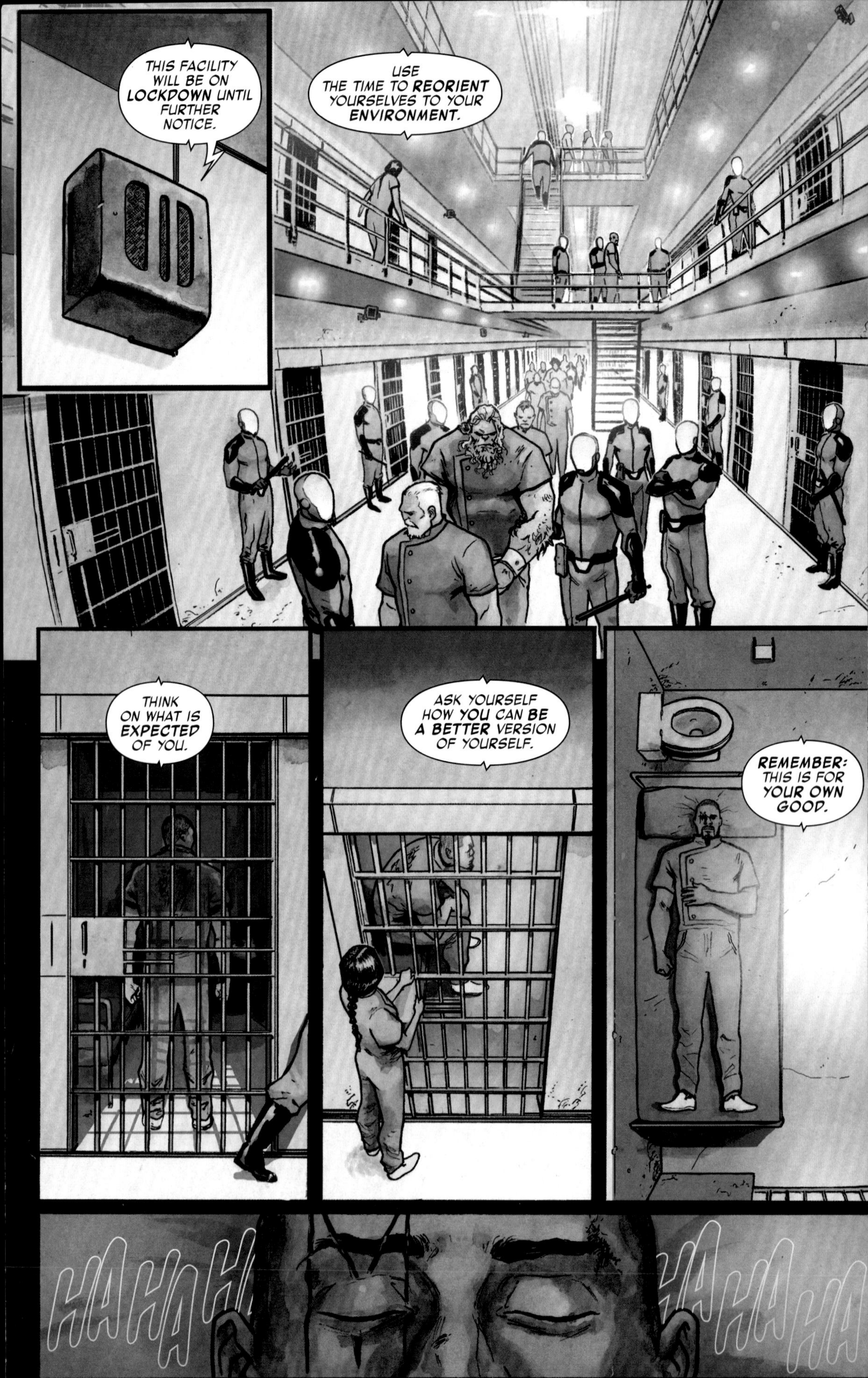
THIS FACILITY WILL BE ON LOCKDOWN UNTIL FURTHER NOTICE.
USE THE TIME TO REORIENT YOURSELVES TO YOUR ENVIRONMENT.
THINK ON WHAT IS EXPECTED OF YOU.
ASK YOURSELF HOW YOU CAN BE A BETTER VERSION OF YOURSELF.
REMEMBER: THIS IS FOR YOUR OWN GOOD.
HAHAHA
HAHAHA

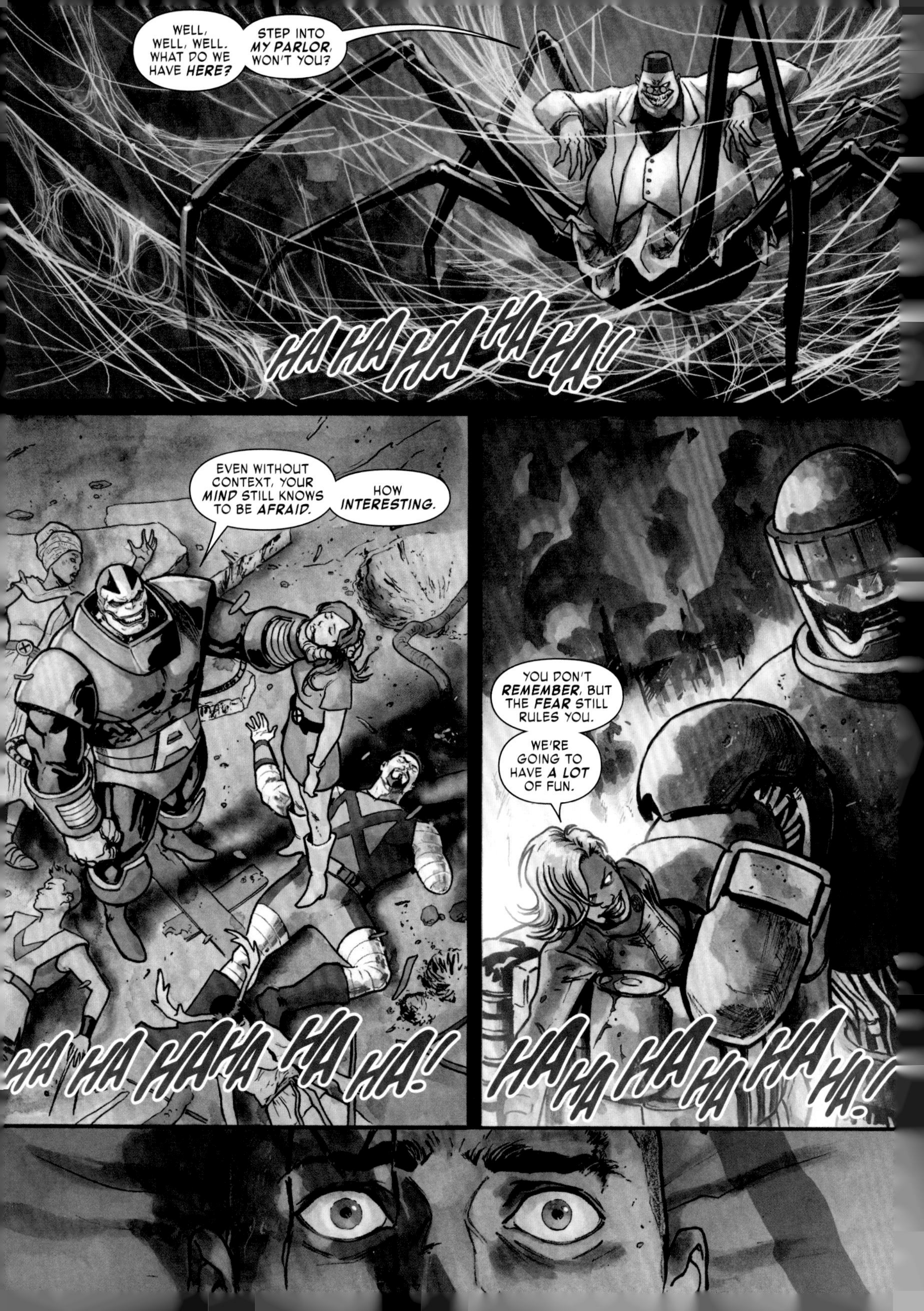
WELL, WELL, WELL. WHAT DO WE HAVE HERE?
STEP INTO MY PARLOR, WON'T YOU?
HA HA HA HA HA HA!
EVEN WITHOUT CONTEXT, YOUR MIND STILL KNOWS TO BE AFRAID.
HOW INTERESTING.
HA HA HAHA HA HA!
YOU DON'T REMEMBER, BUT THE FEAR STILL RULES YOU.
WE'RE GOING TO HAVE A LOT OF FUN.
HA HA HA HA HA HA HA HA!

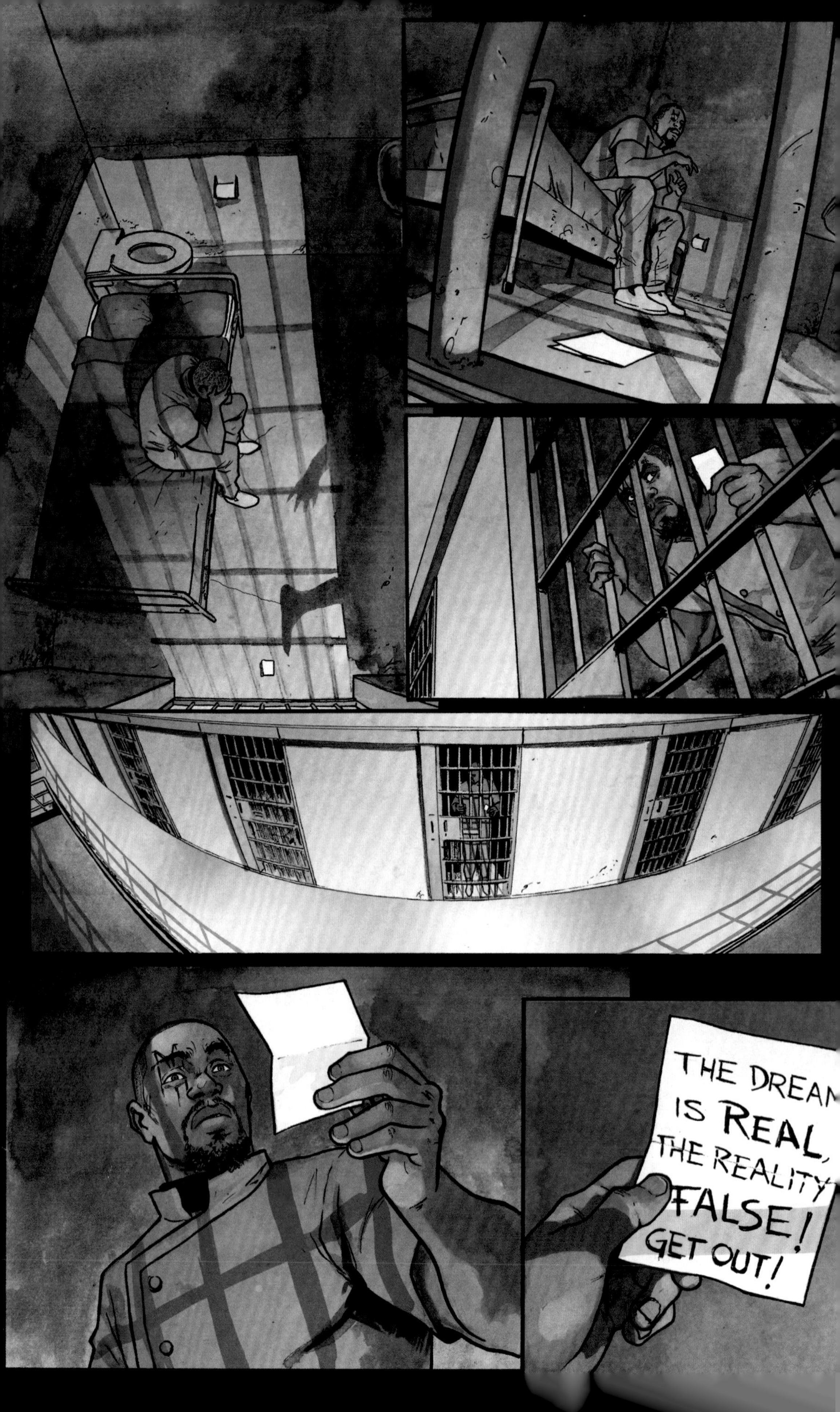
THE DREAM
IS REAL,
THE REALITY
FALSE!
GET OUT!

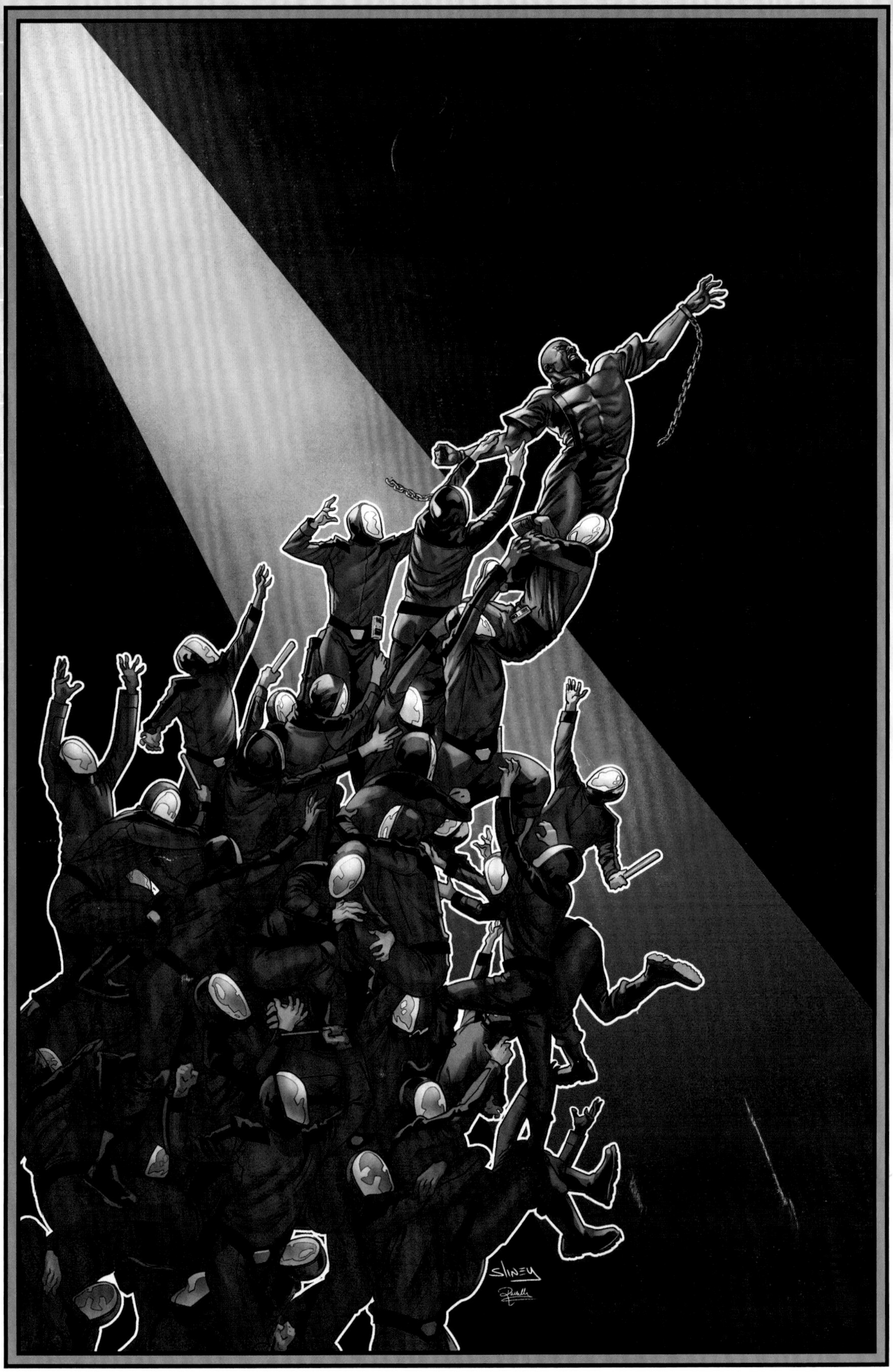
SLINEY

#1 VARIANT BY **WILL SLINEY** & **RACHELLE ROSENBERG**

2

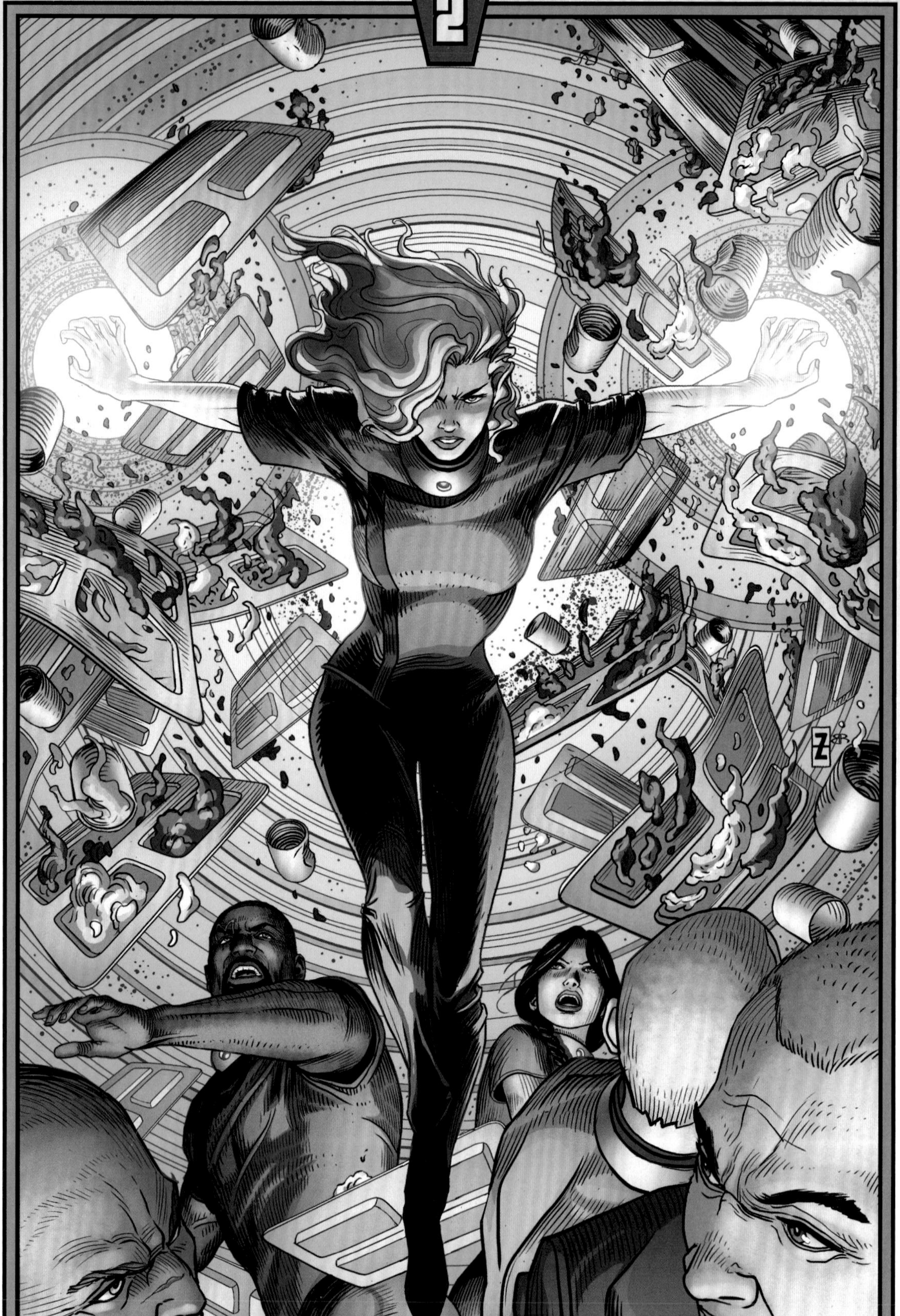

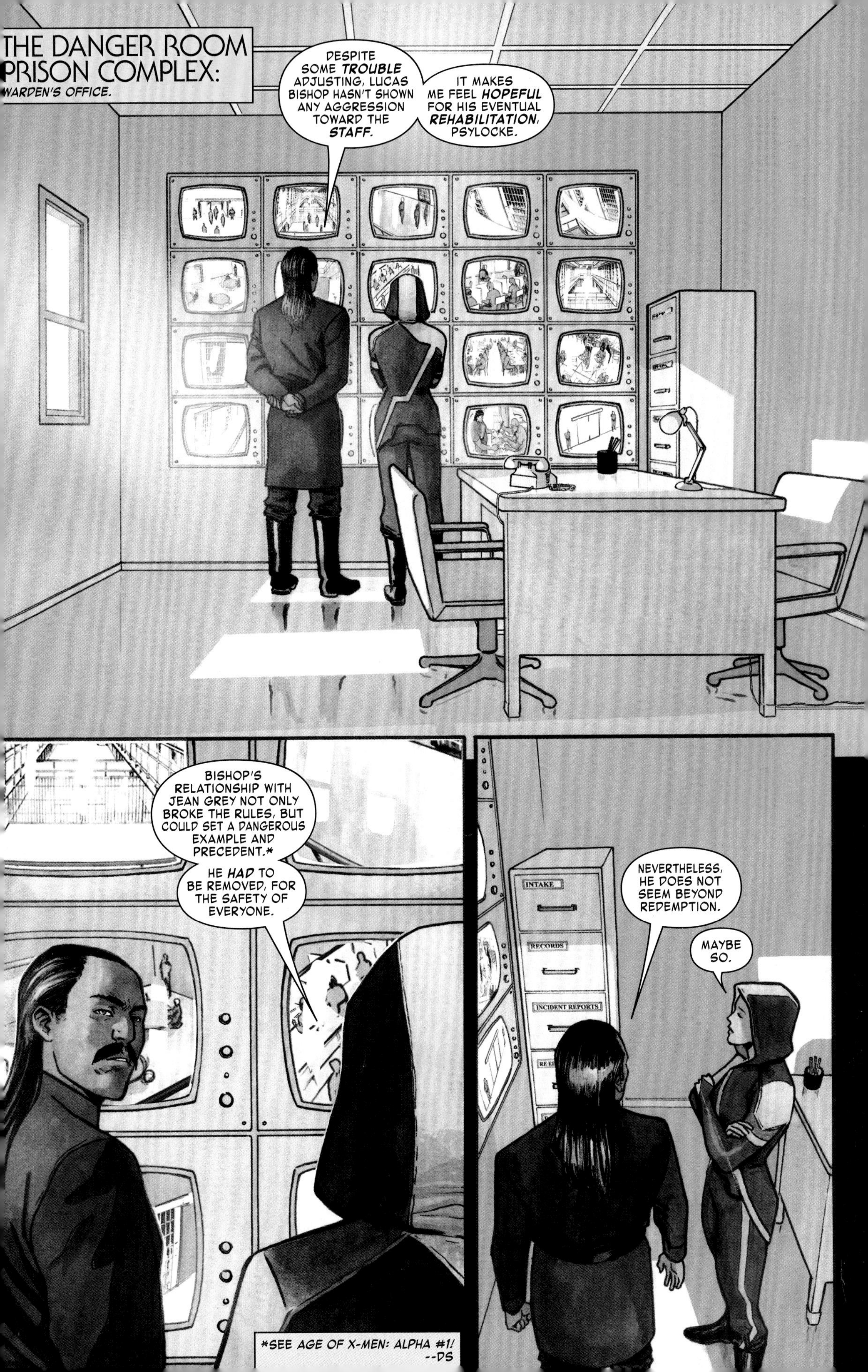
THE DANGER ROOM PRISON COMPLEX:
WARDEN'S OFFICE.
DESPITE SOME TROUBLE ADJUSTING, LUCAS BISHOP HASN'T SHOWN ANY AGGRESSION TOWARD THE STAFF.
IT MAKES ME FEEL HOPEFUL FOR HIS EVENTUAL REHABILITATION, PSYLOCKE.
BISHOP'S RELATIONSHIP WITH JEAN GREY NOT ONLY BROKE THE RULES, BUT COULD SET A DANGEROUS EXAMPLE AND PRECEDENT.*
HE HAD TO BE REMOVED, FOR THE SAFETY OF EVERYONE.
INTAKE
RECORDS
INCIDENT REPORTS
NEVERTHELESS, HE DOES NOT SEEM BEYOND REDEMPTION.
MAYBE SO.
*SEE AGE OF X-MEN: ALPHA #1! --DS

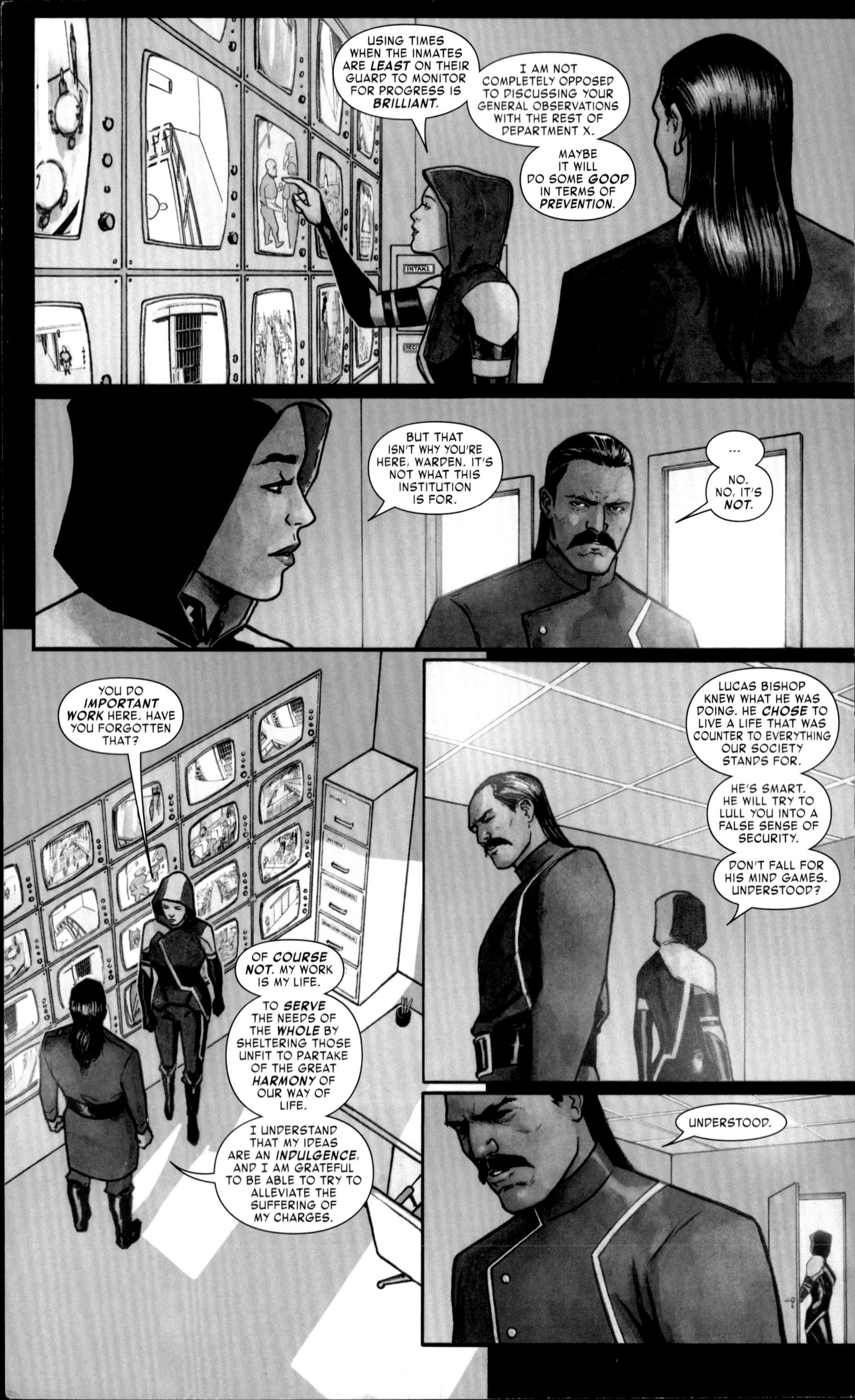

USING TIMES WHEN THE INMATES ARE LEAST ON THEIR GUARD TO MONITOR FOR PROGRESS IS BRILLIANT.
I AM NOT COMPLETELY OPPOSED TO DISCUSSING YOUR GENERAL OBSERVATIONS WITH THE REST OF DEPARTMENT X.
MAYBE IT WILL DO SOME GOOD IN TERMS OF PREVENTION.
INTAKE
BUT THAT ISN'T WHY YOU'RE HERE, WARDEN. IT'S NOT WHAT THIS INSTITUTION IS FOR.
...
NO. NO, IT'S NOT.
YOU DO IMPORTANT WORK HERE. HAVE YOU FORGOTTEN THAT?
OF COURSE NOT. MY WORK IS MY LIFE.
TO SERVE THE NEEDS OF THE WHOLE BY SHELTERING THOSE UNFIT TO PARTAKE OF THE GREAT HARMONY OF OUR WAY OF LIFE.
I UNDERSTAND THAT MY IDEAS ARE AN INDULGENCE, AND I AM GRATEFUL TO BE ABLE TO TRY TO ALLEVIATE THE SUFFERING OF MY CHARGES.
LUCAS BISHOP KNEW WHAT HE WAS DOING. HE CHOSE TO LIVE A LIFE THAT WAS COUNTER TO EVERYTHING OUR SOCIETY STANDS FOR.
HE'S SMART. HE WILL TRY TO LULL YOU INTO A FALSE SENSE OF SECURITY.
DON'T FALL FOR HIS MIND GAMES. UNDERSTOOD?
UNDERSTOOD.

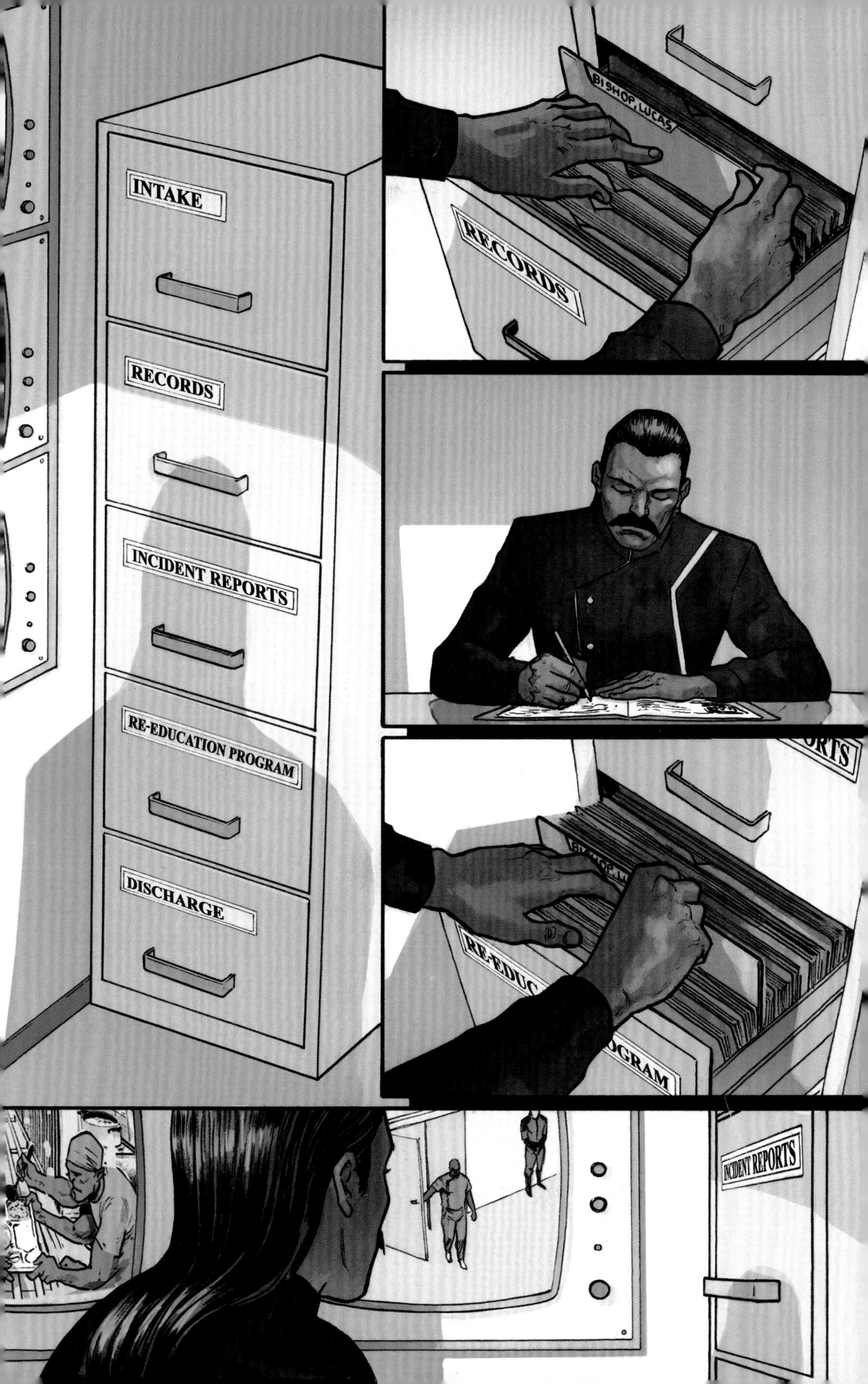
INTAKE
RECORDS
INCIDENT REPORTS
RE-EDUCATION PROGRAM
DISCHARGE
BISHOP, LUCAS
RECORDS
INCIDENT REPORTS

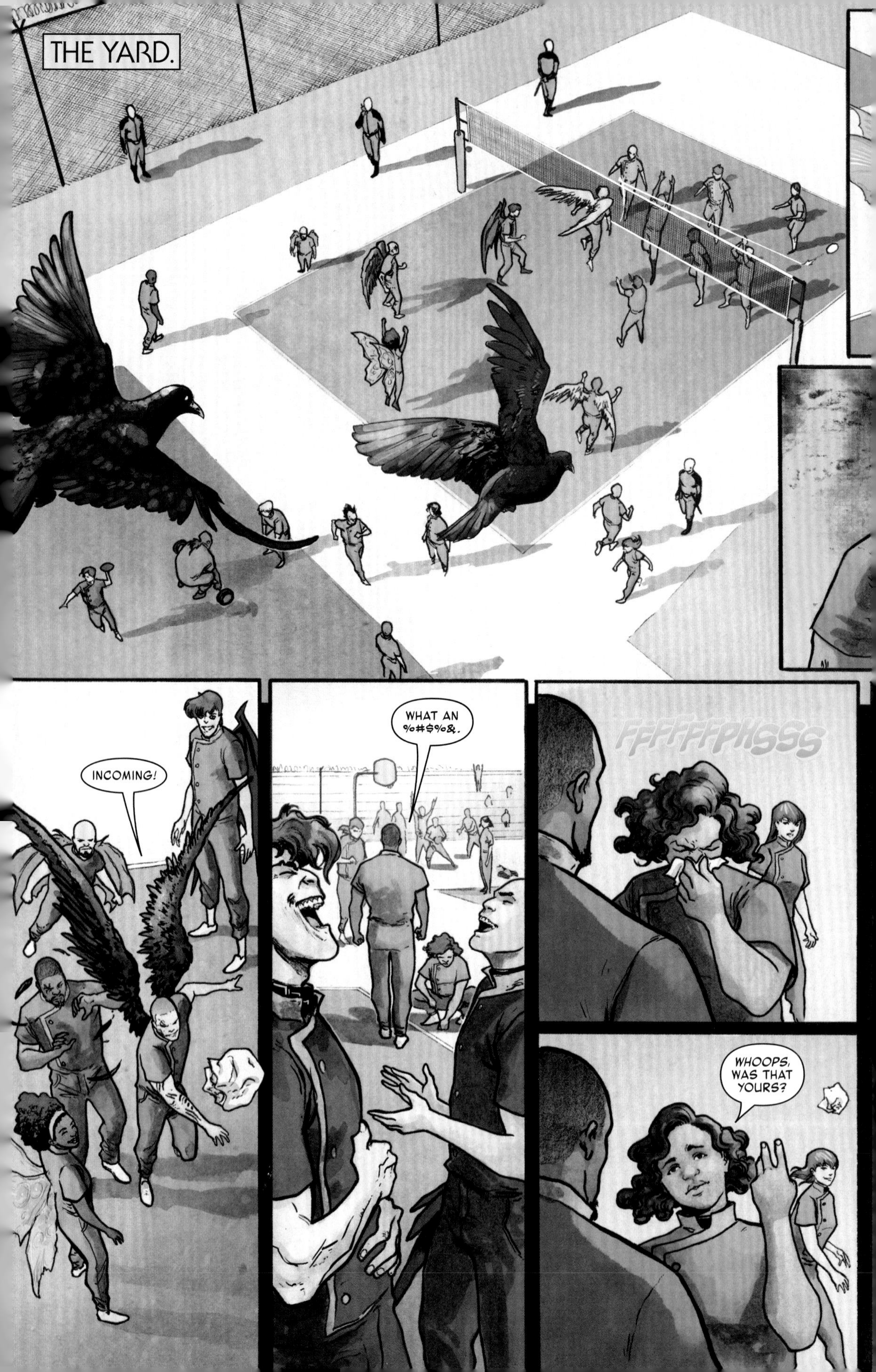
THE YARD.
INCOMING!
WHAT AN %#$%&.
FFFFFFPHSSS
WHOOPS, WAS THAT YOURS?

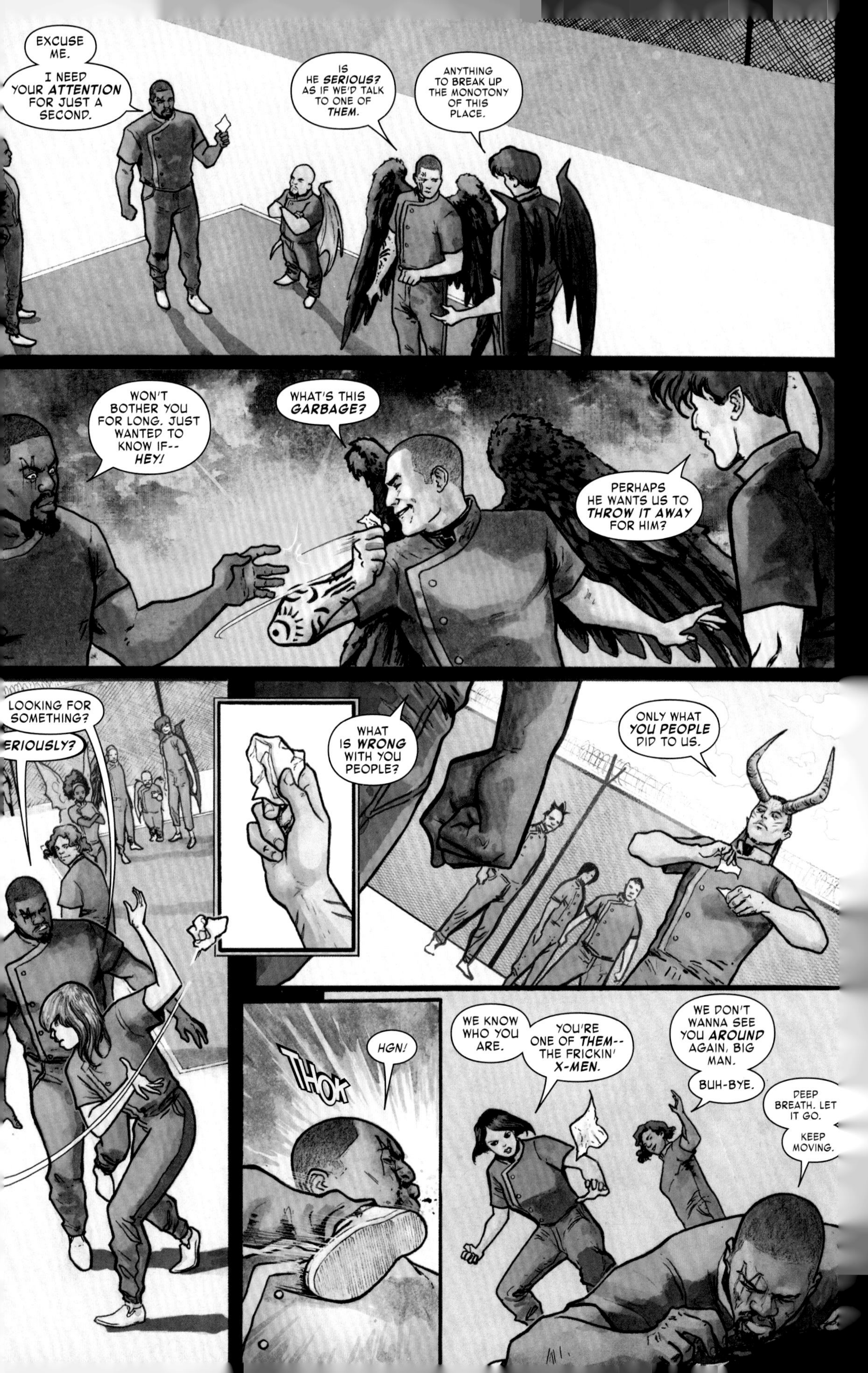
EXCUSE ME.
I NEED YOUR ATTENTION FOR JUST A SECOND.
IS HE SERIOUS? AS IF WE'D TALK TO ONE OF THEM.
ANYTHING TO BREAK UP THE MONOTONY OF THIS PLACE.
WON'T BOTHER YOU FOR LONG. JUST WANTED TO KNOW IF-- HEY!
WHAT'S THIS GARBAGE?
PERHAPS HE WANTS US TO THROW IT AWAY FOR HIM?
LOOKING FOR SOMETHING?
ERIOUSLY?
WHAT IS WRONG WITH YOU PEOPLE?
ONLY WHAT YOU PEOPLE DID TO US.
THOK
HGN!
WE KNOW WHO YOU ARE.
YOU'RE ONE OF THEM-- THE FRICKIN' X-MEN.
WE DON'T WANNA SEE YOU AROUND AGAIN, BIG MAN.
BUH-BYE.
DEEP BREATH. LET IT GO.
KEEP MOVING.

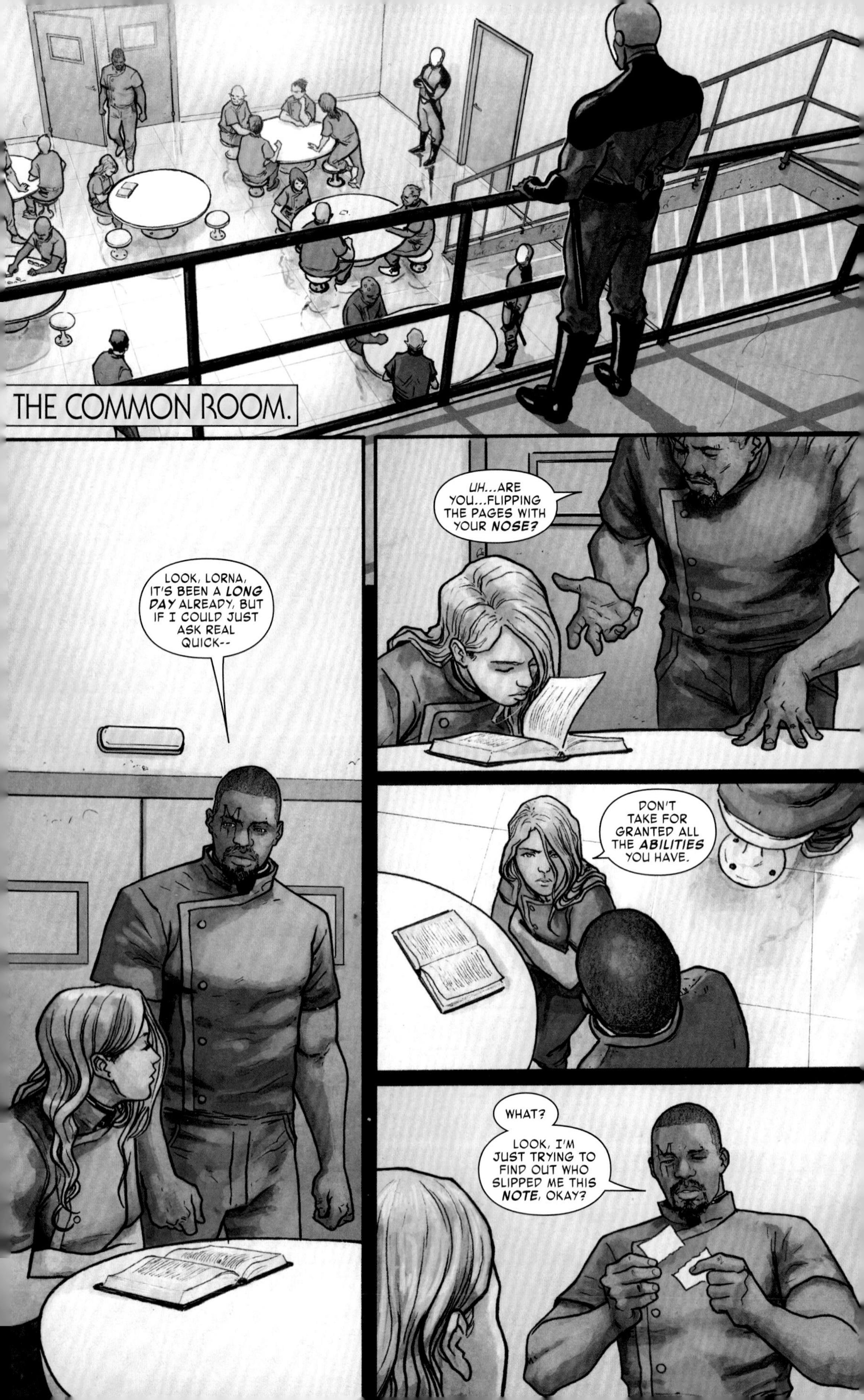
THE COMMON ROOM.
LOOK, LORNA, IT'S BEEN A LONG DAY ALREADY, BUT IF I COULD JUST ASK REAL QUICK--
UH...ARE YOU...FLIPPING THE PAGES WITH YOUR NOSE?
DON'T TAKE FOR GRANTED ALL THE ABILITIES YOU HAVE.
WHAT?
LOOK, I'M JUST TRYING TO FIND OUT WHO SLIPPED ME THIS NOTE, OKAY?

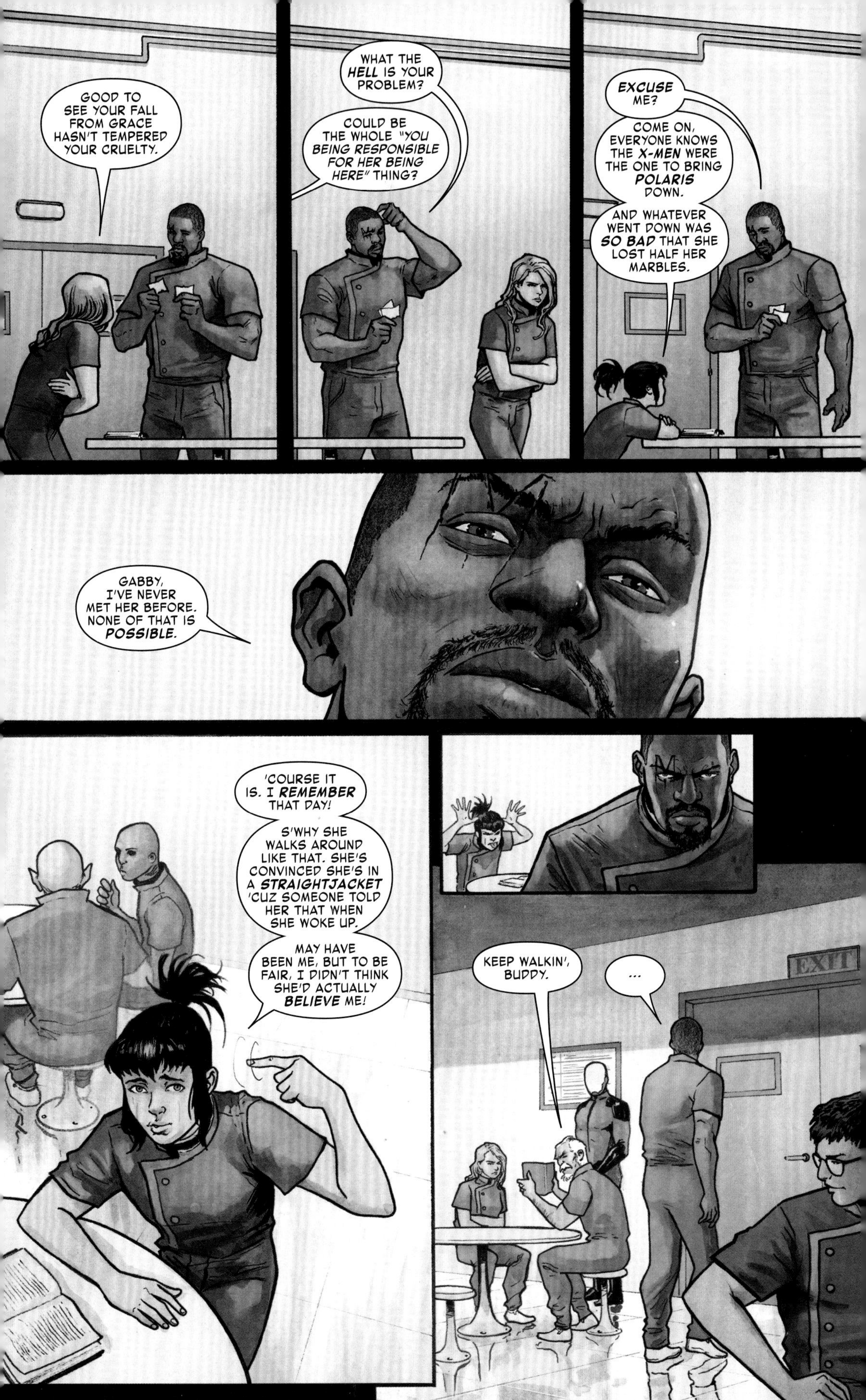
GOOD TO SEE YOUR FALL FROM GRACE HASN'T TEMPERED YOUR CRUELTY.
WHAT THE HELL IS YOUR PROBLEM?
COULD BE THE WHOLE "YOU BEING RESPONSIBLE FOR HER BEING HERE" THING?
EXCUSE ME?
COME ON, EVERYONE KNOWS THE X-MEN WERE THE ONE TO BRING POLARIS DOWN.
AND WHATEVER WENT DOWN WAS SO BAD THAT SHE LOST HALF HER MARBLES.
GABBY, I'VE NEVER MET HER BEFORE. NONE OF THAT IS POSSIBLE.
'COURSE IT IS. I REMEMBER THAT DAY!
S'WHY SHE WALKS AROUND LIKE THAT. SHE'S CONVINCED SHE'S IN A STRAIGHTJACKET 'CUZ SOMEONE TOLD HER THAT WHEN SHE WOKE UP.
MAY HAVE BEEN ME, BUT TO BE FAIR, I DIDN'T THINK SHE'D ACTUALLY BELIEVE ME!
KEEP WALKIN', BUDDY.
...
EXIT

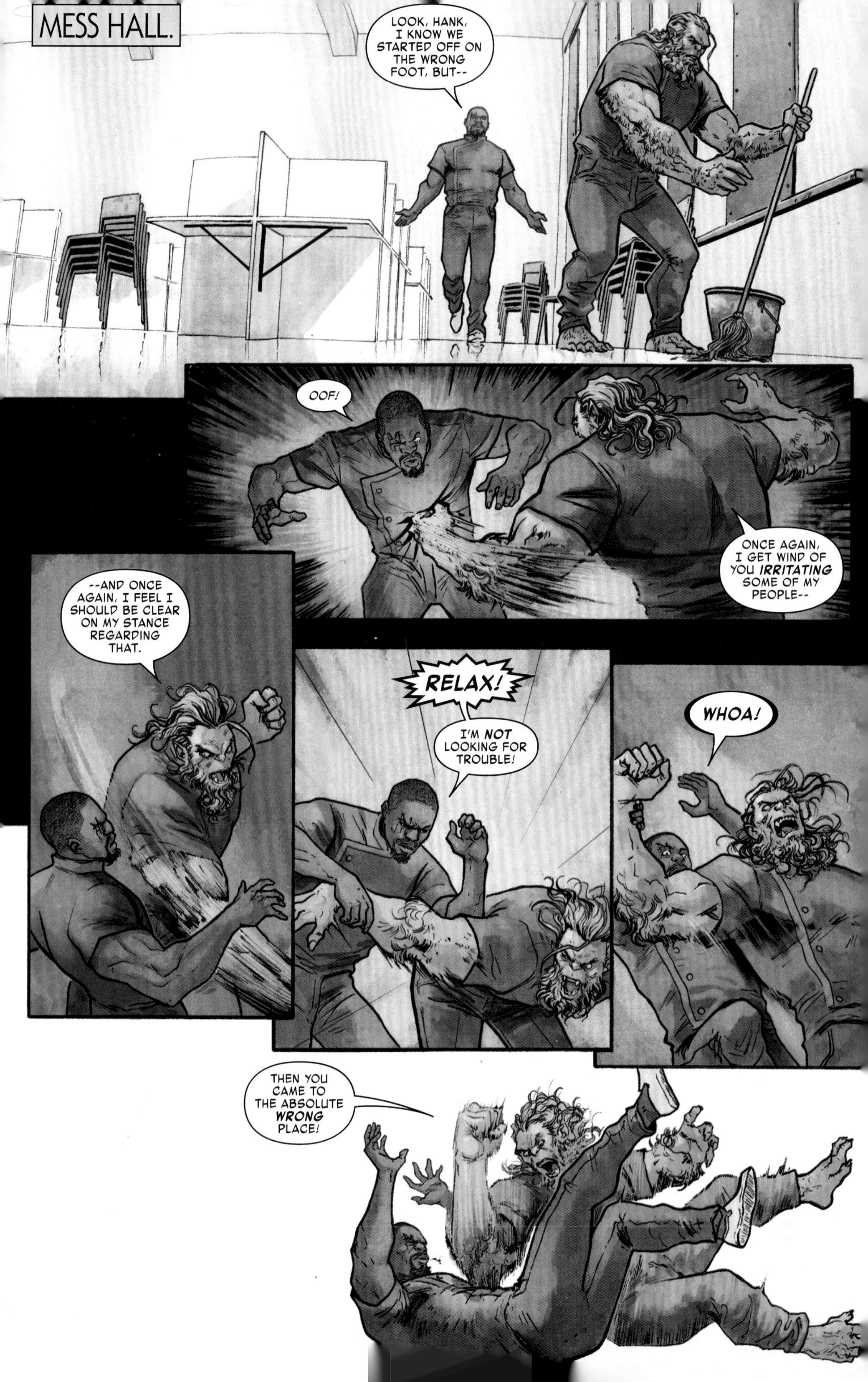
MESS HALL.
LOOK, HANK, I KNOW WE STARTED OFF ON THE WRONG FOOT, BUT--
OOF!
ONCE AGAIN, I GET WIND OF YOU IRRITATING SOME OF MY PEOPLE--
--AND ONCE AGAIN, I FEEL I SHOULD BE CLEAR ON MY STANCE REGARDING THAT.
RELAX!
I'M NOT LOOKING FOR TROUBLE!
WHOA!
THEN YOU CAME TO THE ABSOLUTE WRONG PLACE!

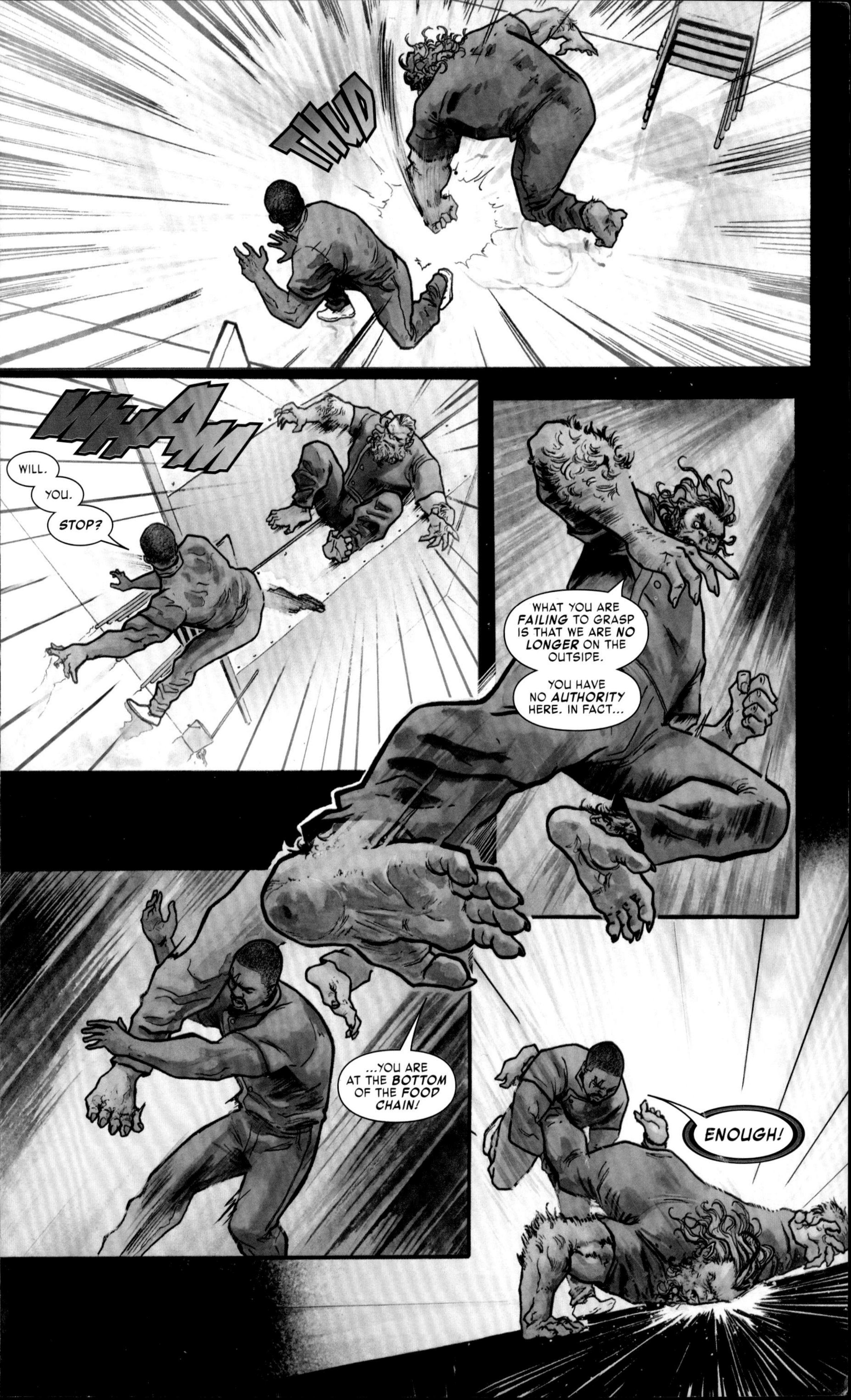
THUD
WHAM
WILL.
YOU.
STOP?
WHAT YOU ARE FAILING TO GRASP IS THAT WE ARE NO LONGER ON THE OUTSIDE.
YOU HAVE NO AUTHORITY HERE. IN FACT...
...YOU ARE AT THE BOTTOM OF THE FOOD CHAIN!
ENOUGH!

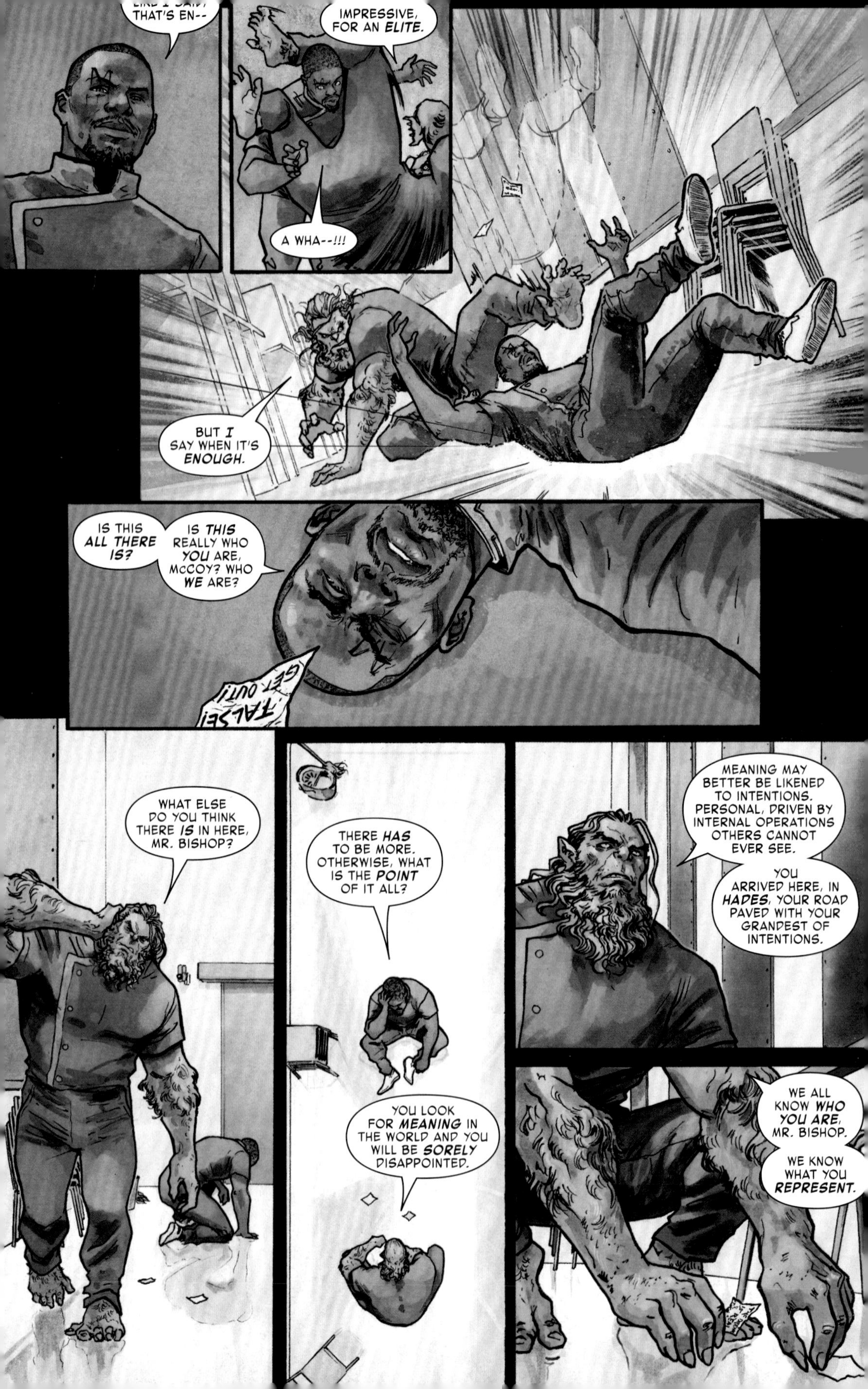
THAT'S EN--
IMPRESSIVE, FOR AN *ELITE.*
A WHA--!!!
BUT *I* SAY WHEN IT'S *ENOUGH.*
IS THIS *ALL THERE IS?*
IS *THIS* REALLY WHO *YOU* ARE, McCOY? WHO *WE* ARE?
GET OUT!
FALSE!
WHAT ELSE DO YOU THINK THERE *IS* IN HERE, MR. BISHOP?
THERE *HAS* TO BE MORE. OTHERWISE, WHAT IS THE *POINT* OF IT ALL?
YOU LOOK FOR *MEANING* IN THE WORLD AND YOU WILL BE *SORELY* DISAPPOINTED.
MEANING MAY BETTER BE LIKENED TO INTENTIONS. PERSONAL, DRIVEN BY INTERNAL OPERATIONS OTHERS CANNOT EVER SEE.
YOU ARRIVED HERE, IN *HADES*, YOUR ROAD PAVED WITH YOUR GRANDEST OF INTENTIONS.
WE ALL KNOW *WHO YOU ARE*, MR. BISHOP.
WE KNOW WHAT YOU *REPRESENT.*

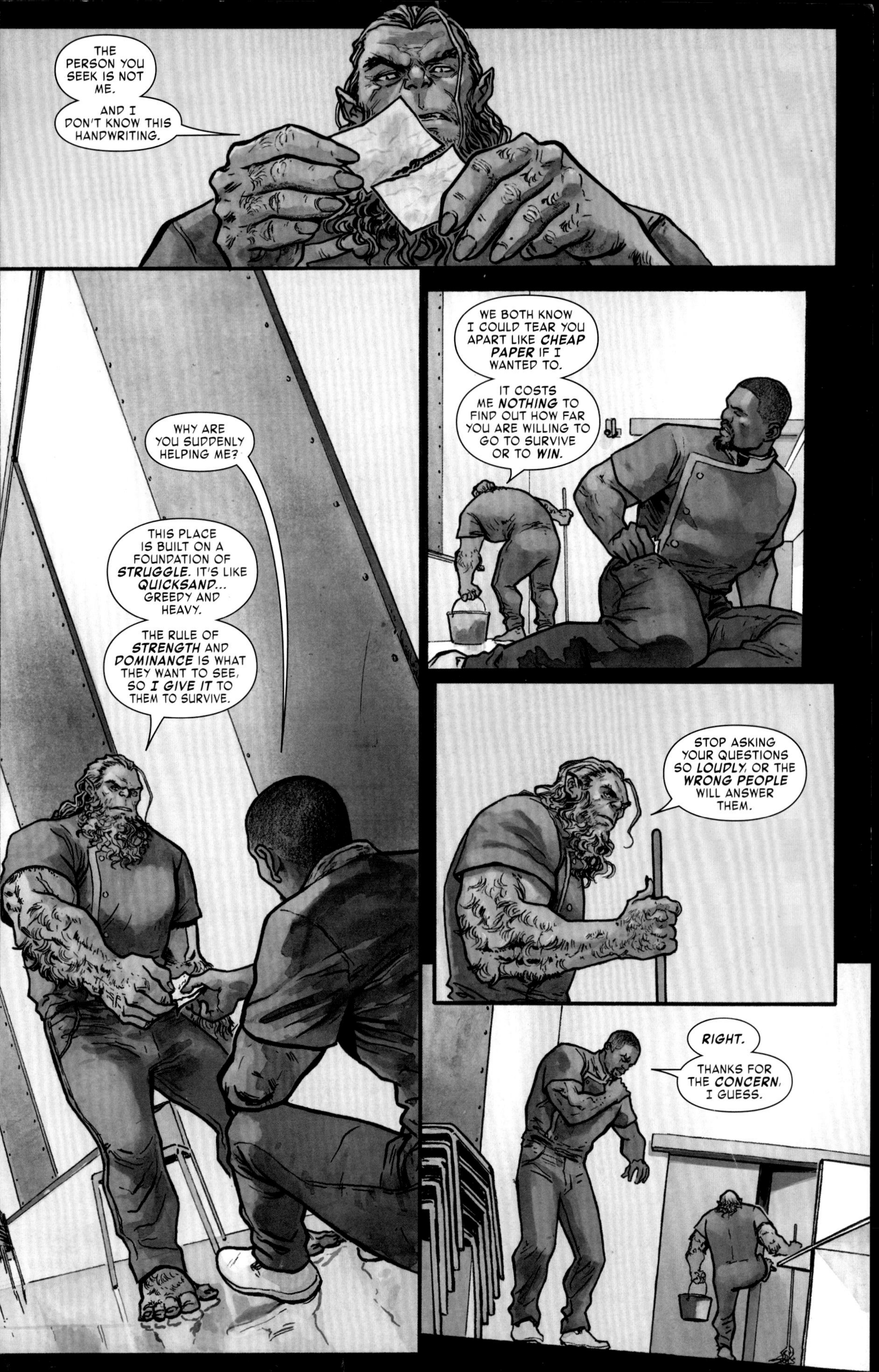
THE PERSON YOU SEEK IS NOT ME.
AND I DON'T KNOW THIS HANDWRITING.
WHY ARE YOU SUDDENLY HELPING ME?
THIS PLACE IS BUILT ON A FOUNDATION OF STRUGGLE. IT'S LIKE QUICKSAND... GREEDY AND HEAVY.
THE RULE OF STRENGTH AND DOMINANCE IS WHAT THEY WANT TO SEE, SO I GIVE IT TO THEM TO SURVIVE.
WE BOTH KNOW I COULD TEAR YOU APART LIKE CHEAP PAPER IF I WANTED TO.
IT COSTS ME NOTHING TO FIND OUT HOW FAR YOU ARE WILLING TO GO TO SURVIVE OR TO WIN.
STOP ASKING YOUR QUESTIONS SO LOUDLY, OR THE WRONG PEOPLE WILL ANSWER THEM.
RIGHT.
THANKS FOR THE CONCERN, I GUESS.

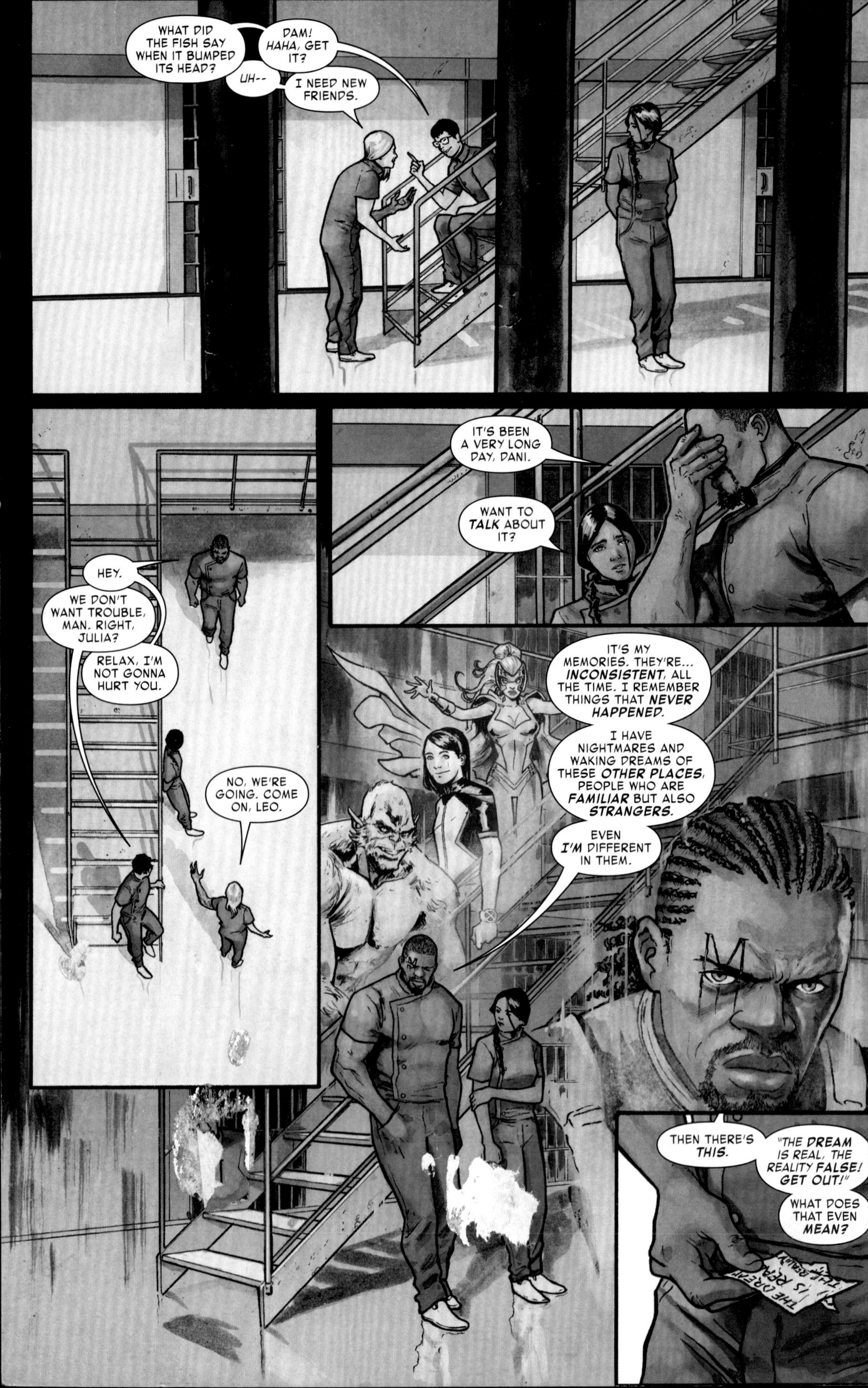
WHAT DID THE FISH SAY WHEN IT BUMPED ITS HEAD?
DAM! HAHA, GET IT?
UH--
I NEED NEW FRIENDS.
HEY.
WE DON'T WANT TROUBLE, MAN. RIGHT, JULIA?
RELAX, I'M NOT GONNA HURT YOU.
NO, WE'RE GOING. COME ON, LEO.
IT'S BEEN A VERY LONG DAY, DANI.
WANT TO TALK ABOUT IT?
IT'S MY MEMORIES. THEY'RE... INCONSISTENT, ALL THE TIME. I REMEMBER THINGS THAT NEVER HAPPENED.
I HAVE NIGHTMARES AND WAKING DREAMS OF THESE OTHER PLACES, PEOPLE WHO ARE FAMILIAR BUT ALSO STRANGERS.
EVEN I'M DIFFERENT IN THEM.
THEN THERE'S THIS.
"THE DREAM IS REAL, THE REALITY FALSE! GET OUT!"
WHAT DOES THAT EVEN MEAN?

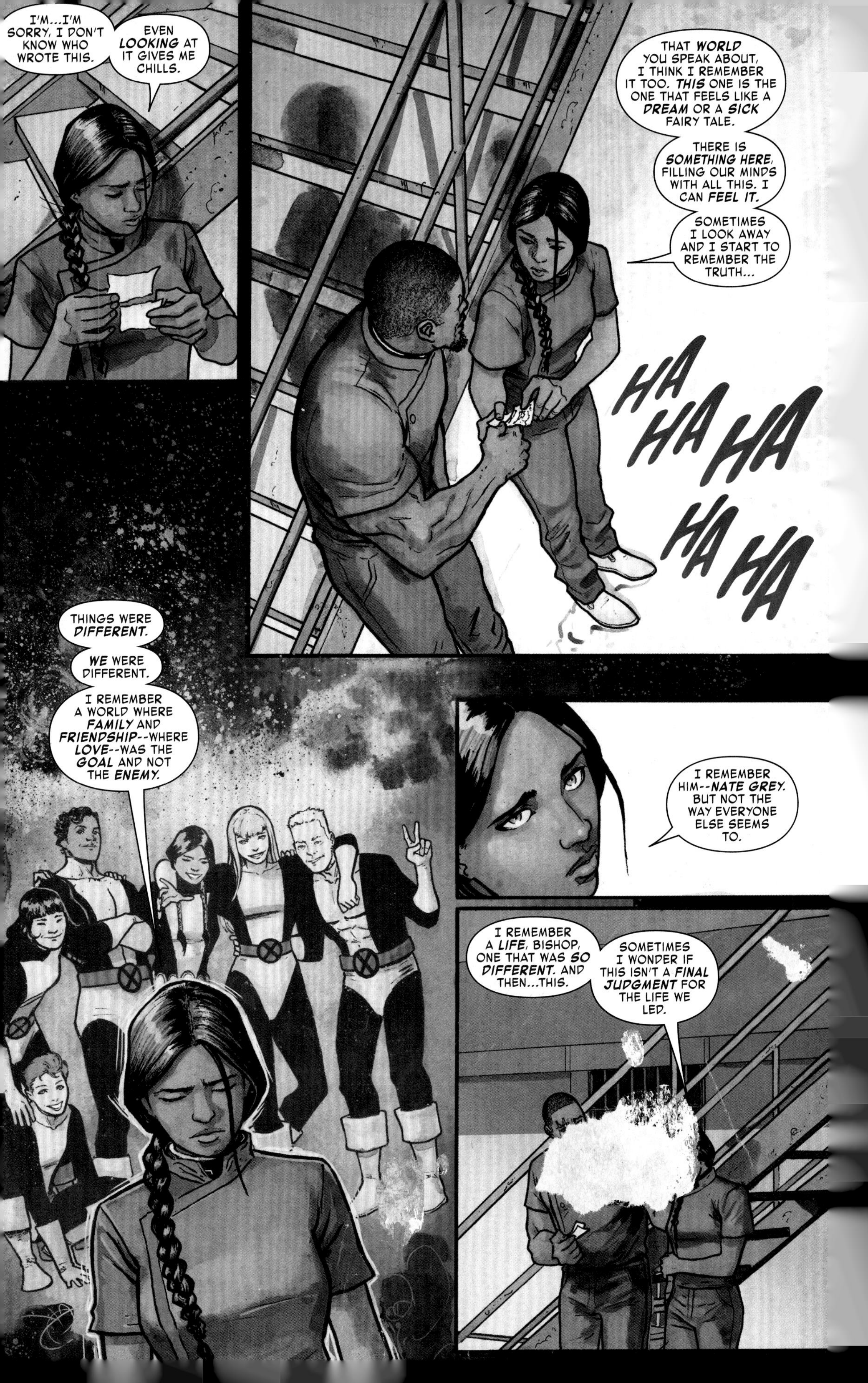
I'M...I'M SORRY, I DON'T KNOW WHO WROTE THIS.
EVEN LOOKING AT IT GIVES ME CHILLS.
THAT WORLD YOU SPEAK ABOUT, I THINK I REMEMBER IT TOO. THIS ONE IS THE ONE THAT FEELS LIKE A DREAM OR A SICK FAIRY TALE.
THERE IS SOMETHING HERE, FILLING OUR MINDS WITH ALL THIS. I CAN FEEL IT.
SOMETIMES I LOOK AWAY AND I START TO REMEMBER THE TRUTH...
HA HA HA HA HA HA
THINGS WERE DIFFERENT.
WE WERE DIFFERENT.
I REMEMBER A WORLD WHERE FAMILY AND FRIENDSHIP--WHERE LOVE--WAS THE GOAL AND NOT THE ENEMY.
I REMEMBER HIM--NATE GREY. BUT NOT THE WAY EVERYONE ELSE SEEMS TO.
I REMEMBER A LIFE, BISHOP, ONE THAT WAS SO DIFFERENT. AND THEN...THIS.
SOMETIMES I WONDER IF THIS ISN'T A FINAL JUDGMENT FOR THE LIFE WE LED.

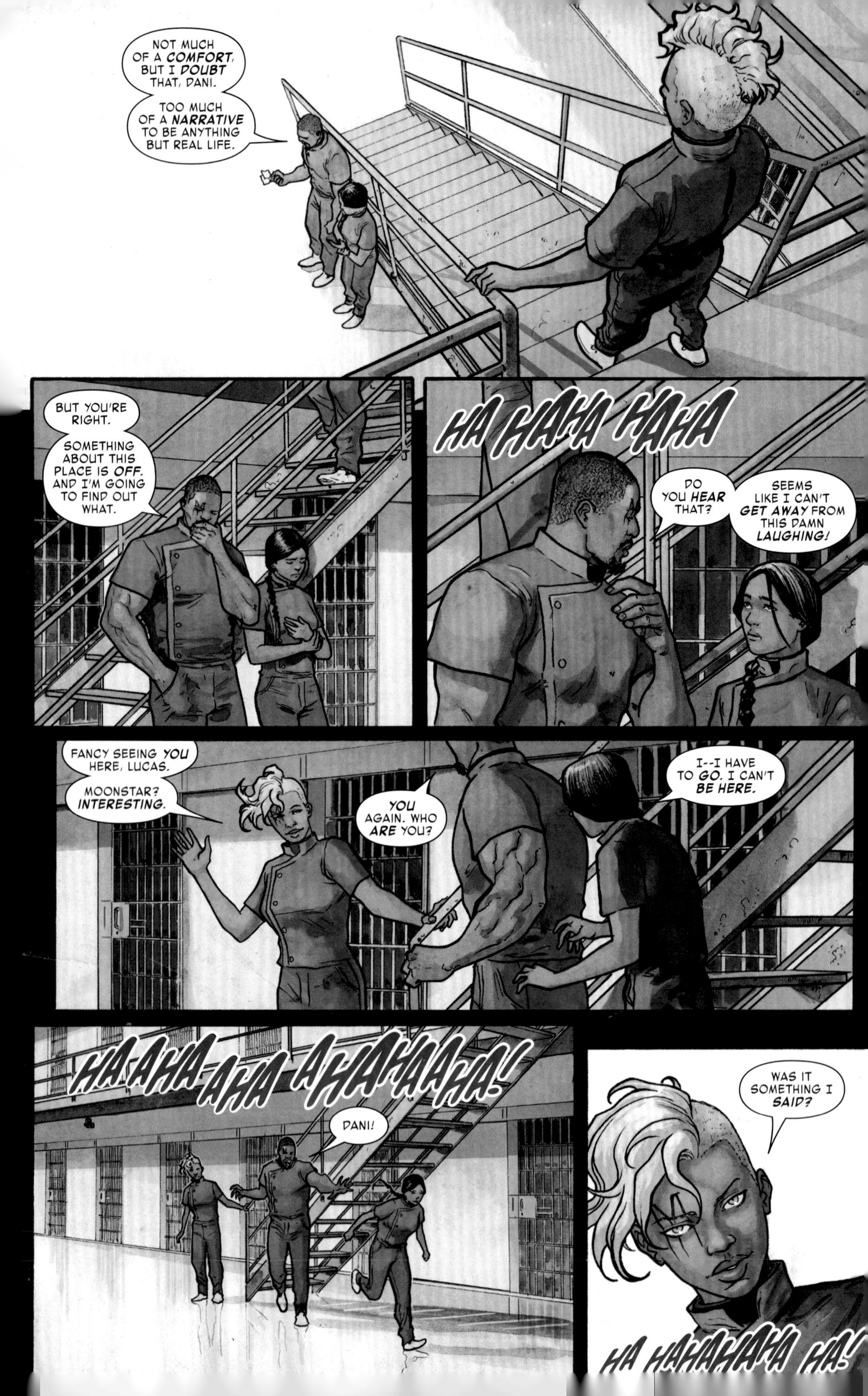
NOT MUCH OF A COMFORT, BUT I DOUBT THAT, DANI.
TOO MUCH OF A NARRATIVE TO BE ANYTHING BUT REAL LIFE.
BUT YOU'RE RIGHT.
SOMETHING ABOUT THIS PLACE IS OFF. AND I'M GOING TO FIND OUT WHAT.
HA HAHA HAHA
DO YOU HEAR THAT?
SEEMS LIKE I CAN'T GET AWAY FROM THIS DAMN LAUGHING!
FANCY SEEING YOU HERE, LUCAS.
MOONSTAR? INTERESTING.
YOU AGAIN. WHO ARE YOU?
I--I HAVE TO GO. I CAN'T BE HERE.
HA AHA AHA AHAHAAAHA!
DANI!
WAS IT SOMETHING I SAID?
HA HAHAHAHA HA!

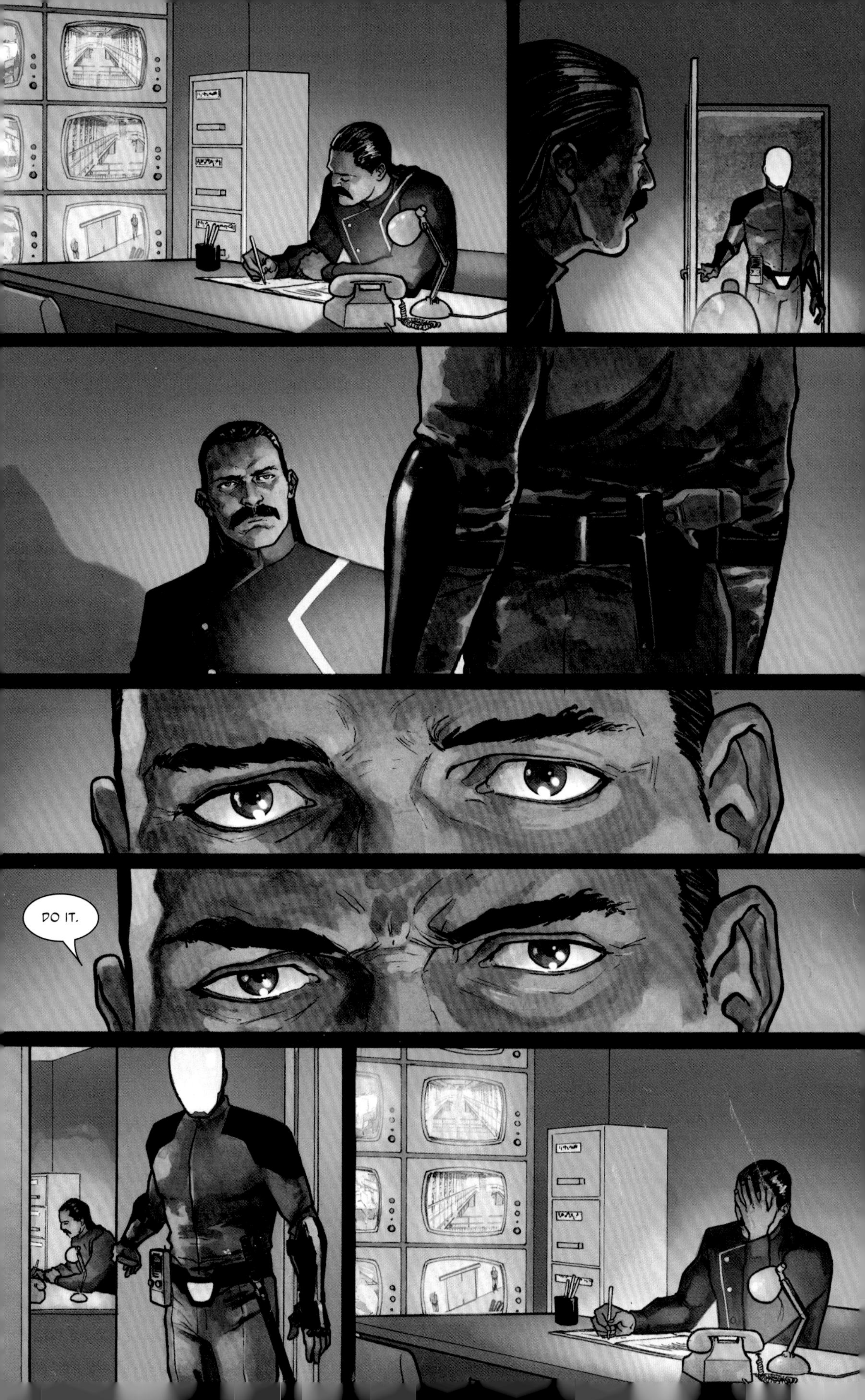
DO IT.

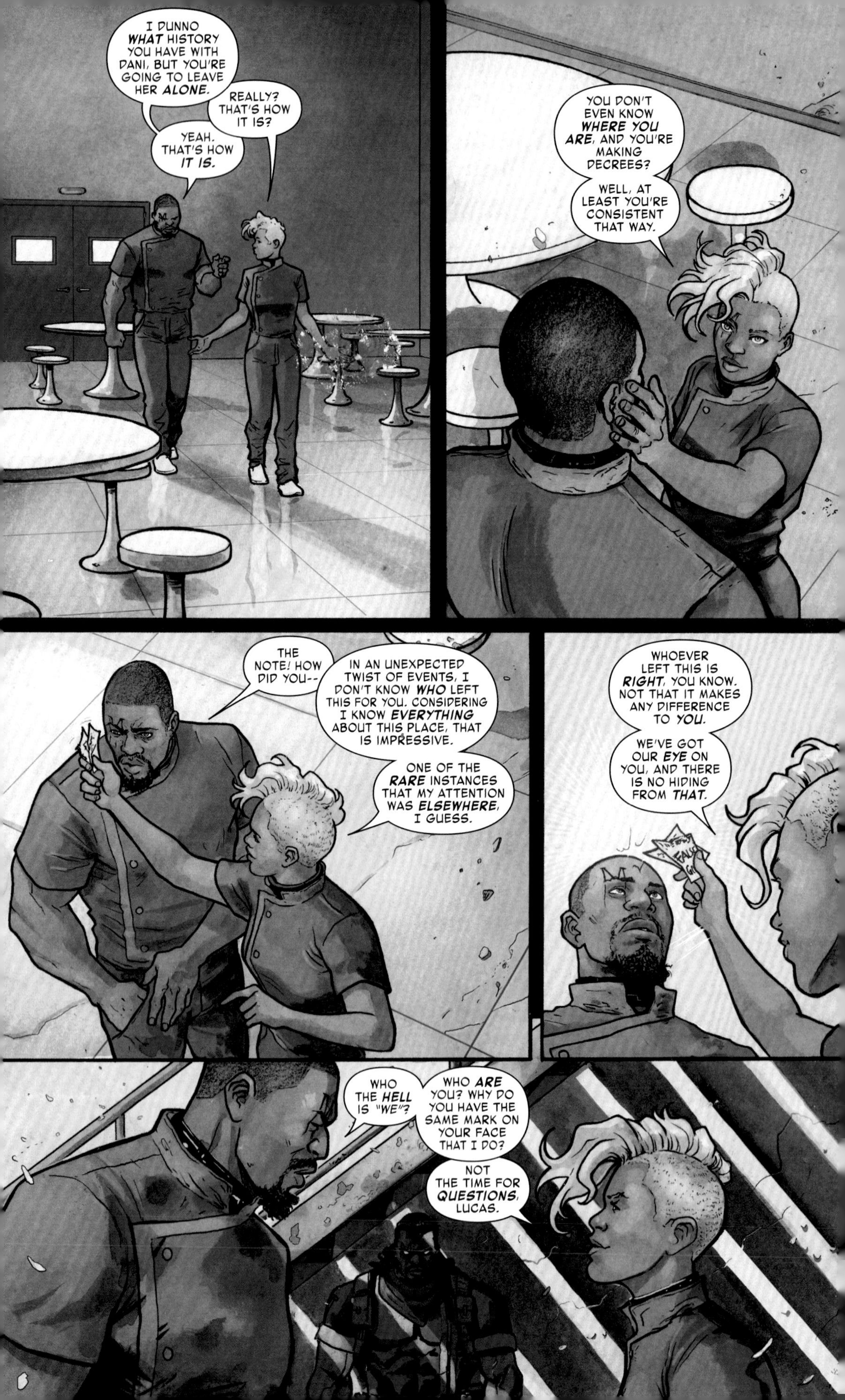
I DUNNO WHAT HISTORY YOU HAVE WITH DANI, BUT YOU'RE GOING TO LEAVE HER ALONE.
REALLY? THAT'S HOW IT IS?
YEAH. THAT'S HOW IT IS.
YOU DON'T EVEN KNOW WHERE YOU ARE, AND YOU'RE MAKING DECREES?
WELL, AT LEAST YOU'RE CONSISTENT THAT WAY.
THE NOTE! HOW DID YOU--
IN AN UNEXPECTED TWIST OF EVENTS, I DON'T KNOW WHO LEFT THIS FOR YOU. CONSIDERING I KNOW EVERYTHING ABOUT THIS PLACE, THAT IS IMPRESSIVE.
ONE OF THE RARE INSTANCES THAT MY ATTENTION WAS ELSEWHERE, I GUESS.
WHOEVER LEFT THIS IS RIGHT, YOU KNOW. NOT THAT IT MAKES ANY DIFFERENCE TO YOU.
WE'VE GOT OUR EYE ON YOU, AND THERE IS NO HIDING FROM THAT.
WHO THE HELL IS "WE"?
WHO ARE YOU? WHY DO YOU HAVE THE SAME MARK ON YOUR FACE THAT I DO?
NOT THE TIME FOR QUESTIONS, LUCAS.

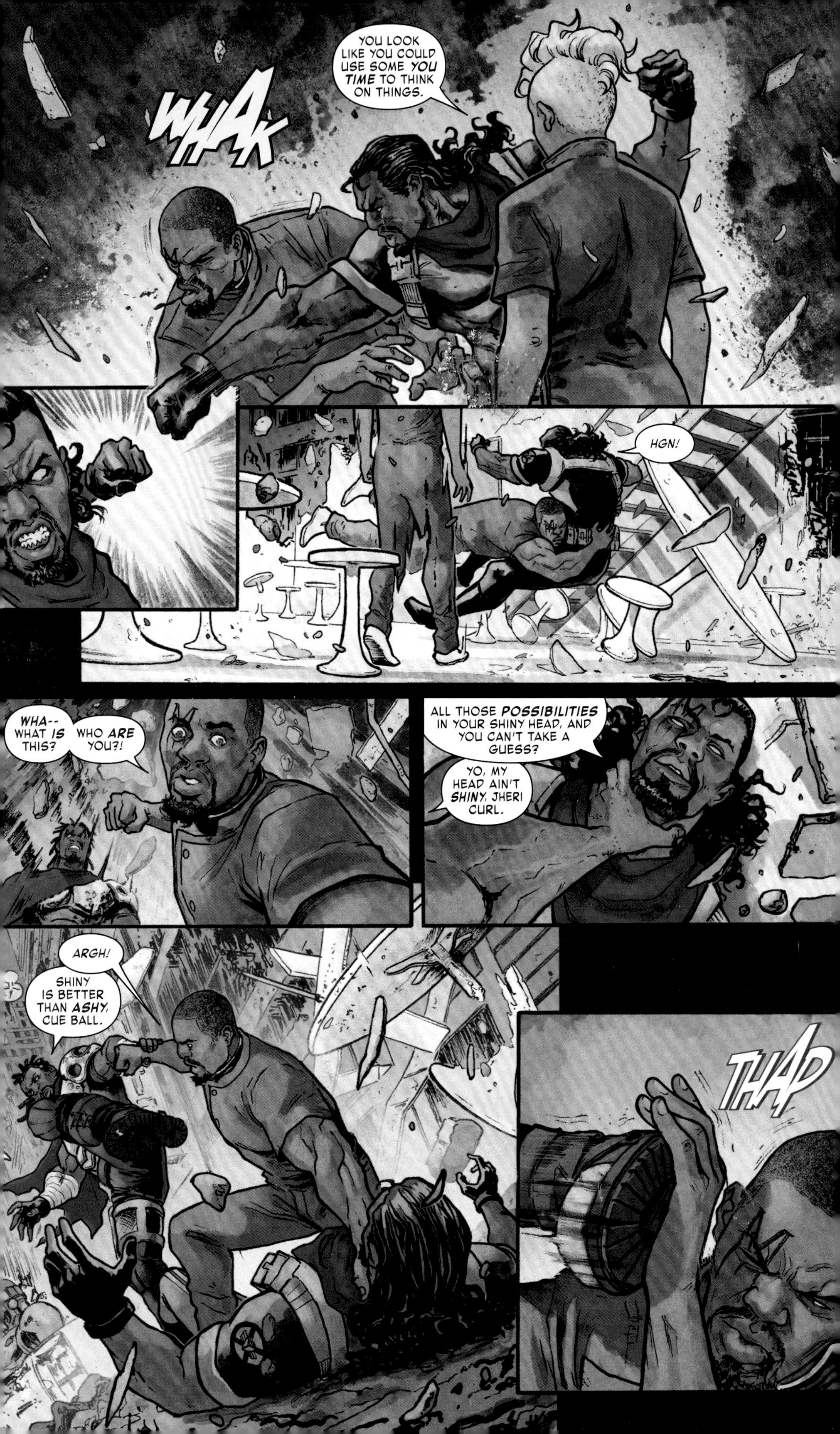

YOU LOOK LIKE YOU COULD USE SOME *YOU TIME* TO THINK ON THINGS.
WHAK
HGN!
WHA-- WHAT *IS* THIS?
WHO *ARE* YOU?!
ALL THOSE *POSSIBILITIES* IN YOUR SHINY HEAD, AND YOU CAN'T TAKE A GUESS?
YO, MY HEAD AIN'T *SHINY*, JHERI CURL.
ARGH!
SHINY IS BETTER THAN *ASHY*, CUE BALL.
THAP

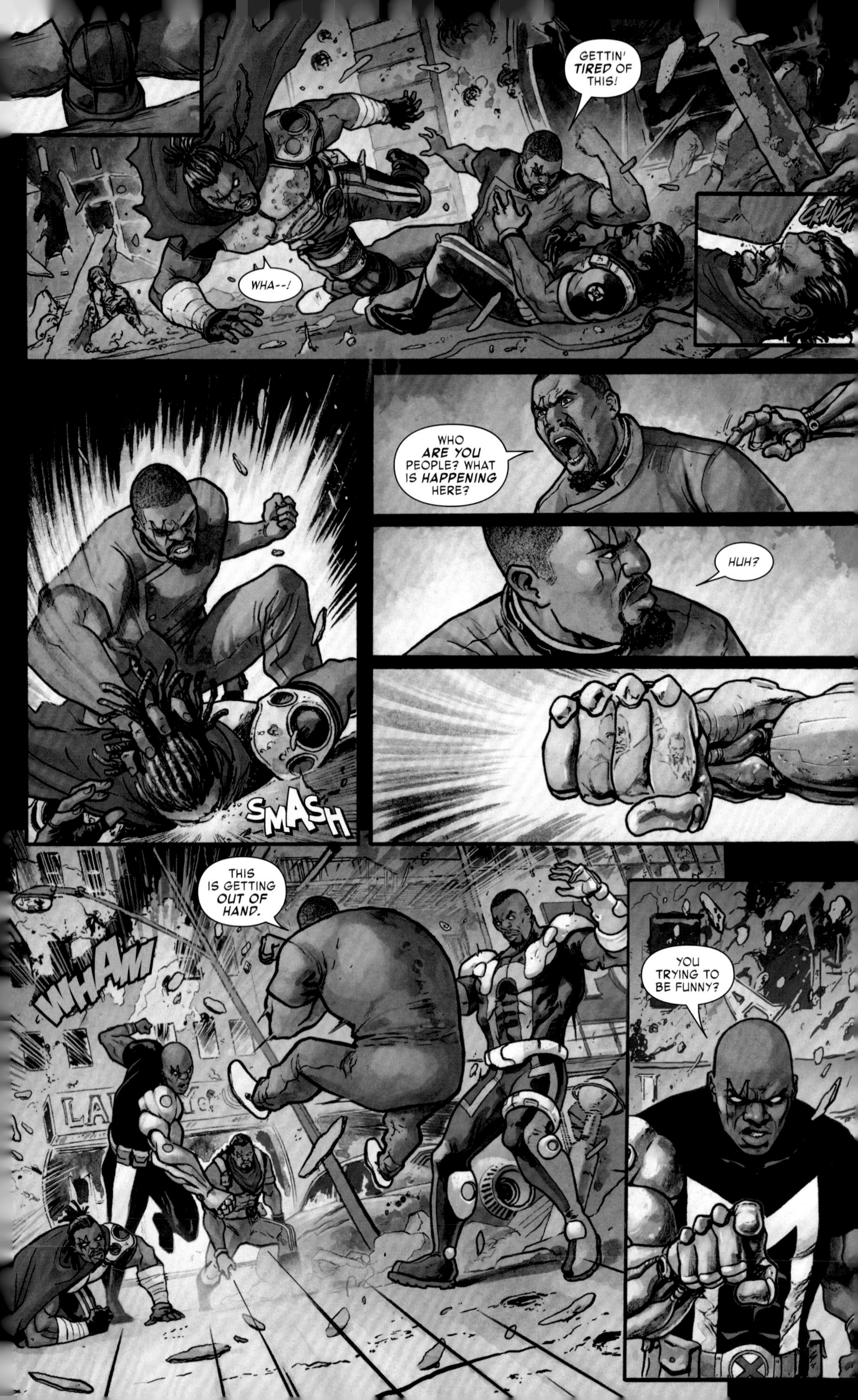
GETTIN' TIRED OF THIS!
WHA--!
CRUNCH
SMASH
WHO ARE YOU PEOPLE? WHAT IS HAPPENING HERE?
HUH?
THIS IS GETTING OUT OF HAND.
WHAM
YOU TRYING TO BE FUNNY?

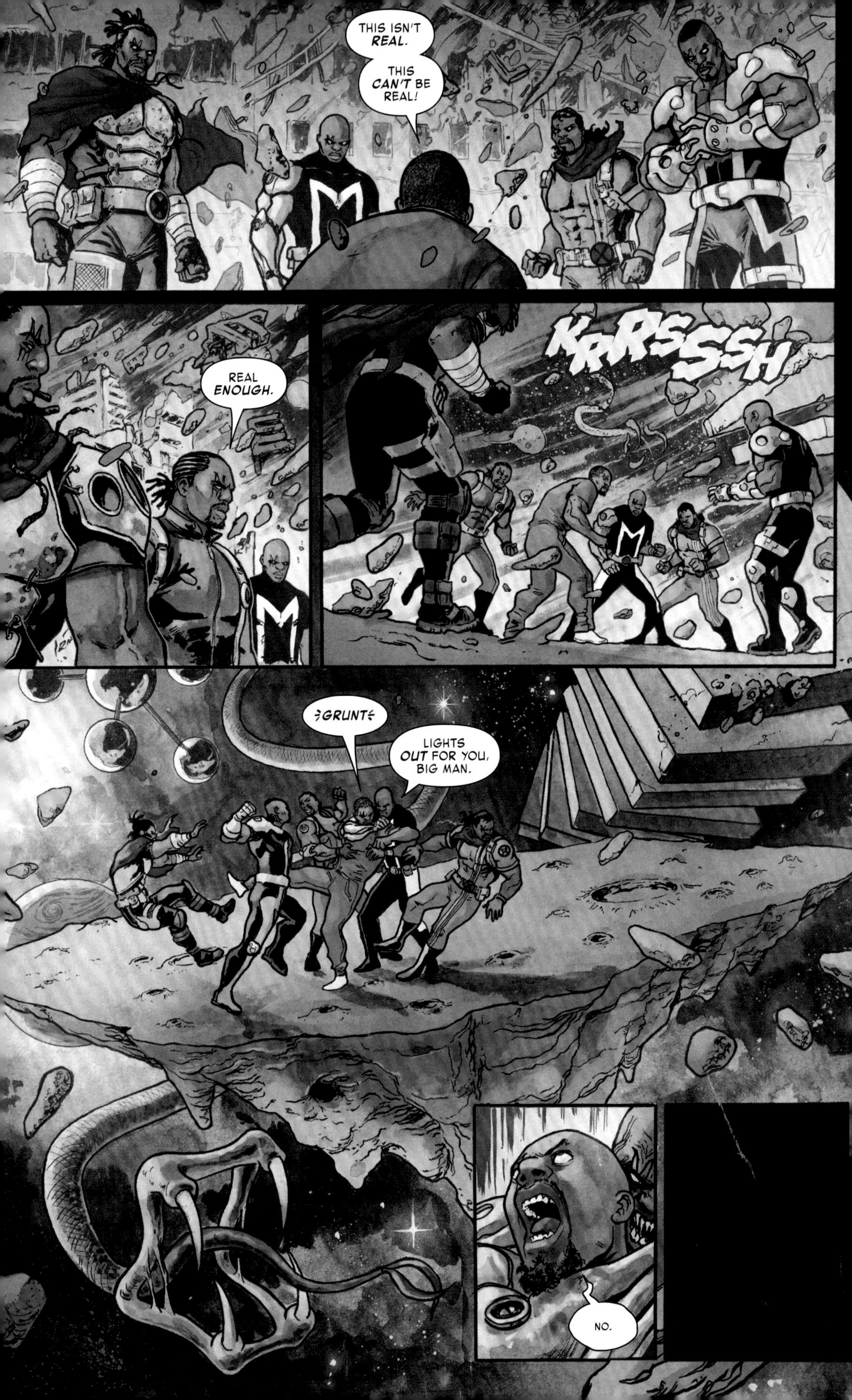

THIS ISN'T REAL.
THIS CAN'T BE REAL!
REAL ENOUGH.
KRRSSSH
GRUNT
LIGHTS OUT FOR YOU, BIG MAN.
NO.

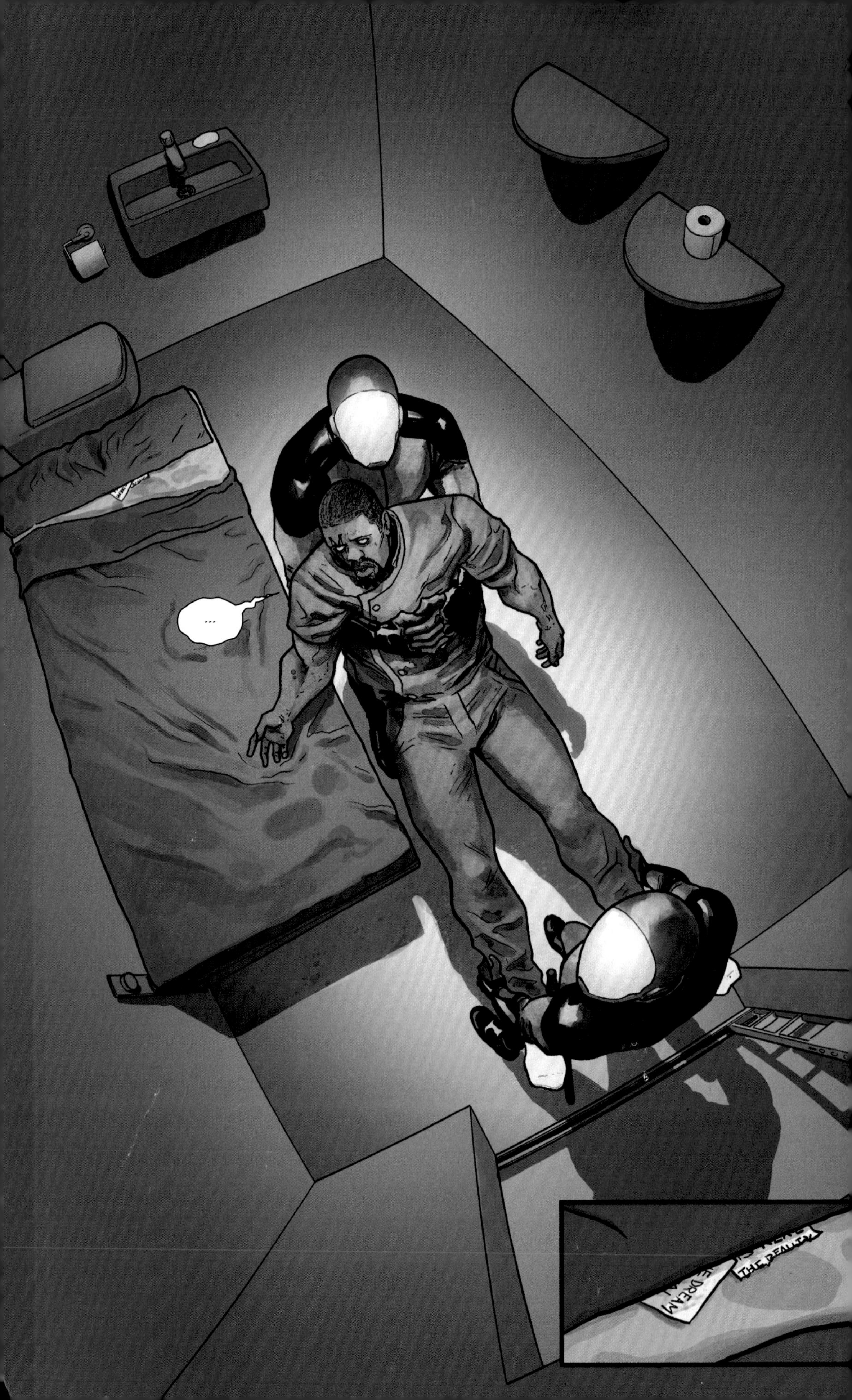
...
DREAM
THE REALITY

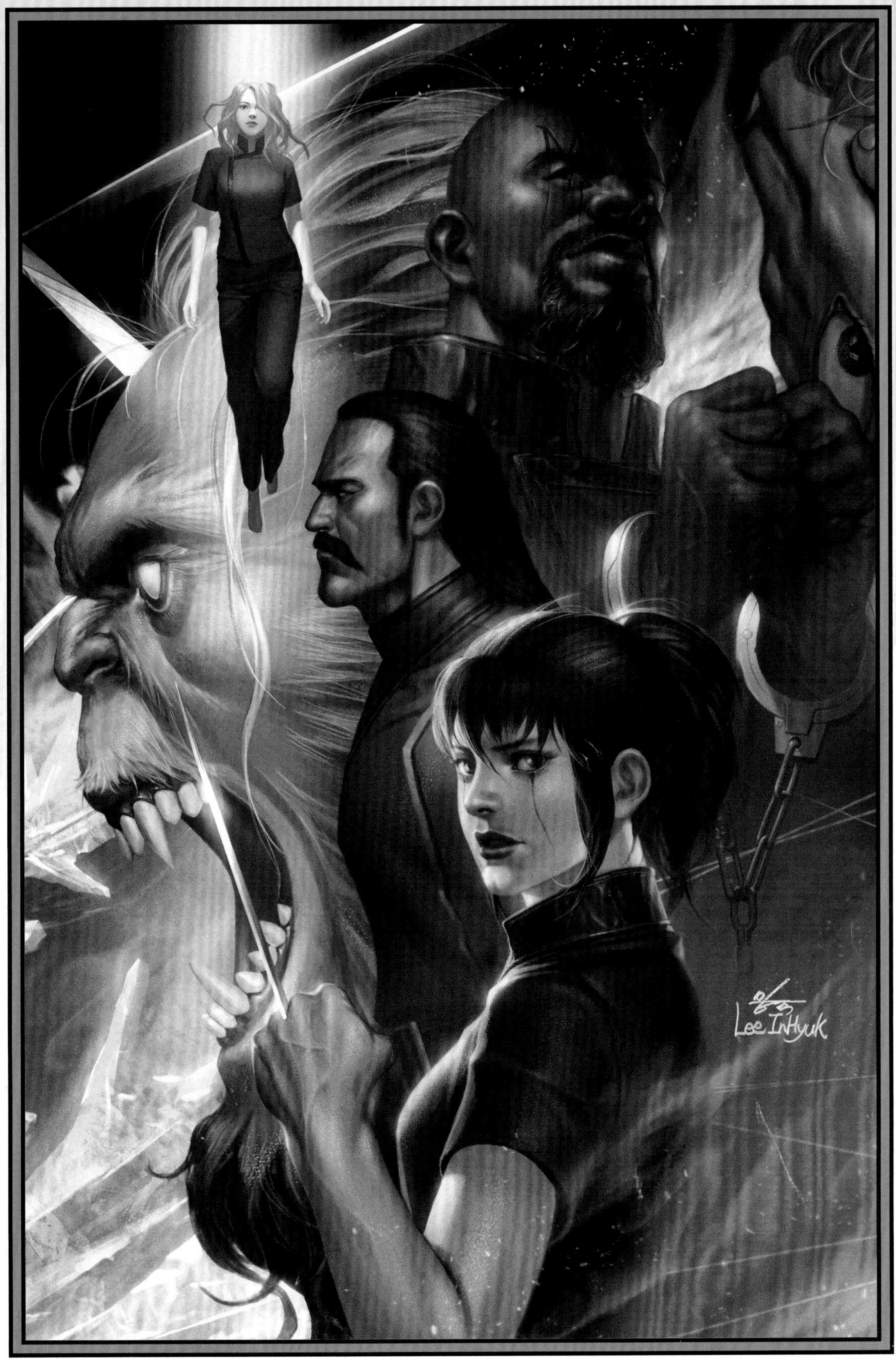
Lee InHyuk

#1 VARIANT BY **INHYUK LEE**

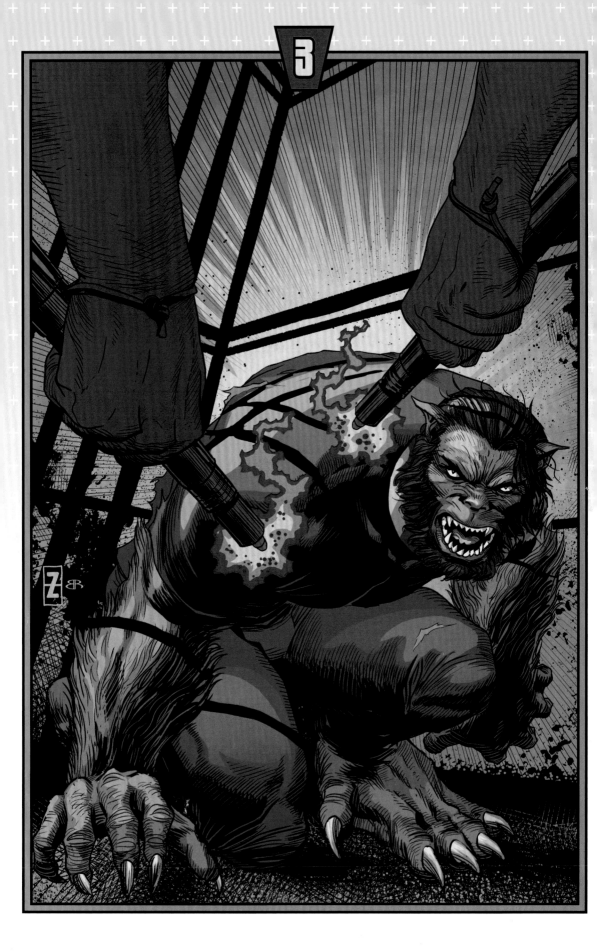

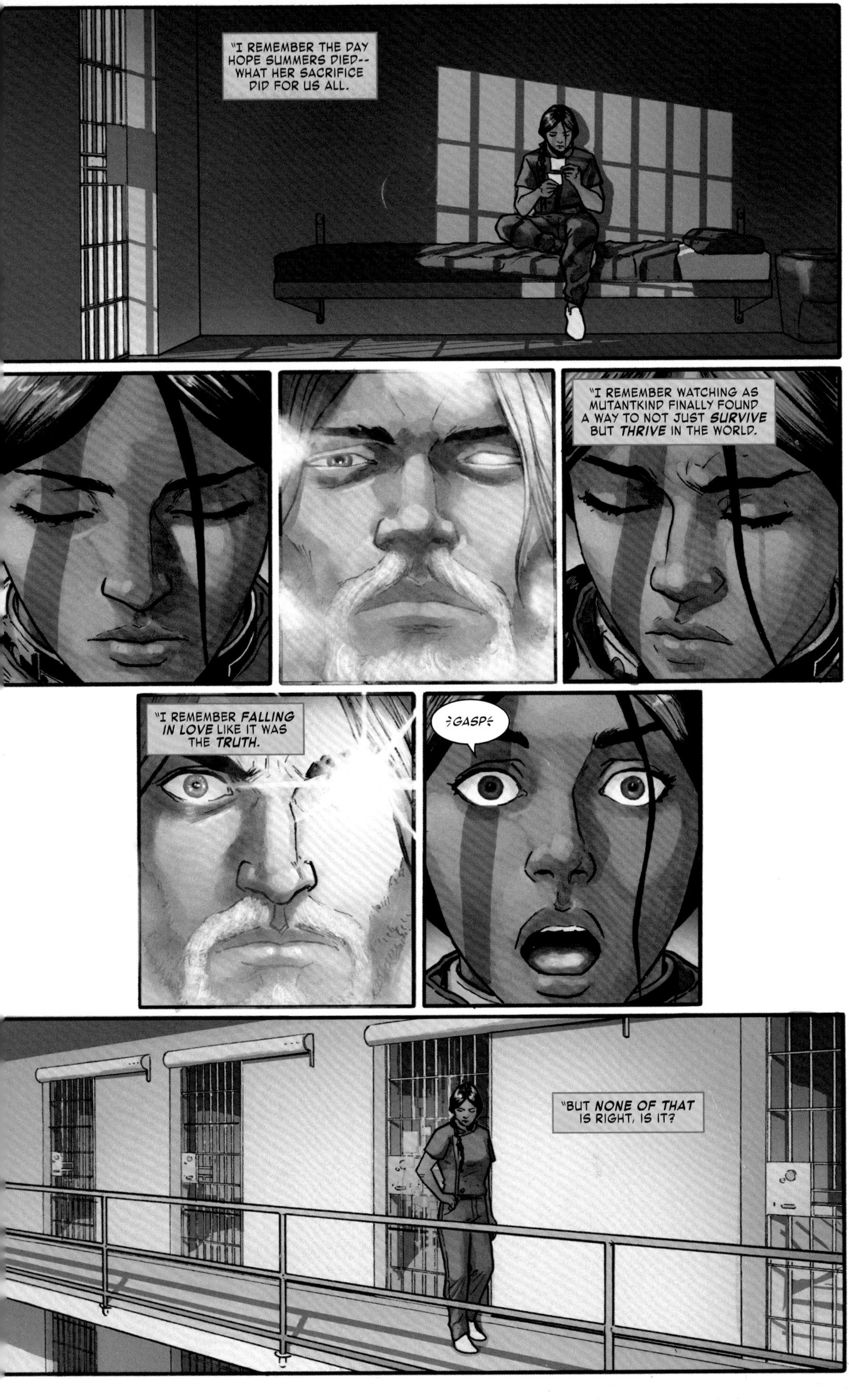
"I REMEMBER THE DAY HOPE SUMMERS DIED-- WHAT HER SACRIFICE DID FOR US ALL.
"I REMEMBER WATCHING AS MUTANTKIND FINALLY FOUND A WAY TO NOT JUST SURVIVE BUT THRIVE IN THE WORLD.
"I REMEMBER FALLING IN LOVE LIKE IT WAS THE TRUTH.
GASP
"BUT NONE OF THAT IS RIGHT, IS IT?

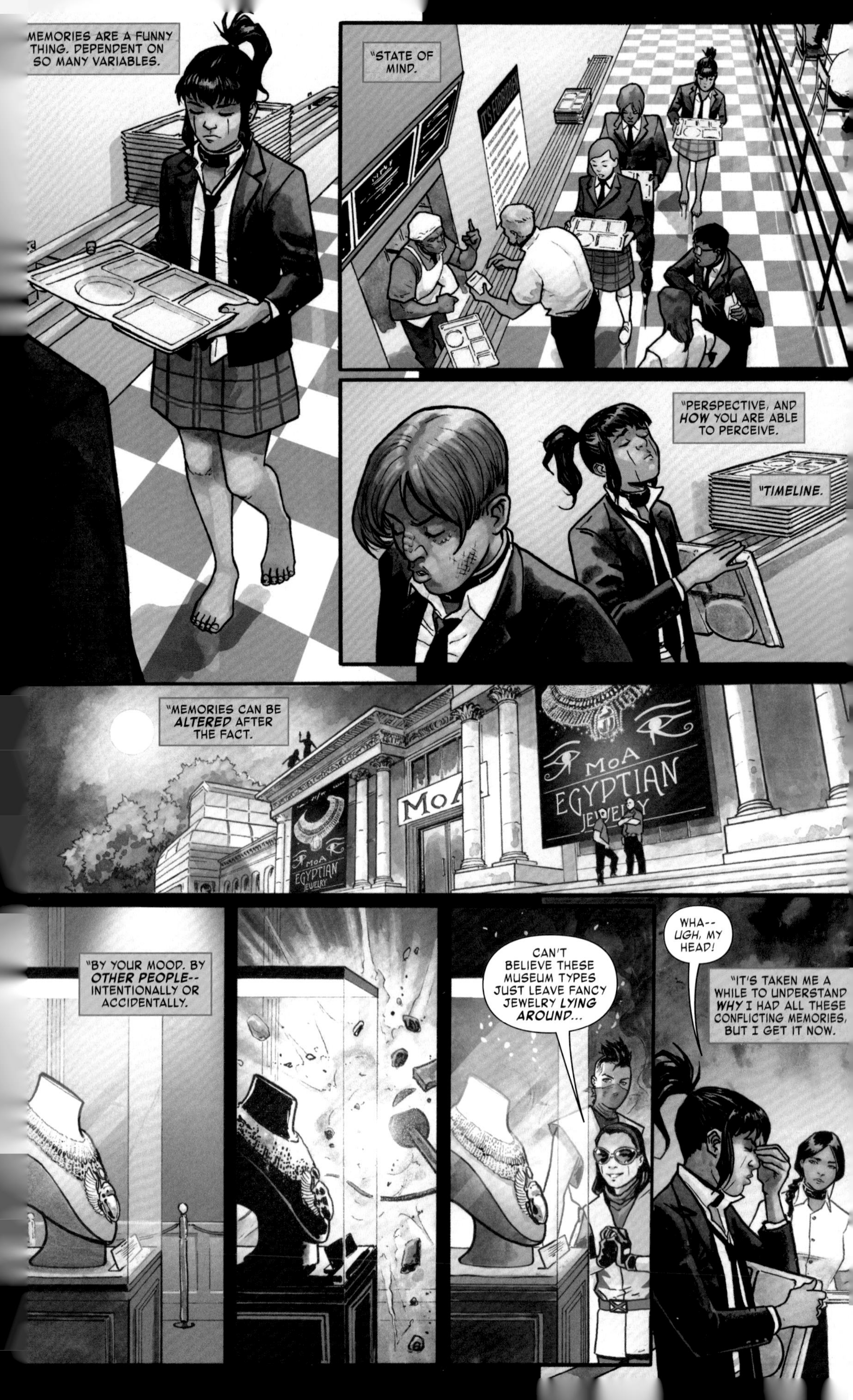
MEMORIES ARE A FUNNY THING. DEPENDENT ON SO MANY VARIABLES.
"STATE OF MIND.
"PERSPECTIVE, AND HOW YOU ARE ABLE TO PERCEIVE.
"TIMELINE.
"MEMORIES CAN BE ALTERED AFTER THE FACT.
MoA
MoA EGYPTIAN JEWELRY
"BY YOUR MOOD. BY OTHER PEOPLE-- INTENTIONALLY OR ACCIDENTALLY.
CAN'T BELIEVE THESE MUSEUM TYPES JUST LEAVE FANCY JEWELRY LYING AROUND...
WHA-- UGH, MY HEAD!
"IT'S TAKEN ME A WHILE TO UNDERSTAND WHY I HAD ALL THESE CONFLICTING MEMORIES, BUT I GET IT NOW.

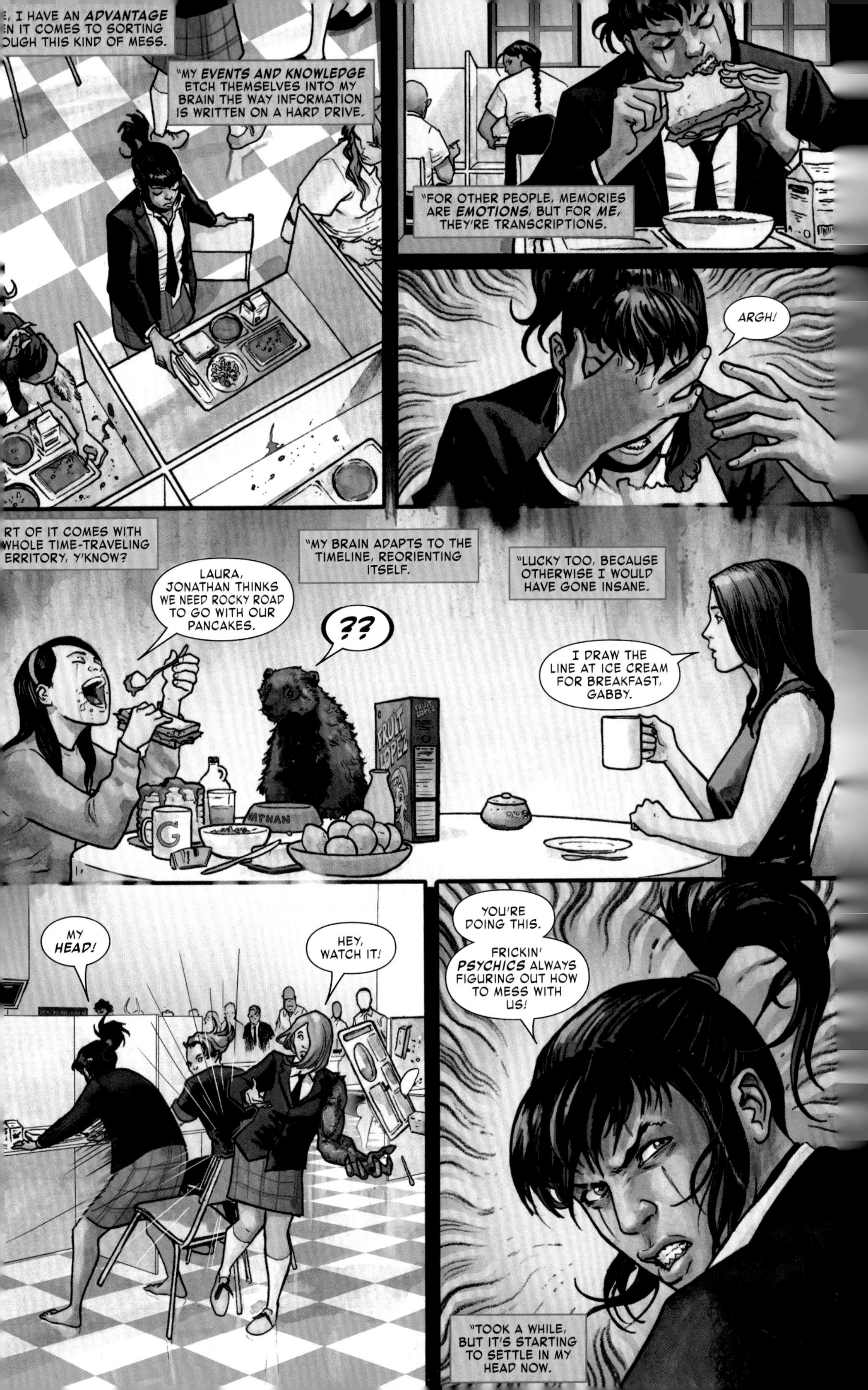

E, I HAVE AN ADVANTAGE EN IT COMES TO SORTING OUGH THIS KIND OF MESS.
"MY EVENTS AND KNOWLEDGE ETCH THEMSELVES INTO MY BRAIN THE WAY INFORMATION IS WRITTEN ON A HARD DRIVE.
"FOR OTHER PEOPLE, MEMORIES ARE EMOTIONS, BUT FOR ME, THEY'RE TRANSCRIPTIONS.
ARGH!
RT OF IT COMES WITH WHOLE TIME-TRAVELING ERRITORY, Y'KNOW?
"MY BRAIN ADAPTS TO THE TIMELINE, REORIENTING ITSELF.
"LUCKY TOO, BECAUSE OTHERWISE I WOULD HAVE GONE INSANE.
LAURA, JONATHAN THINKS WE NEED ROCKY ROAD TO GO WITH OUR PANCAKES.
??
I DRAW THE LINE AT ICE CREAM FOR BREAKFAST, GABBY.
MY HEAD!
HEY, WATCH IT!
YOU'RE DOING THIS.
FRICKIN' PSYCHICS ALWAYS FIGURING OUT HOW TO MESS WITH US!
"TOOK A WHILE, BUT IT'S STARTING TO SETTLE IN MY HEAD NOW.

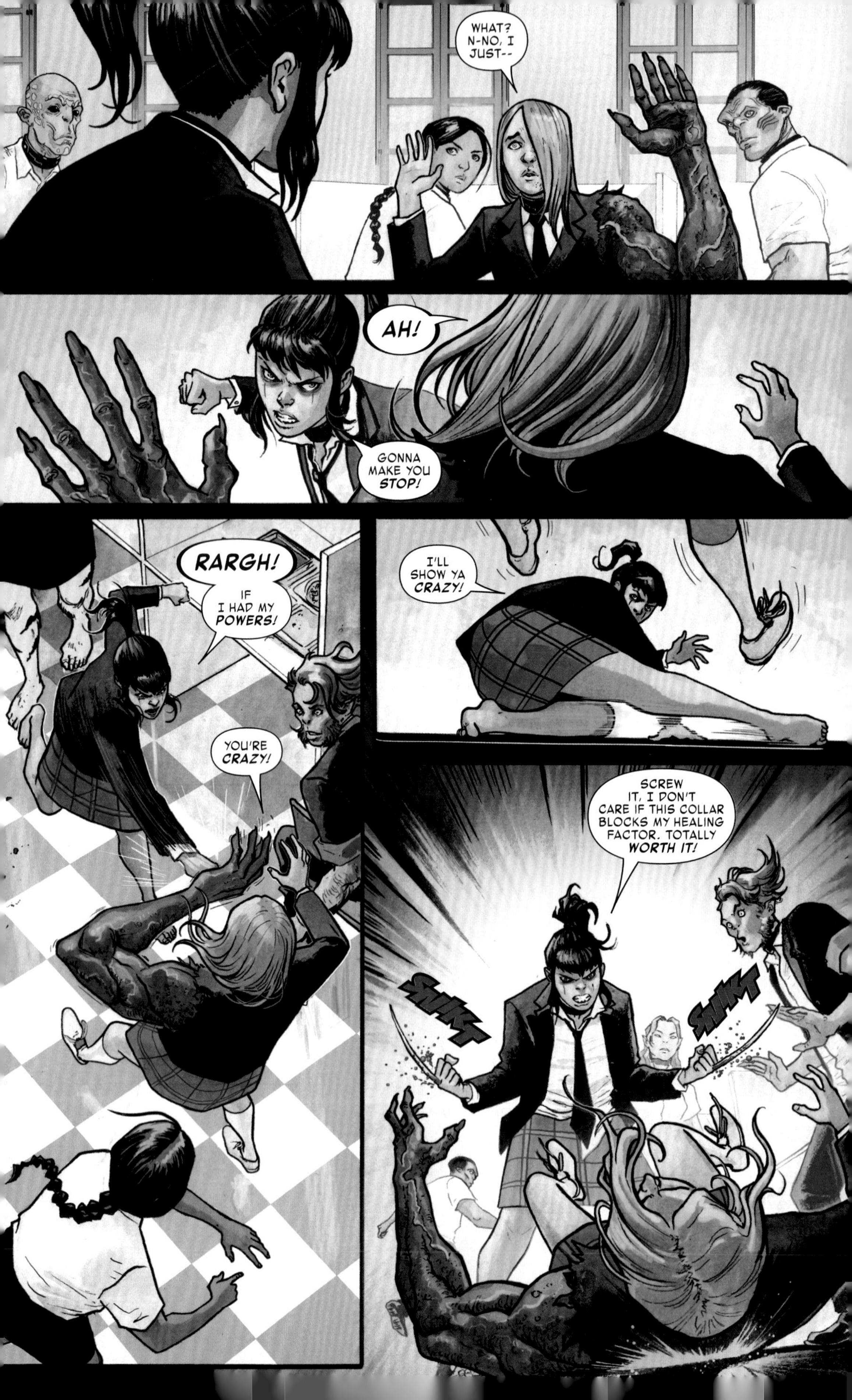
WHAT? N-NO, I JUST--
AH!
GONNA MAKE YOU STOP!
RARGH!
IF I HAD MY POWERS!
YOU'RE CRAZY!
I'LL SHOW YA CRAZY!
SCREW IT, I DON'T CARE IF THIS COLLAR BLOCKS MY HEALING FACTOR. TOTALLY WORTH IT!
SNIKT
SNIKT

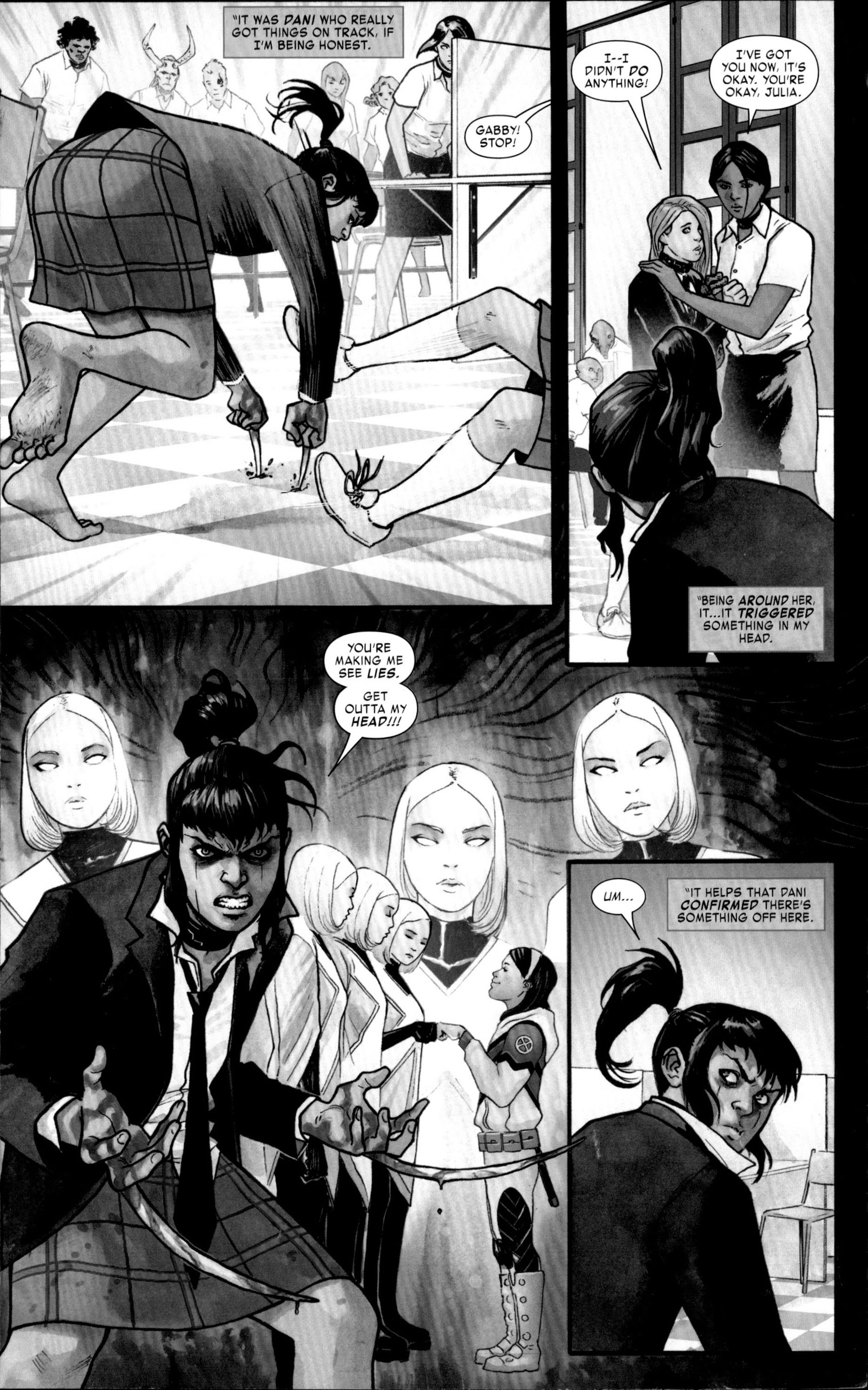
"IT WAS DANI WHO REALLY GOT THINGS ON TRACK, IF I'M BEING HONEST.
GABBY! STOP!
I--I DIDN'T DO ANYTHING!
I'VE GOT YOU NOW, IT'S OKAY. YOU'RE OKAY, JULIA.
"BEING AROUND HER, IT...IT TRIGGERED SOMETHING IN MY HEAD.
YOU'RE MAKING ME SEE LIES.
GET OUTTA MY HEAD!!!
UM...
"IT HELPS THAT DANI CONFIRMED THERE'S SOMETHING OFF HERE.

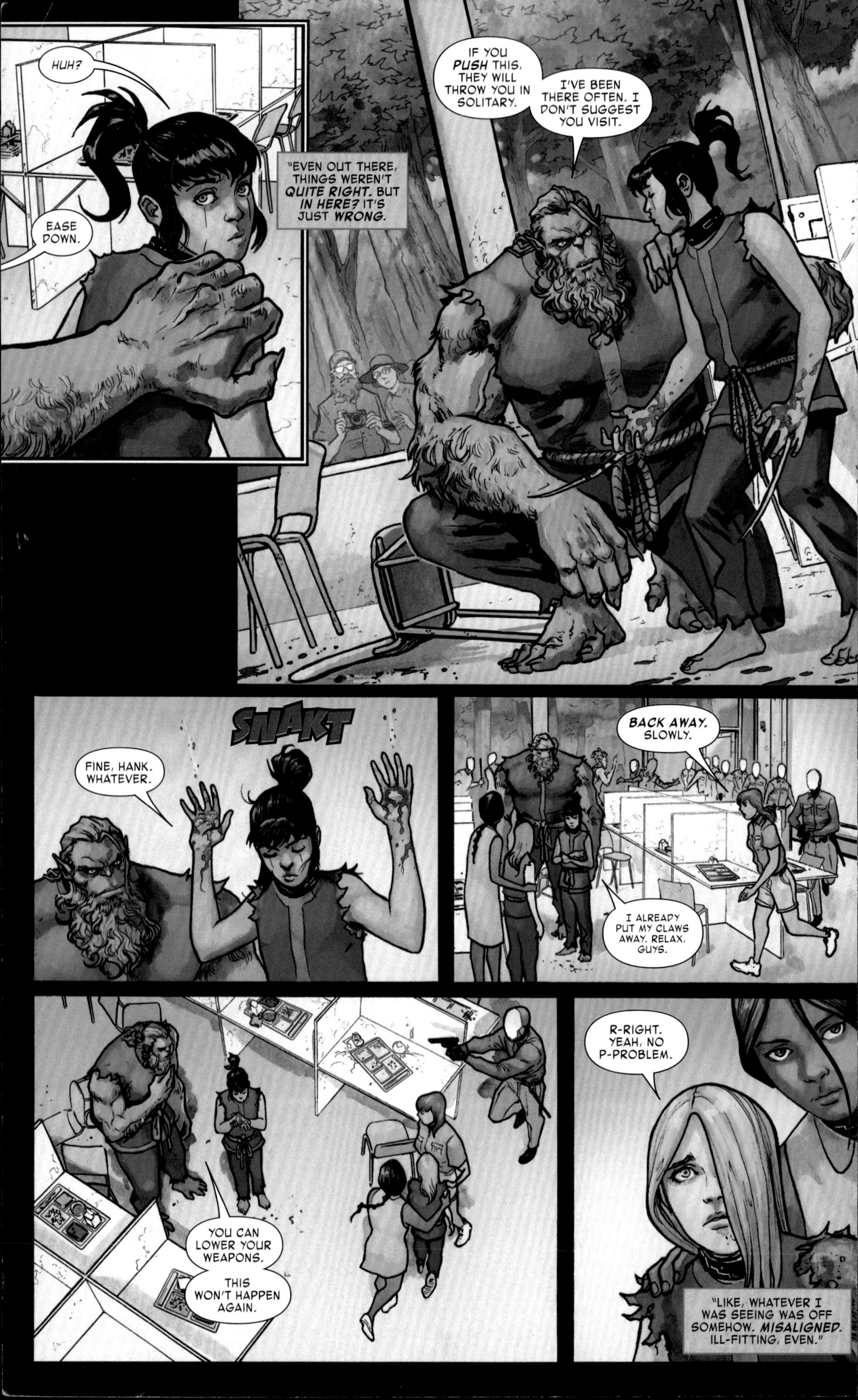
HUH?
EASE DOWN.
"EVEN OUT THERE, THINGS WEREN'T QUITE RIGHT. BUT IN HERE? IT'S JUST WRONG.
IF YOU PUSH THIS, THEY WILL THROW YOU IN SOLITARY.
I'VE BEEN THERE OFTEN. I DON'T SUGGEST YOU VISIT.
SNAKT
FINE, HANK. WHATEVER.
BACK AWAY. SLOWLY.
I ALREADY PUT MY CLAWS AWAY. RELAX, GUYS.
YOU CAN LOWER YOUR WEAPONS.
THIS WON'T HAPPEN AGAIN.
R-RIGHT. YEAH, NO P-PROBLEM.
"LIKE, WHATEVER I WAS SEEING WAS OFF SOMEHOW. MISALIGNED. ILL-FITTING, EVEN."

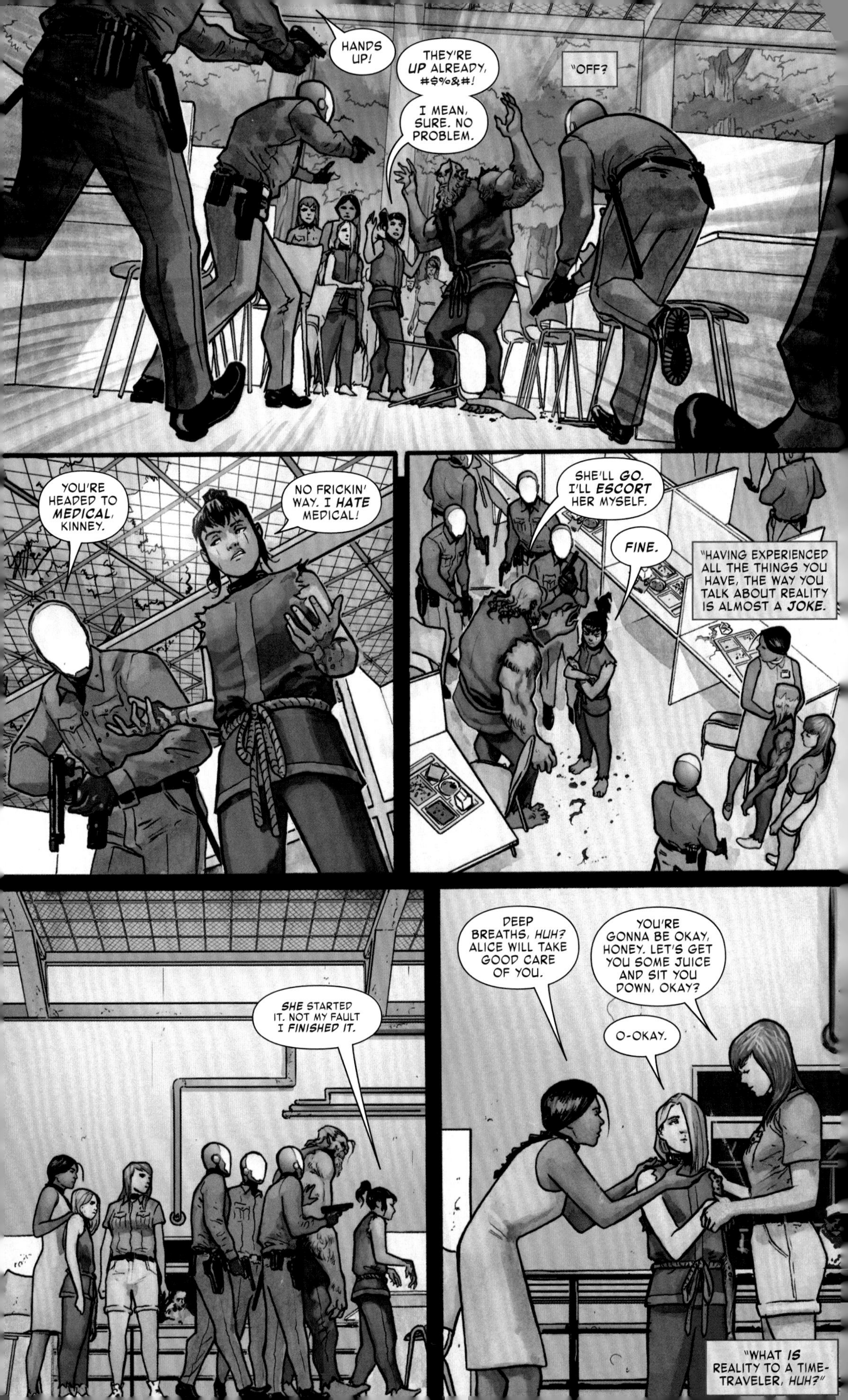
HANDS UP!
THEY'RE UP ALREADY, #$%&#!
I MEAN, SURE. NO PROBLEM.
"OFF?
YOU'RE HEADED TO MEDICAL, KINNEY.
NO FRICKIN' WAY. I HATE MEDICAL!
SHE'LL GO. I'LL ESCORT HER MYSELF.
FINE.
"HAVING EXPERIENCED ALL THE THINGS YOU HAVE, THE WAY YOU TALK ABOUT REALITY IS ALMOST A JOKE.
SHE STARTED IT. NOT MY FAULT I FINISHED IT.
DEEP BREATHS, HUH? ALICE WILL TAKE GOOD CARE OF YOU.
YOU'RE GONNA BE OKAY, HONEY. LET'S GET YOU SOME JUICE AND SIT YOU DOWN, OKAY?
O-OKAY.
"WHAT IS REALITY TO A TIME-TRAVELER, HUH?"

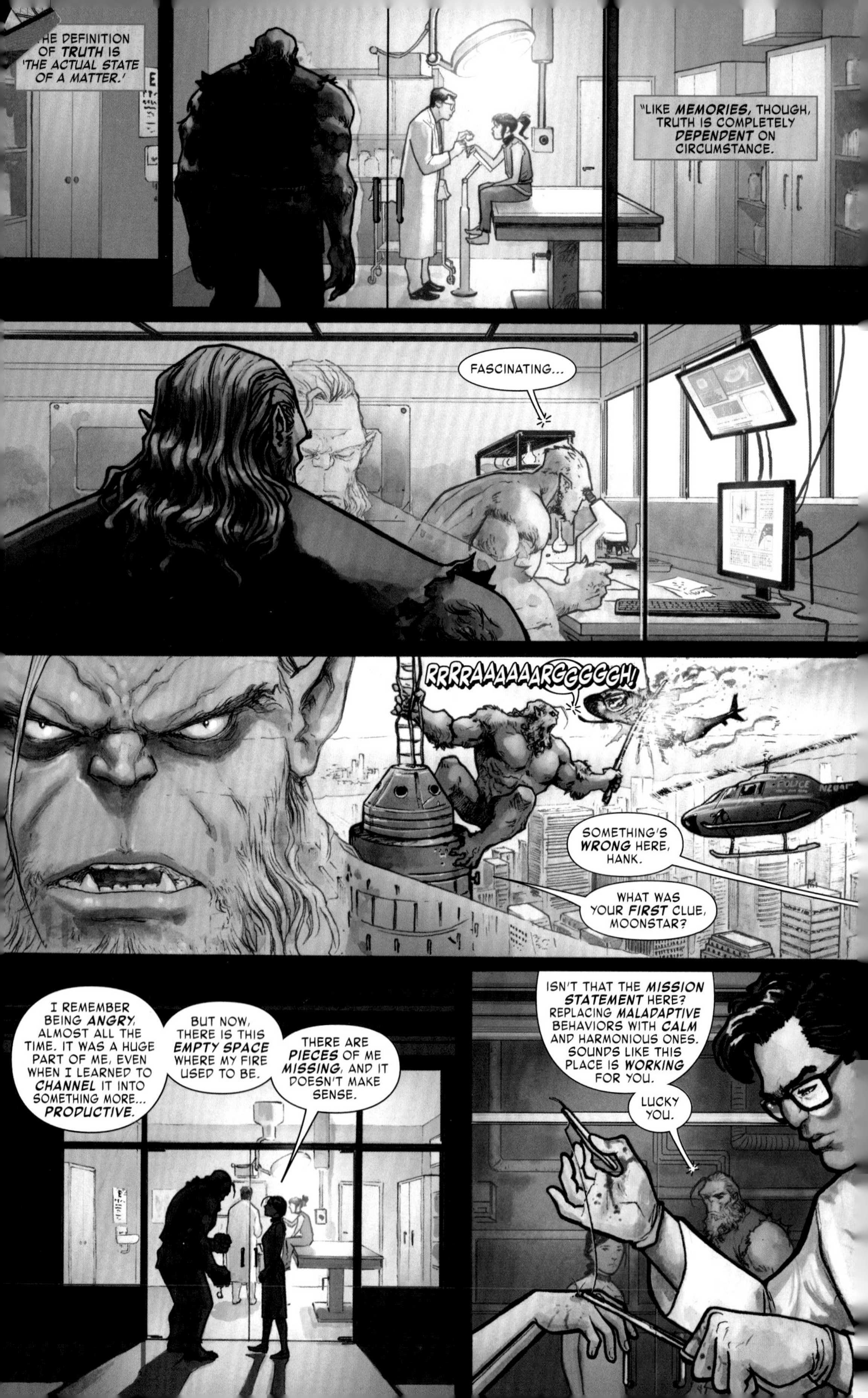
THE DEFINITION OF TRUTH IS 'THE ACTUAL STATE OF A MATTER.'
"LIKE MEMORIES, THOUGH, TRUTH IS COMPLETELY DEPENDENT ON CIRCUMSTANCE.
FASCINATING...
RRRRAAAAAARGGGGGH!
SOMETHING'S WRONG HERE, HANK.
WHAT WAS YOUR FIRST CLUE, MOONSTAR?
I REMEMBER BEING ANGRY, ALMOST ALL THE TIME. IT WAS A HUGE PART OF ME, EVEN WHEN I LEARNED TO CHANNEL IT INTO SOMETHING MORE... PRODUCTIVE.
BUT NOW, THERE IS THIS EMPTY SPACE WHERE MY FIRE USED TO BE.
THERE ARE PIECES OF ME MISSING, AND IT DOESN'T MAKE SENSE.
ISN'T THAT THE MISSION STATEMENT HERE? REPLACING MALADAPTIVE BEHAVIORS WITH CALM AND HARMONIOUS ONES. SOUNDS LIKE THIS PLACE IS WORKING FOR YOU.
LUCKY YOU.

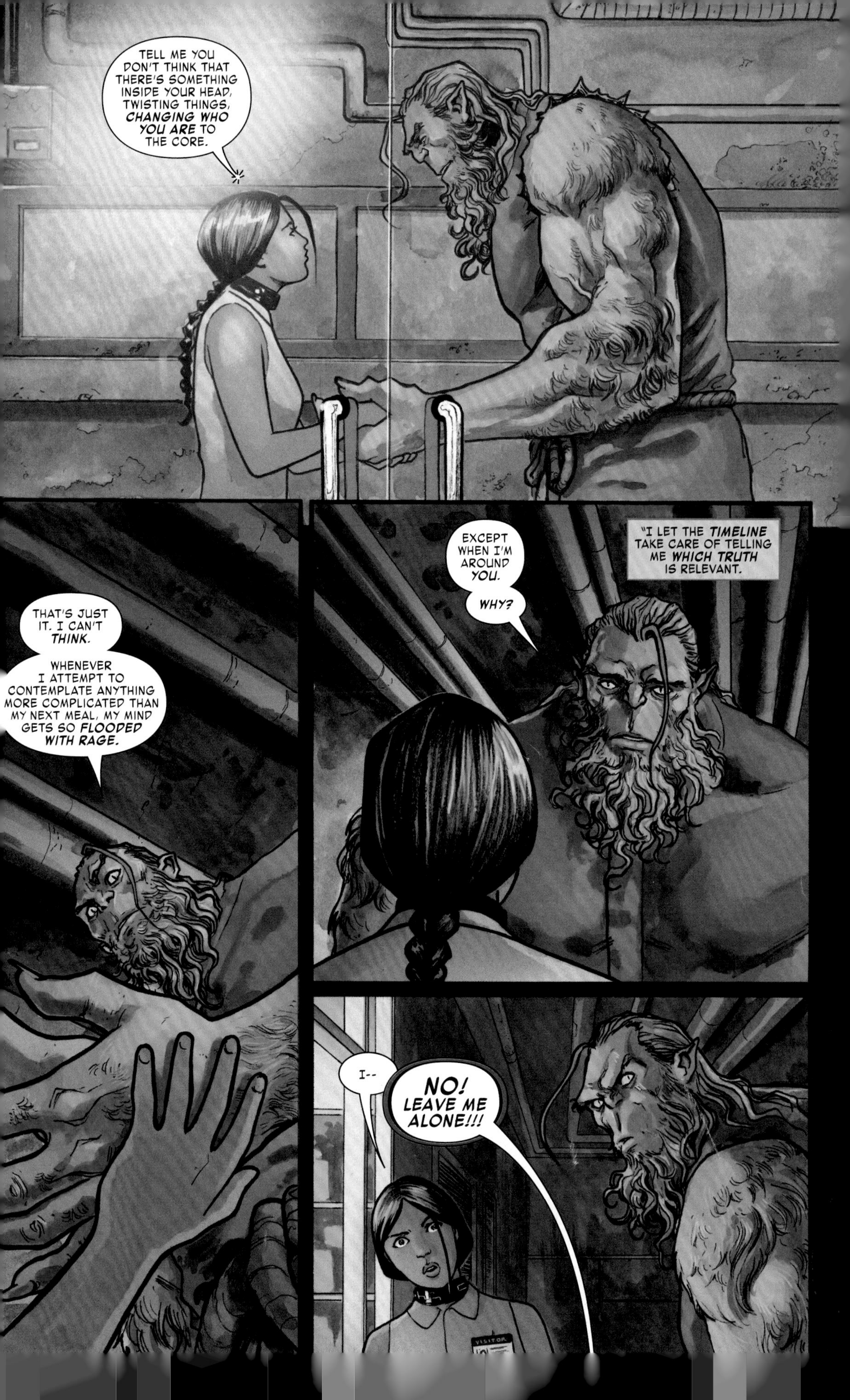
TELL ME YOU DON'T THINK THAT THERE'S SOMETHING INSIDE YOUR HEAD, TWISTING THINGS, *CHANGING WHO YOU ARE* TO THE CORE.
THAT'S JUST IT. I CAN'T *THINK.*
WHENEVER I ATTEMPT TO CONTEMPLATE ANYTHING MORE COMPLICATED THAN MY NEXT MEAL, MY MIND GETS SO *FLOODED WITH RAGE.*
"I LET THE *TIMELINE* TAKE CARE OF TELLING ME *WHICH TRUTH* IS RELEVANT.
EXCEPT WHEN I'M AROUND *YOU.*
WHY?
I--
NO! LEAVE ME ALONE!!!
VISITOR

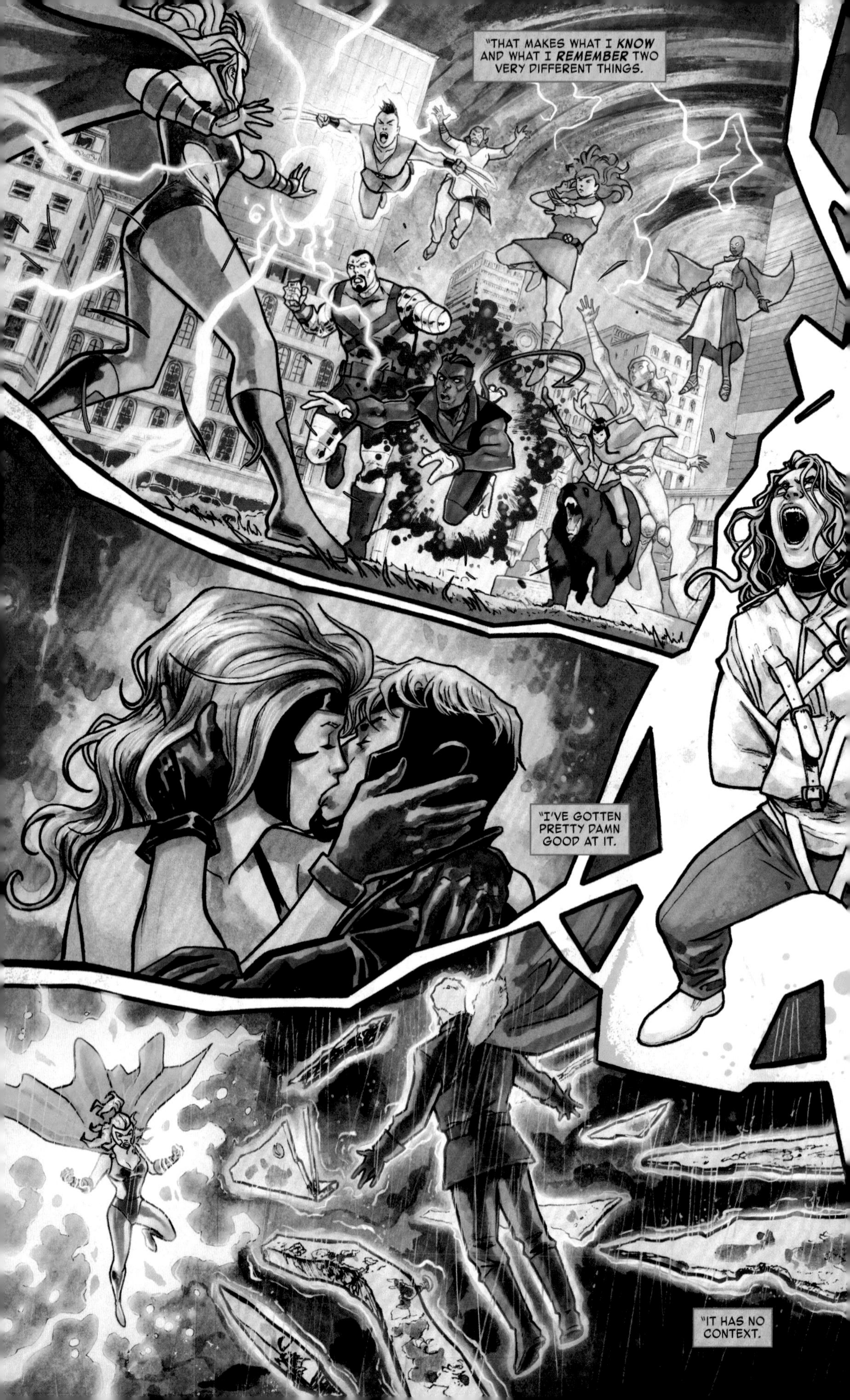
"THAT MAKES WHAT I KNOW AND WHAT I REMEMBER TWO VERY DIFFERENT THINGS.
"I'VE GOTTEN PRETTY DAMN GOOD AT IT.
"IT HAS NO CONTEXT.

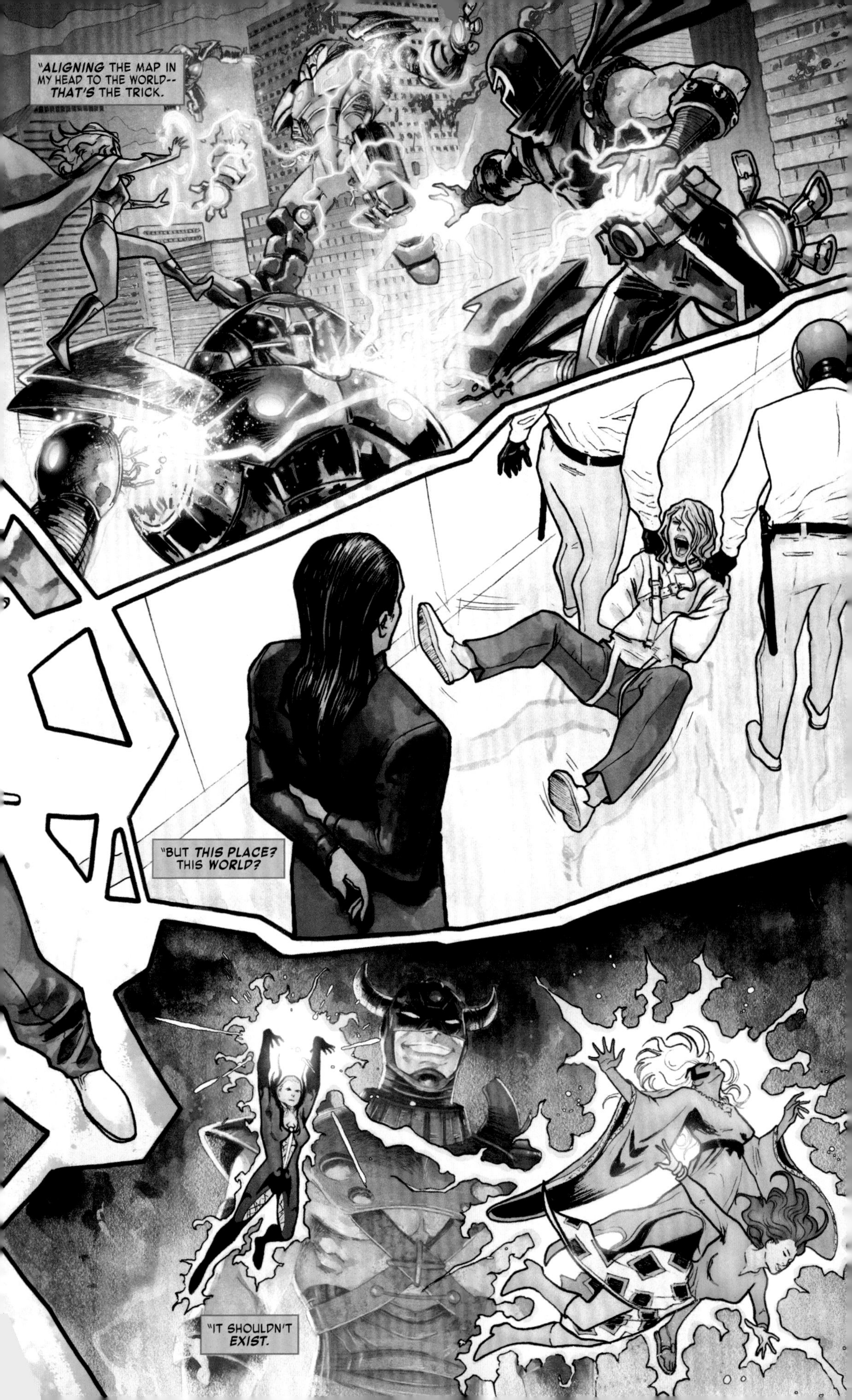
"ALIGNING THE MAP IN MY HEAD TO THE WORLD-- THAT'S THE TRICK.
"BUT THIS PLACE? THIS WORLD?
"IT SHOULDN'T EXIST.

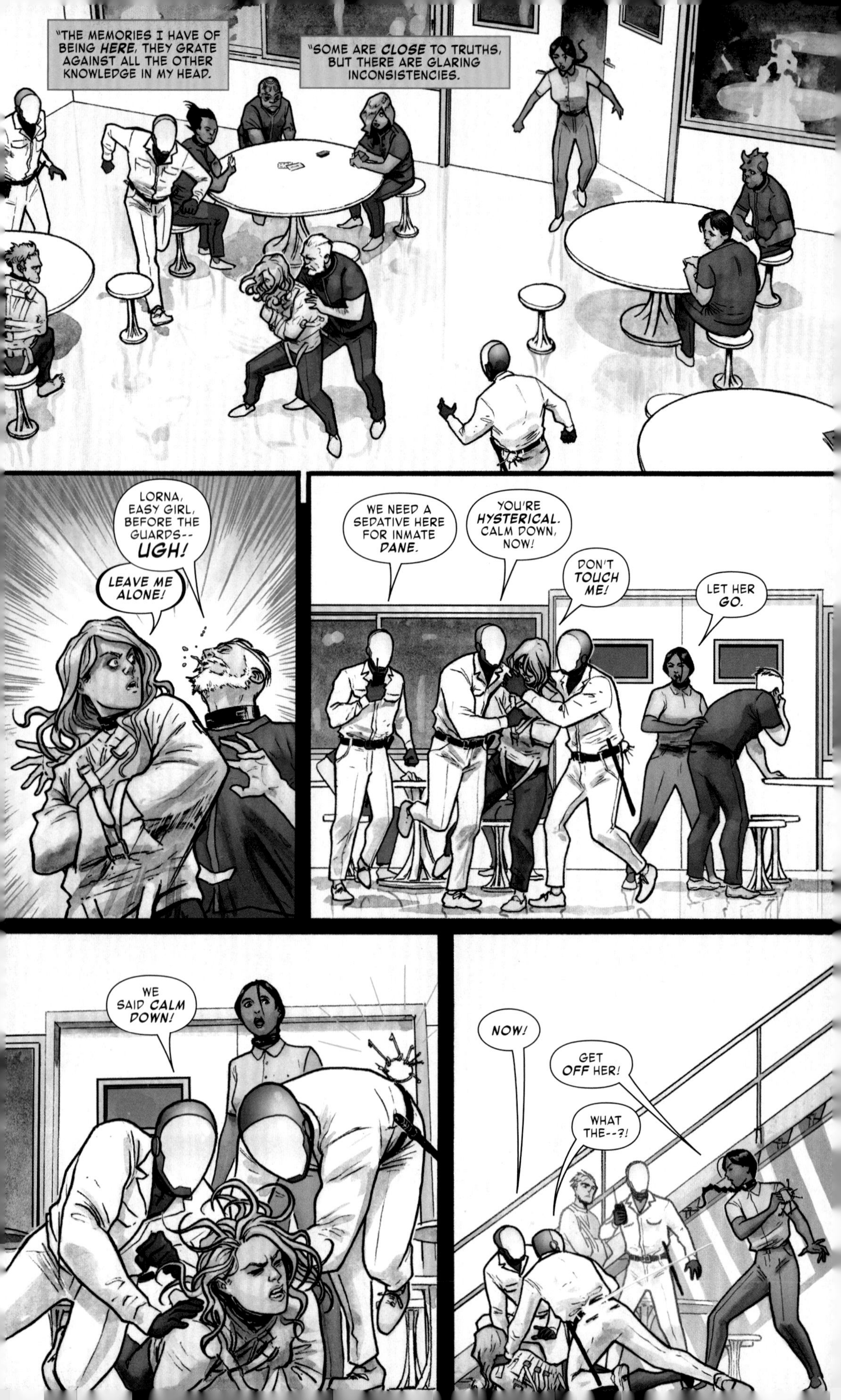
"THE MEMORIES I HAVE OF BEING HERE, THEY GRATE AGAINST ALL THE OTHER KNOWLEDGE IN MY HEAD.
"SOME ARE CLOSE TO TRUTHS, BUT THERE ARE GLARING INCONSISTENCIES.
LORNA, EASY GIRL, BEFORE THE GUARDS-- UGH!
LEAVE ME ALONE!
WE NEED A SEDATIVE HERE FOR INMATE DANE.
YOU'RE HYSTERICAL. CALM DOWN, NOW!
DON'T TOUCH ME!
LET HER GO.
WE SAID CALM DOWN!
NOW!
GET OFF HER!
WHAT THE--?!

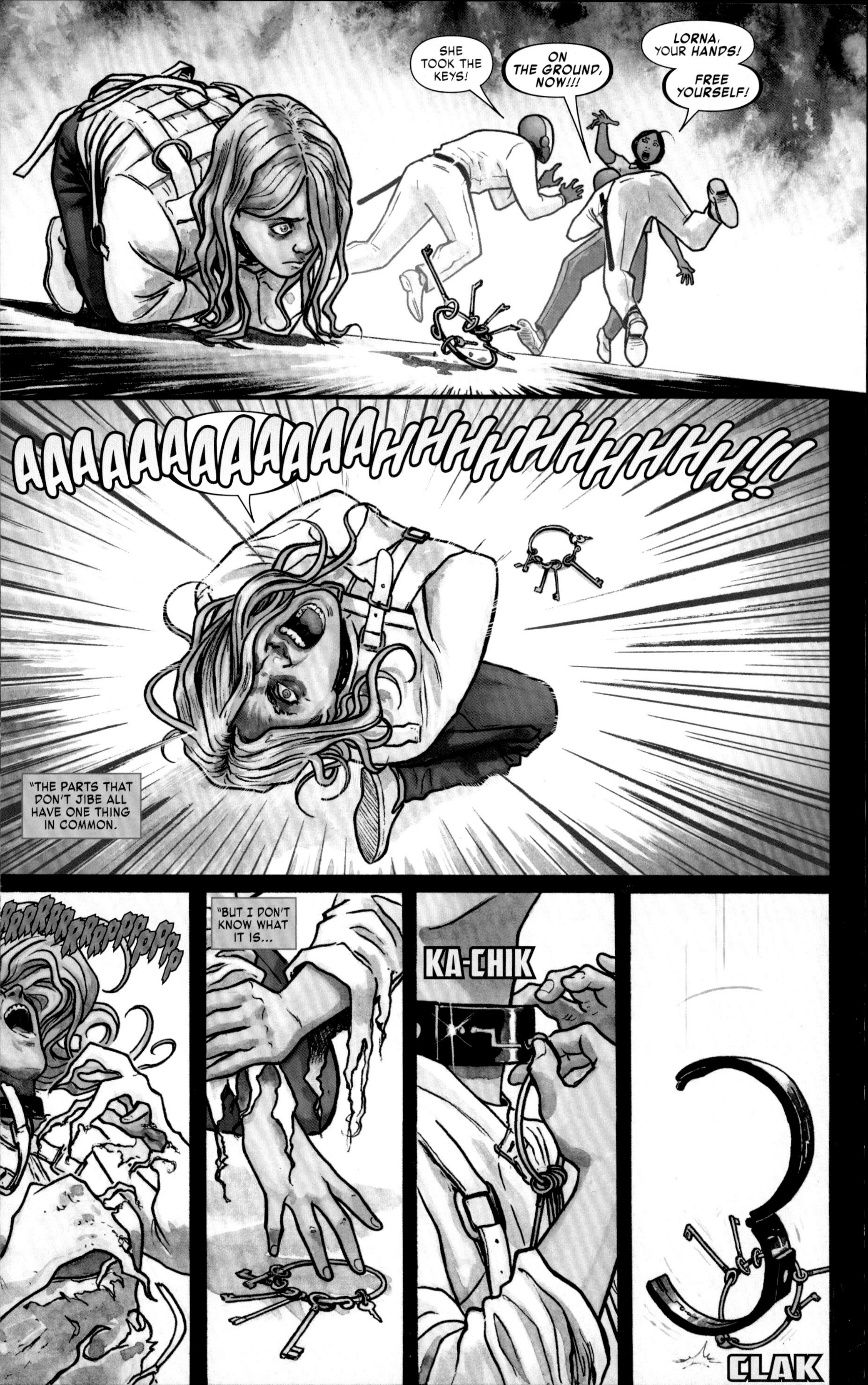
SHE TOOK THE KEYS!
ON THE GROUND, NOW!!!
LORNA, YOUR HANDS!
FREE YOURSELF!
AAAAAAAAAAAAAHHHHHHHHHHHH!!!
"THE PARTS THAT DON'T JIBE ALL HAVE ONE THING IN COMMON.
"BUT I DON'T KNOW WHAT IT IS...
KA-CHIK
CLAK

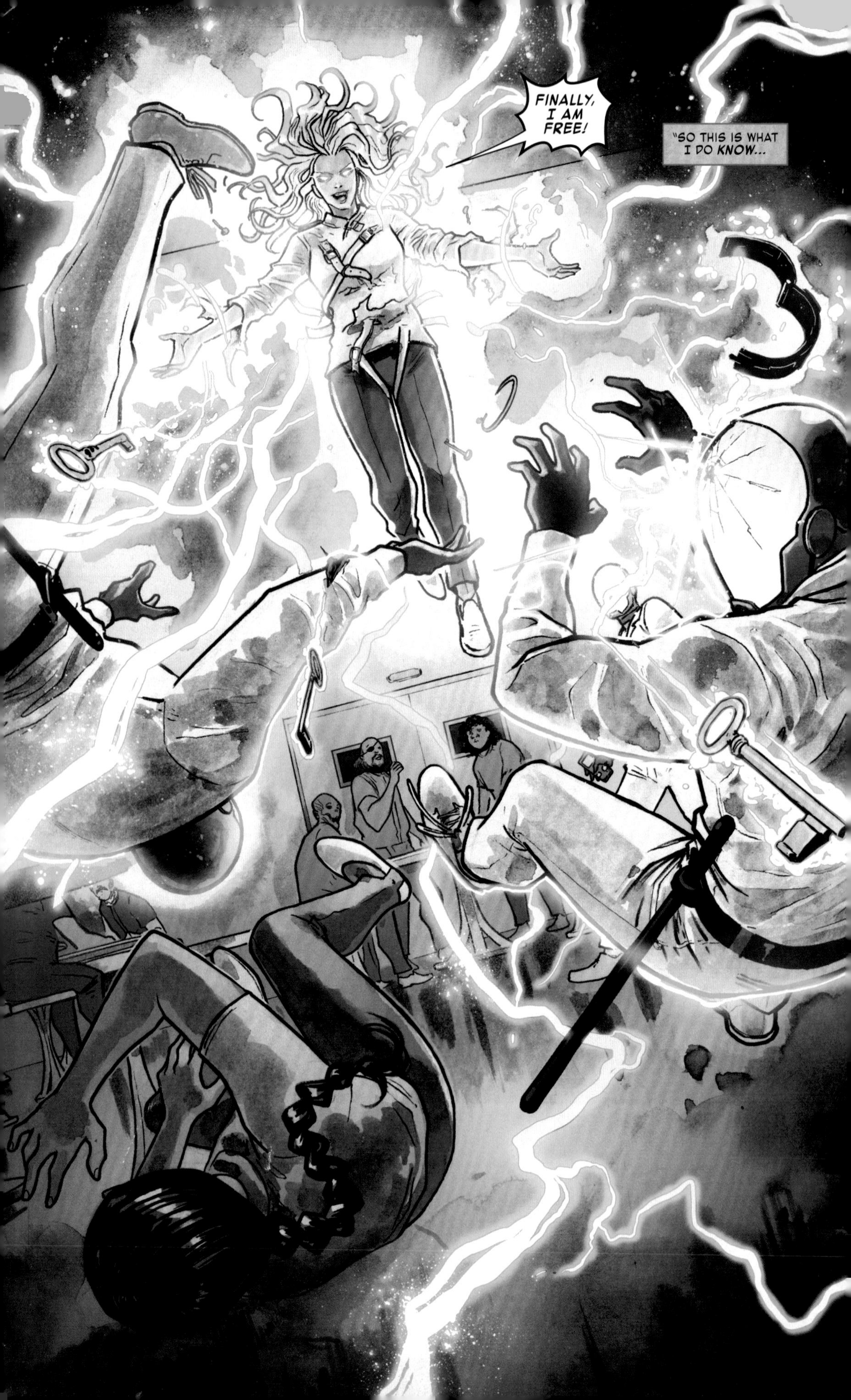
FINALLY, I AM FREE!
"SO THIS IS WHAT I DO KNOW...

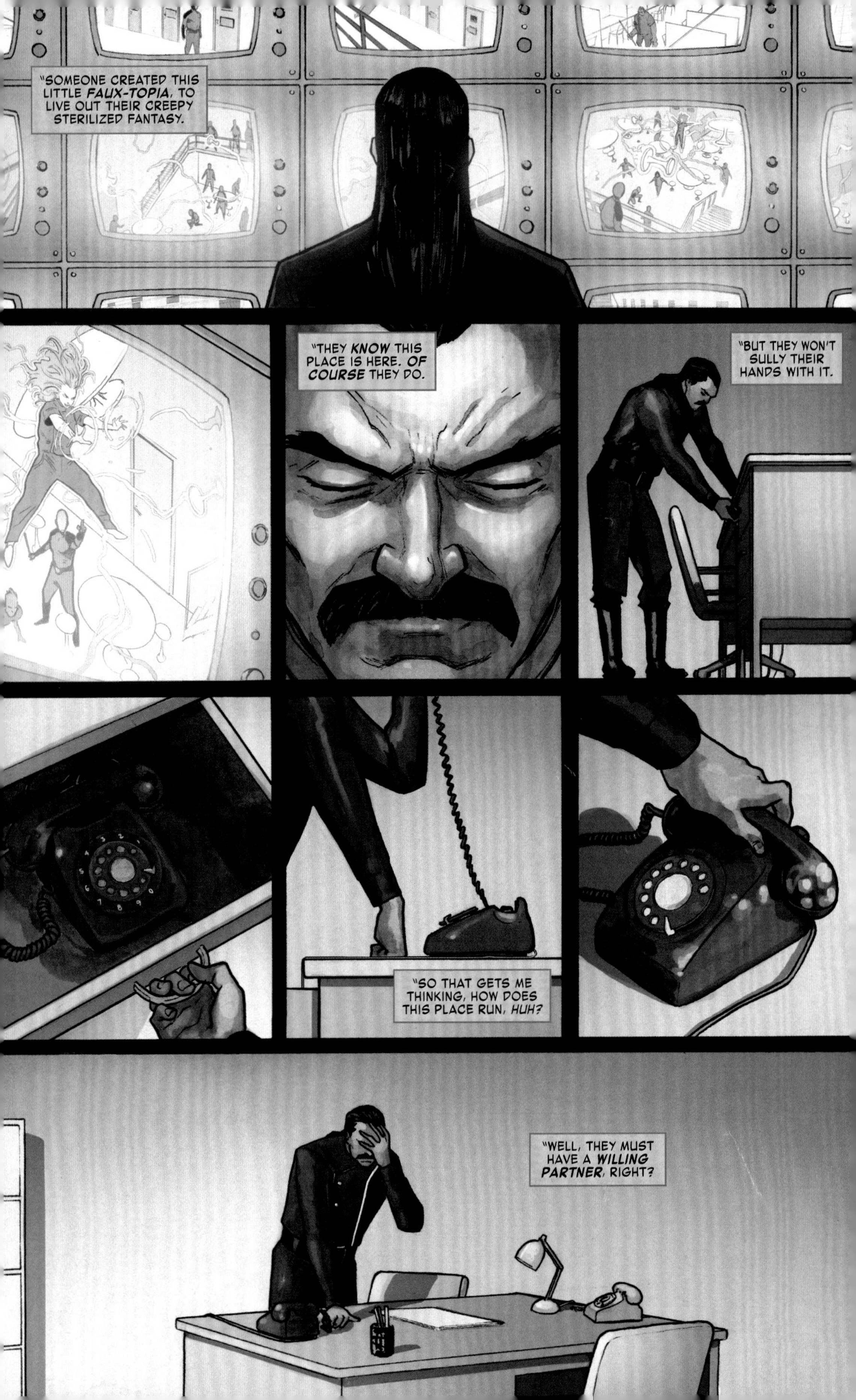
"SOMEONE CREATED THIS LITTLE *FAUX-TOPIA*, TO LIVE OUT THEIR CREEPY STERILIZED FANTASY.
"THEY ***KNOW*** THIS PLACE IS HERE. ***OF COURSE*** THEY DO.
"BUT THEY WON'T SULLY THEIR HANDS WITH IT.
"SO THAT GETS ME THINKING, HOW DOES THIS PLACE RUN, *HUH*?
"WELL, THEY MUST HAVE A ***WILLING PARTNER***, RIGHT?

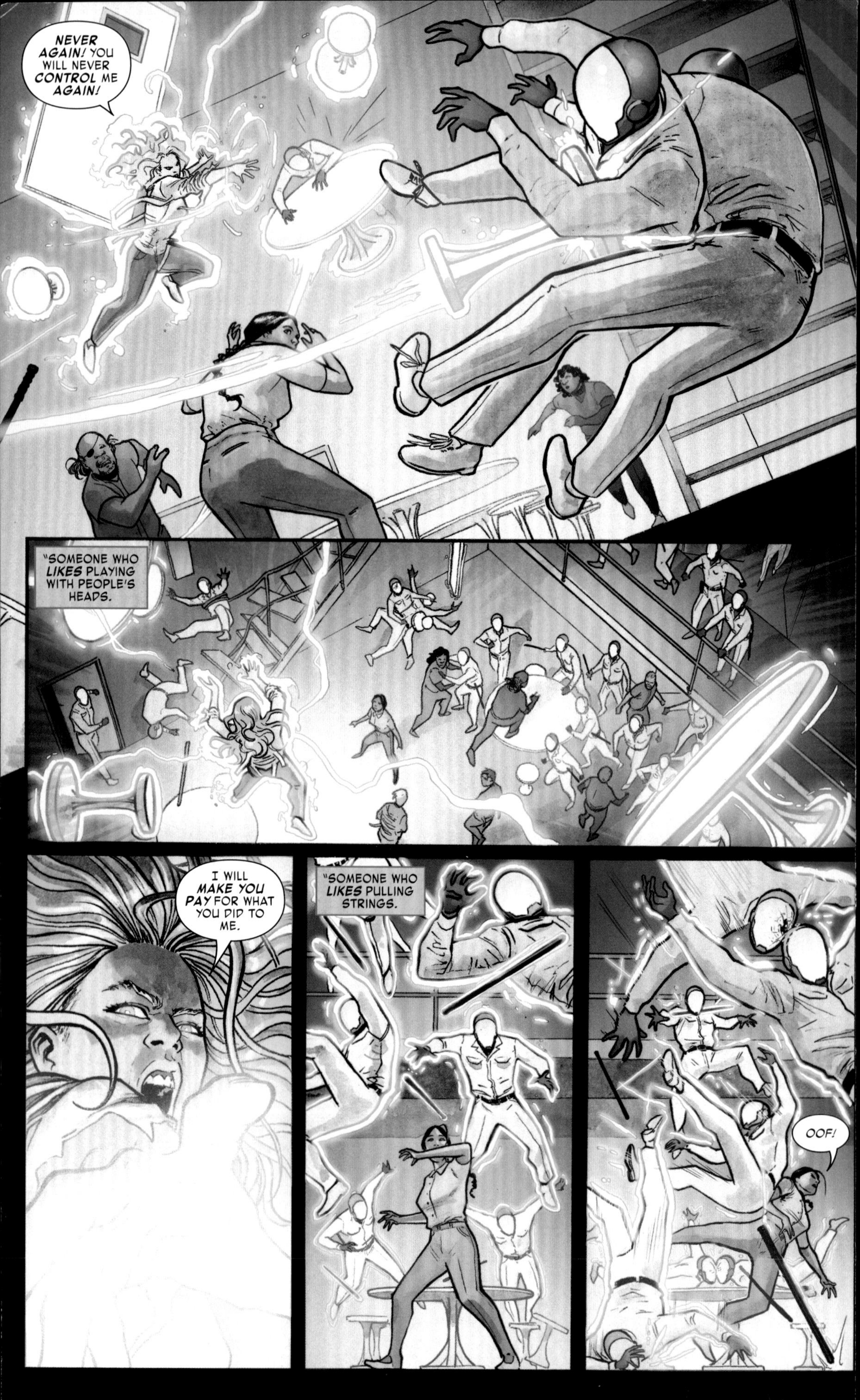
NEVER AGAIN! YOU WILL NEVER CONTROL ME AGAIN!
"SOMEONE WHO LIKES PLAYING WITH PEOPLE'S HEADS.
I WILL MAKE YOU PAY FOR WHAT YOU DID TO ME.
"SOMEONE WHO LIKES PULLING STRINGS.
OOF!

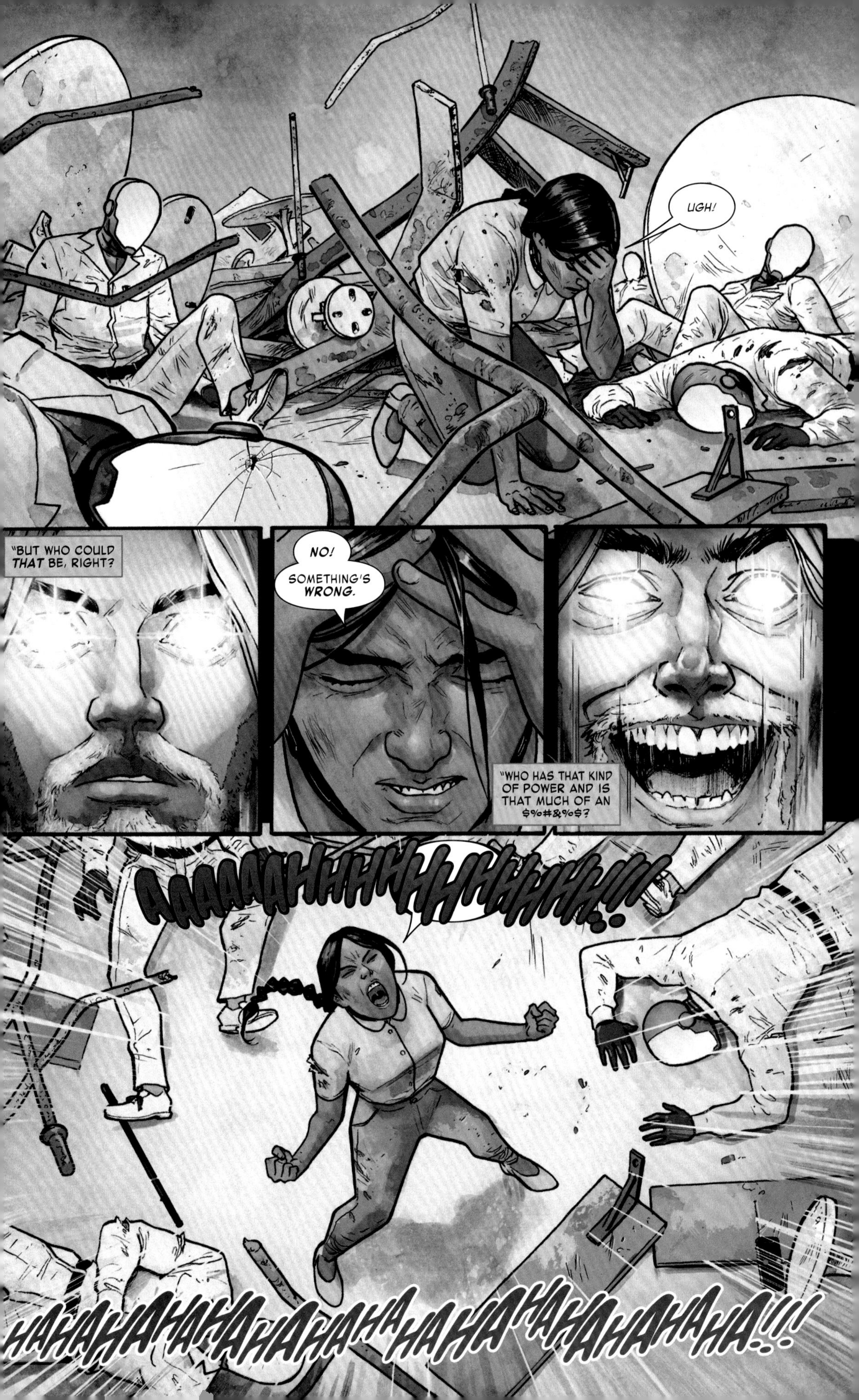
UGH!
"BUT WHO COULD THAT BE, RIGHT?
NO!
SOMETHING'S WRONG.
"WHO HAS THAT KIND OF POWER AND IS THAT MUCH OF AN $%#&%$?
AAAAAAAHHHHHHHHHHHHHH!!!
HAHAHAHAHAHAHAHAHAHAHAHAHAHAHAHAHA!!!

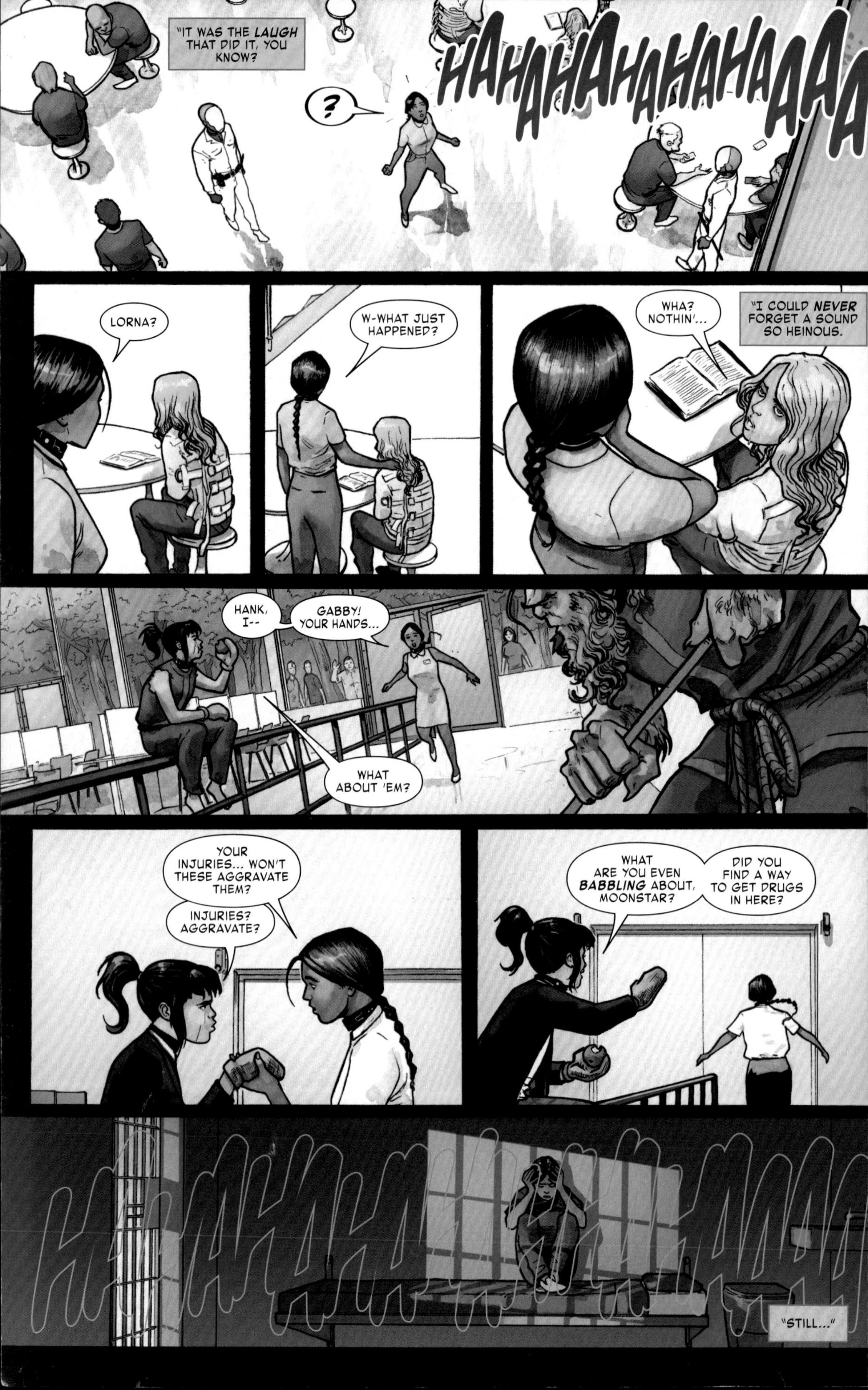
"IT WAS THE LAUGH THAT DID IT, YOU KNOW?
?
HAHAHAHAHAHAHAHAAAA
LORNA?
W-WHAT JUST HAPPENED?
WHA? NOTHIN'...
"I COULD NEVER FORGET A SOUND SO HEINOUS.
HANK, I--
GABBY! YOUR HANDS...
WHAT ABOUT 'EM?
YOUR INJURIES... WON'T THESE AGGRAVATE THEM?
INJURIES? AGGRAVATE?
WHAT ARE YOU EVEN BABBLING ABOUT, MOONSTAR?
DID YOU FIND A WAY TO GET DRUGS IN HERE?
"STILL..."

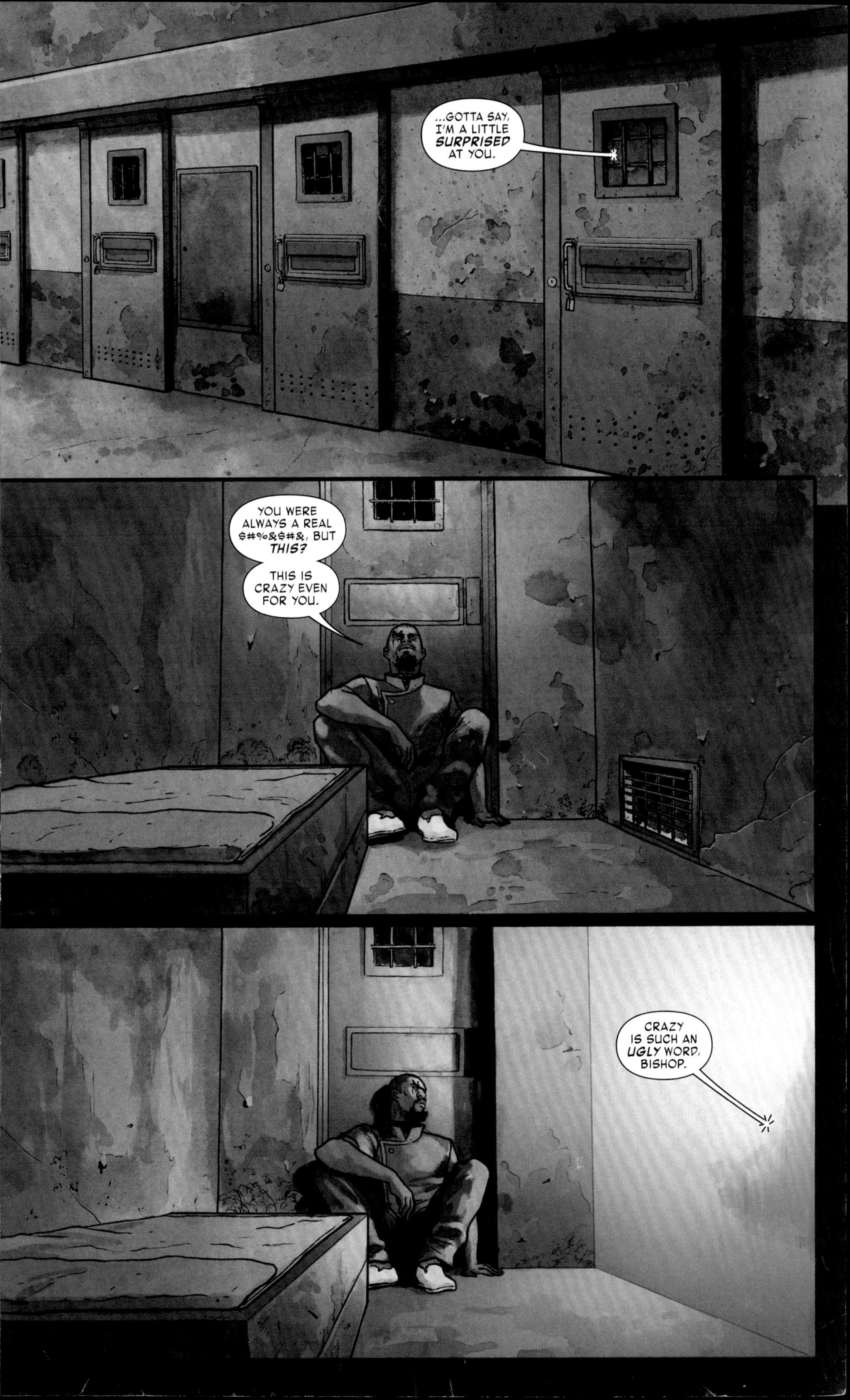
...GOTTA SAY, I'M A LITTLE SURPRISED AT YOU.
YOU WERE ALWAYS A REAL $#%&$#&, BUT THIS?
THIS IS CRAZY EVEN FOR YOU.
CRAZY IS SUCH AN UGLY WORD, BISHOP.

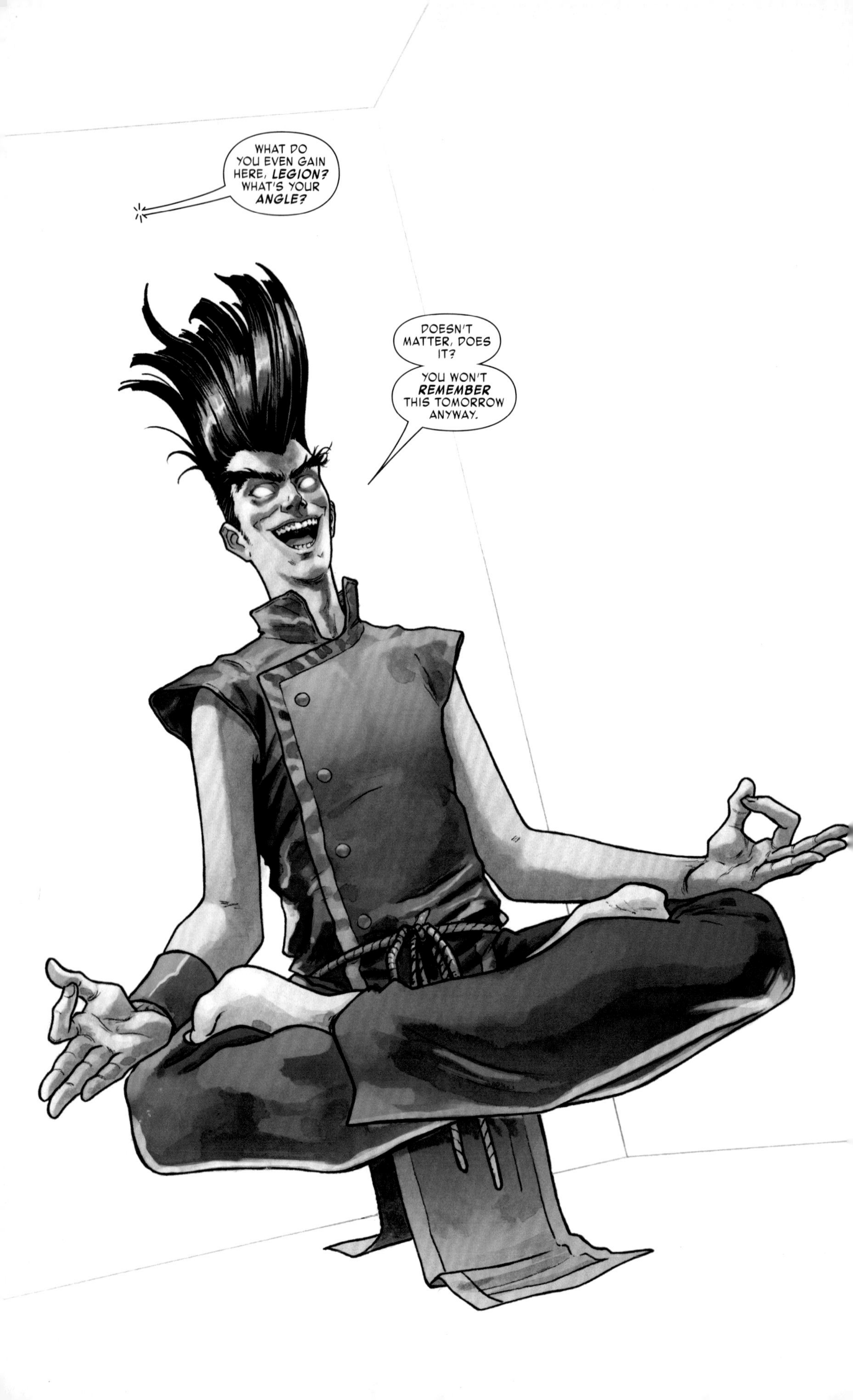
WHAT DO YOU EVEN GAIN HERE, LEGION? WHAT'S YOUR ANGLE?
DOESN'T MATTER, DOES IT?
YOU WON'T REMEMBER THIS TOMORROW ANYWAY.

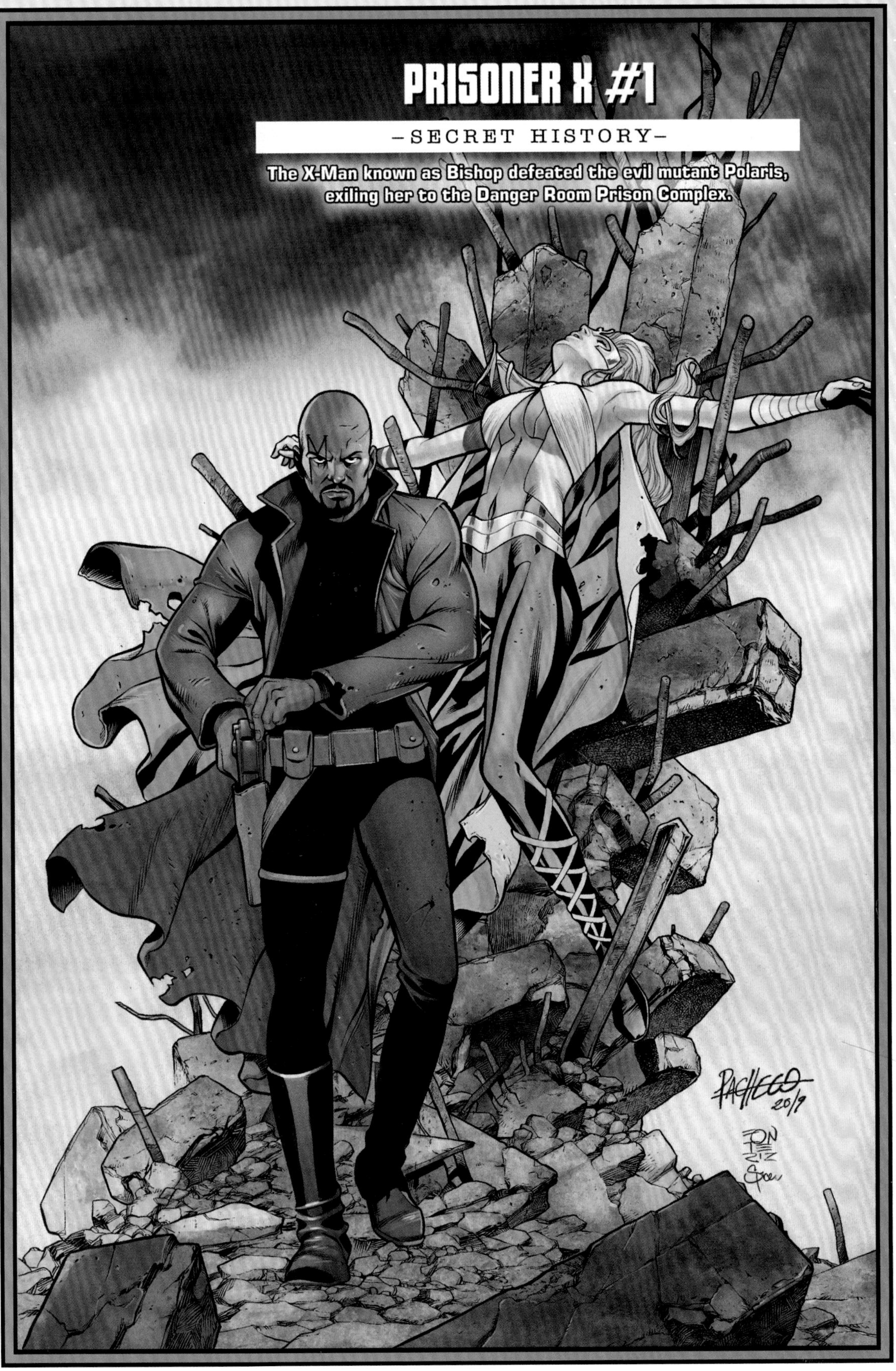
PRISONER X #1
–SECRET HISTORY–
The X-Man known as Bishop defeated the evil mutant Polaris, exiling her to the Danger Room Prison Complex.
PACHECO 20/9

#1 SECRET HISTORY VARIANT BY **CARLOS PACHECO**

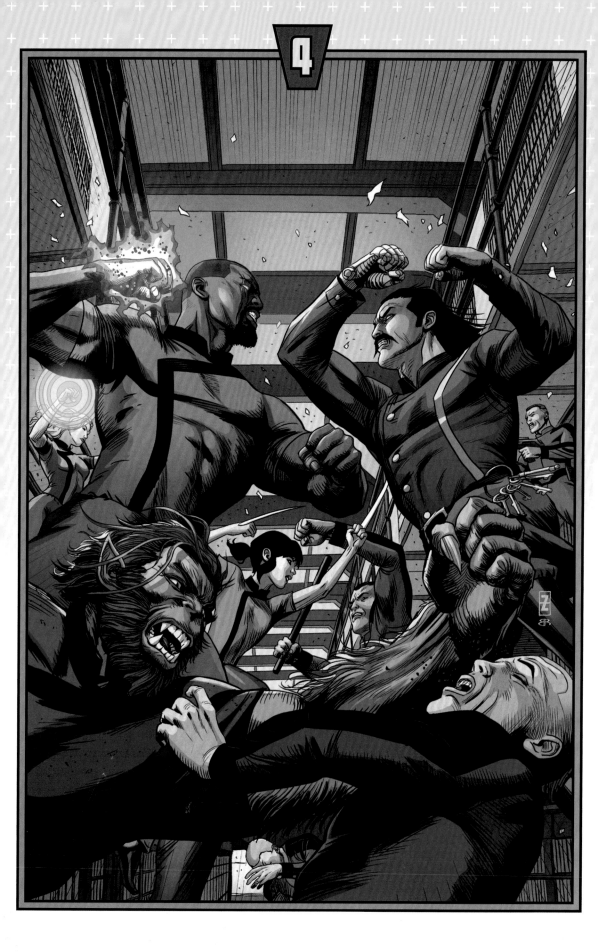

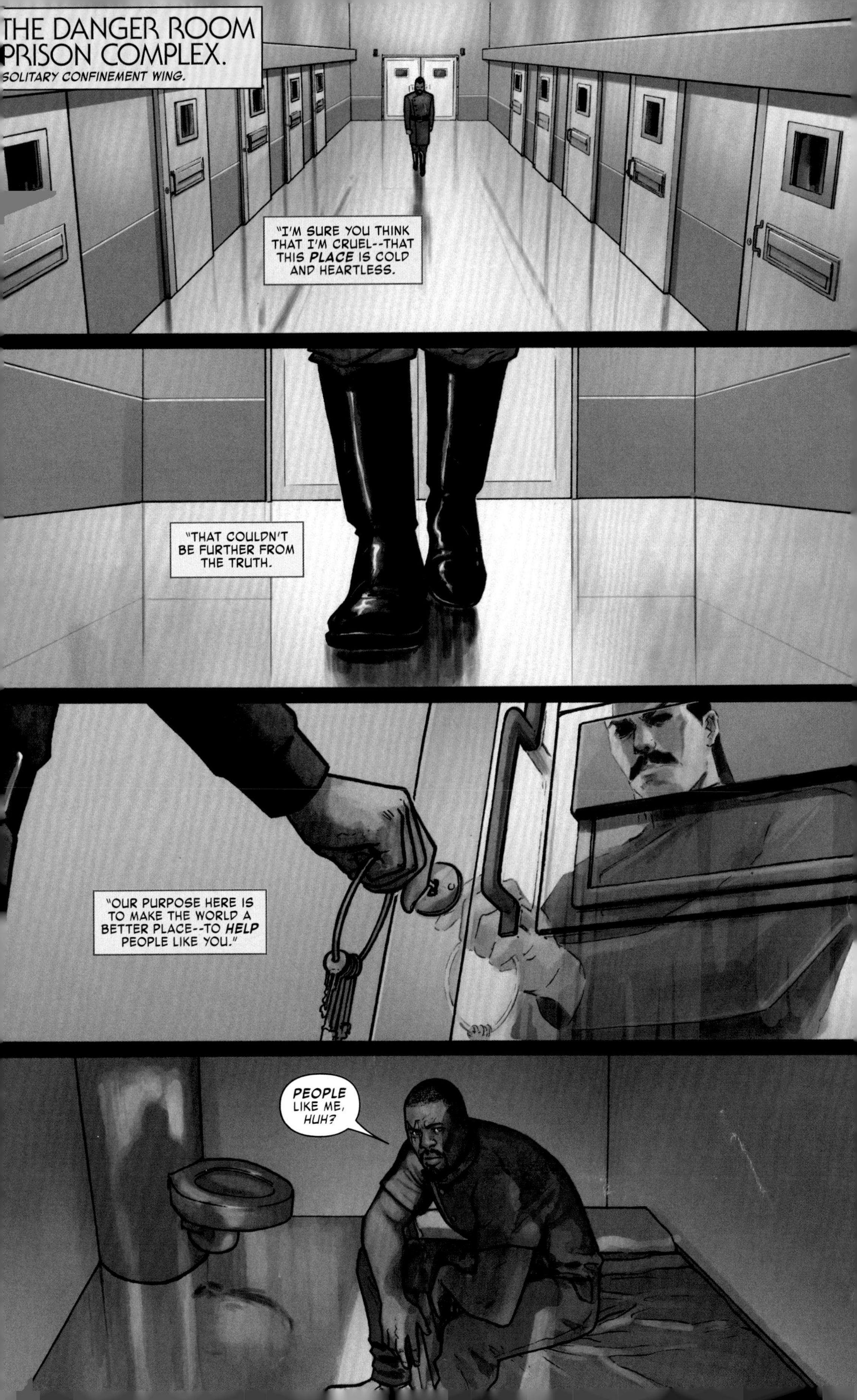
THE DANGER ROOM PRISON COMPLEX.
SOLITARY CONFINEMENT WING.
"I'M SURE YOU THINK THAT I'M CRUEL--THAT THIS PLACE IS COLD AND HEARTLESS.
"THAT COULDN'T BE FURTHER FROM THE TRUTH.
"OUR PURPOSE HERE IS TO MAKE THE WORLD A BETTER PLACE--TO HELP PEOPLE LIKE YOU."
PEOPLE LIKE ME, HUH?

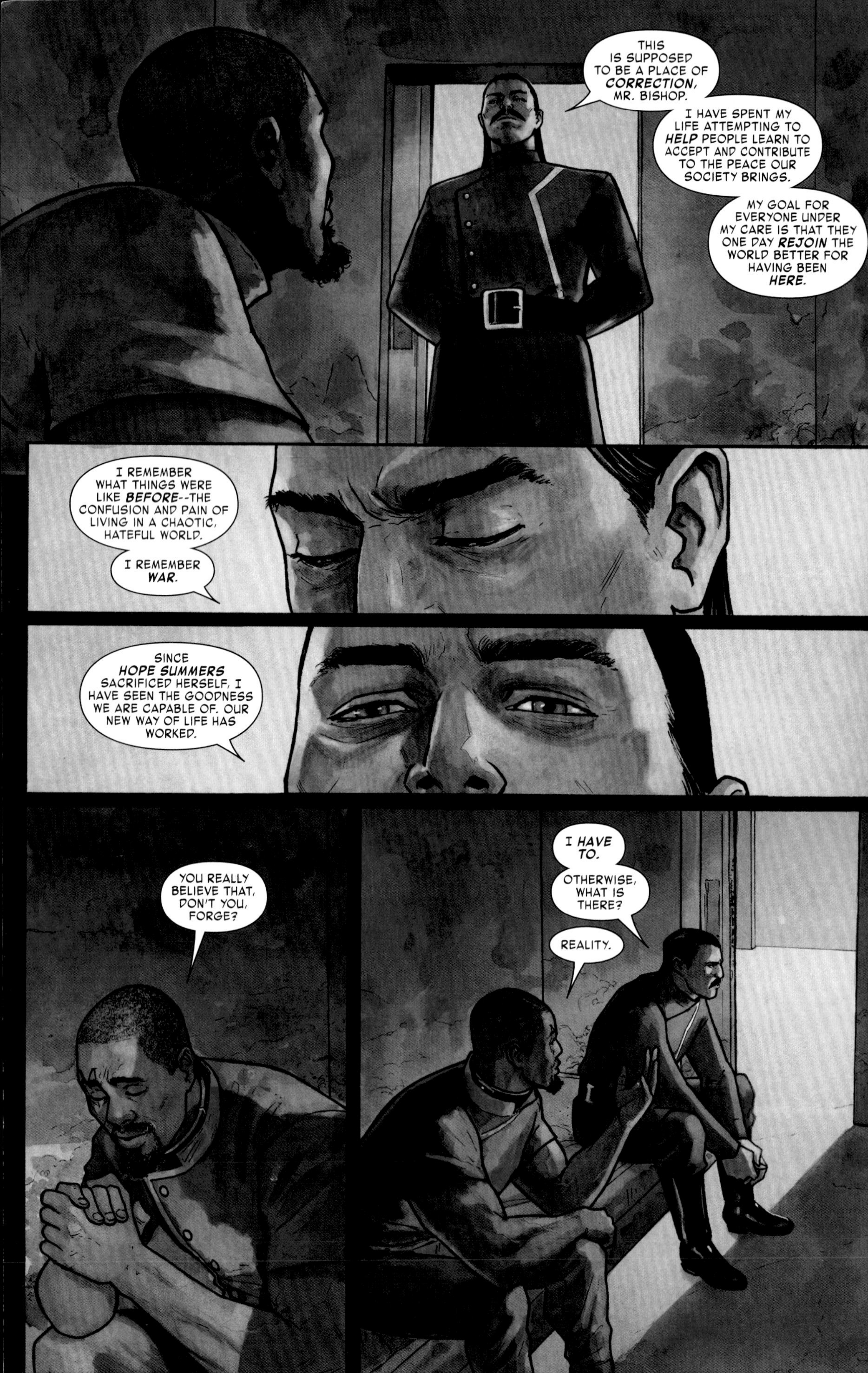
THIS IS SUPPOSED TO BE A PLACE OF CORRECTION, MR. BISHOP.
I HAVE SPENT MY LIFE ATTEMPTING TO HELP PEOPLE LEARN TO ACCEPT AND CONTRIBUTE TO THE PEACE OUR SOCIETY BRINGS.
MY GOAL FOR EVERYONE UNDER MY CARE IS THAT THEY ONE DAY REJOIN THE WORLD BETTER FOR HAVING BEEN HERE.
I REMEMBER WHAT THINGS WERE LIKE BEFORE--THE CONFUSION AND PAIN OF LIVING IN A CHAOTIC, HATEFUL WORLD.
I REMEMBER WAR.
SINCE HOPE SUMMERS SACRIFICED HERSELF, I HAVE SEEN THE GOODNESS WE ARE CAPABLE OF. OUR NEW WAY OF LIFE HAS WORKED.
YOU REALLY BELIEVE THAT, DON'T YOU, FORGE?
I HAVE TO.
OTHERWISE, WHAT IS THERE?
REALITY.

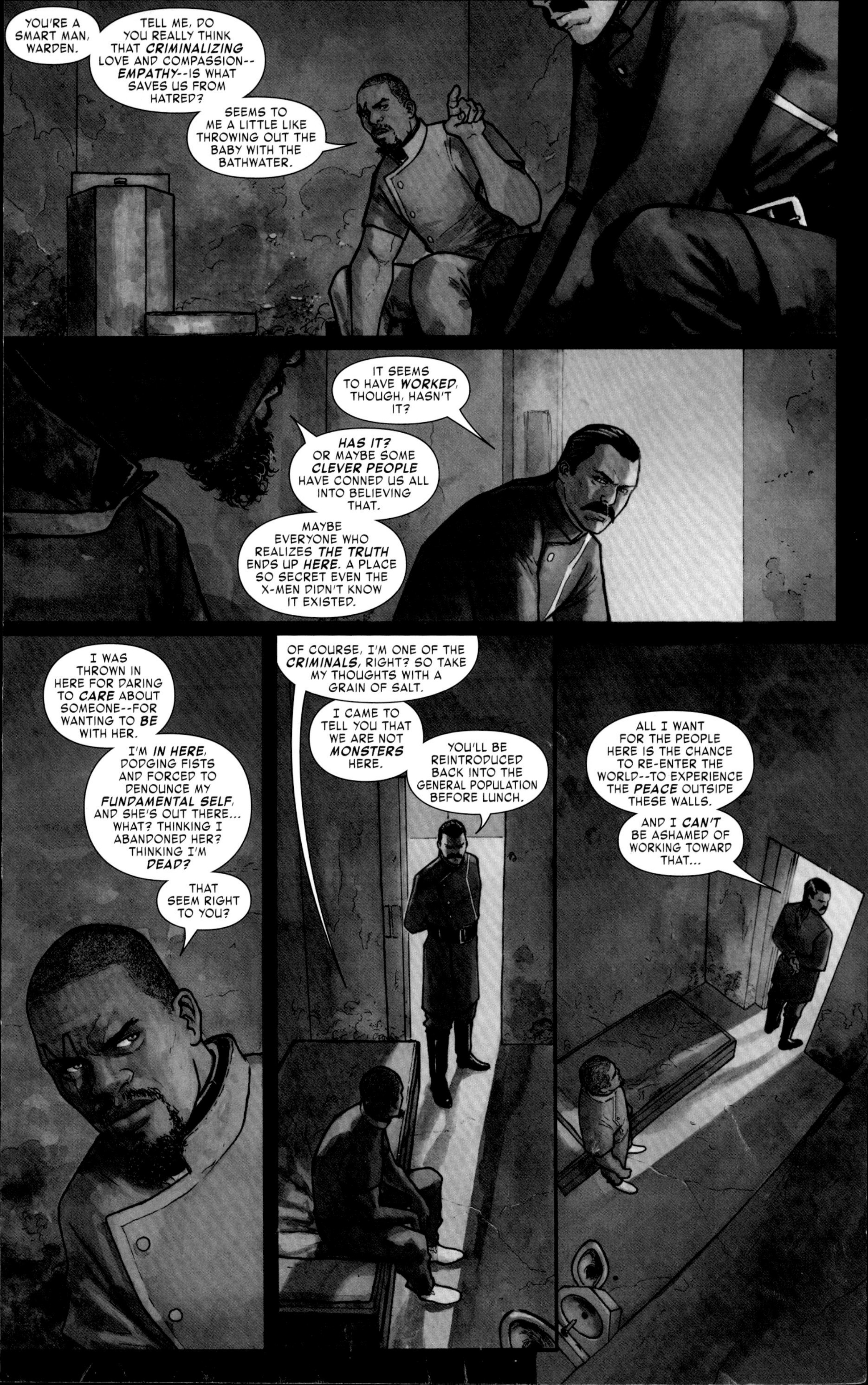

YOU'RE A SMART MAN, WARDEN.
TELL ME, DO YOU REALLY THINK THAT CRIMINALIZING LOVE AND COMPASSION-- EMPATHY--IS WHAT SAVES US FROM HATRED?
SEEMS TO ME A LITTLE LIKE THROWING OUT THE BABY WITH THE BATHWATER.
IT SEEMS TO HAVE WORKED, THOUGH, HASN'T IT?
HAS IT? OR MAYBE SOME CLEVER PEOPLE HAVE CONNED US ALL INTO BELIEVING THAT.
MAYBE EVERYONE WHO REALIZES THE TRUTH ENDS UP HERE. A PLACE SO SECRET EVEN THE X-MEN DIDN'T KNOW IT EXISTED.
I WAS THROWN IN HERE FOR DARING TO CARE ABOUT SOMEONE--FOR WANTING TO BE WITH HER.
I'M IN HERE, DODGING FISTS AND FORCED TO DENOUNCE MY FUNDAMENTAL SELF, AND SHE'S OUT THERE... WHAT? THINKING I ABANDONED HER? THINKING I'M DEAD?
THAT SEEM RIGHT TO YOU?
OF COURSE, I'M ONE OF THE CRIMINALS, RIGHT? SO TAKE MY THOUGHTS WITH A GRAIN OF SALT.
I CAME TO TELL YOU THAT WE ARE NOT MONSTERS HERE.
YOU'LL BE REINTRODUCED BACK INTO THE GENERAL POPULATION BEFORE LUNCH.
ALL I WANT FOR THE PEOPLE HERE IS THE CHANCE TO RE-ENTER THE WORLD--TO EXPERIENCE THE PEACE OUTSIDE THESE WALLS.
AND I CAN'T BE ASHAMED OF WORKING TOWARD THAT...

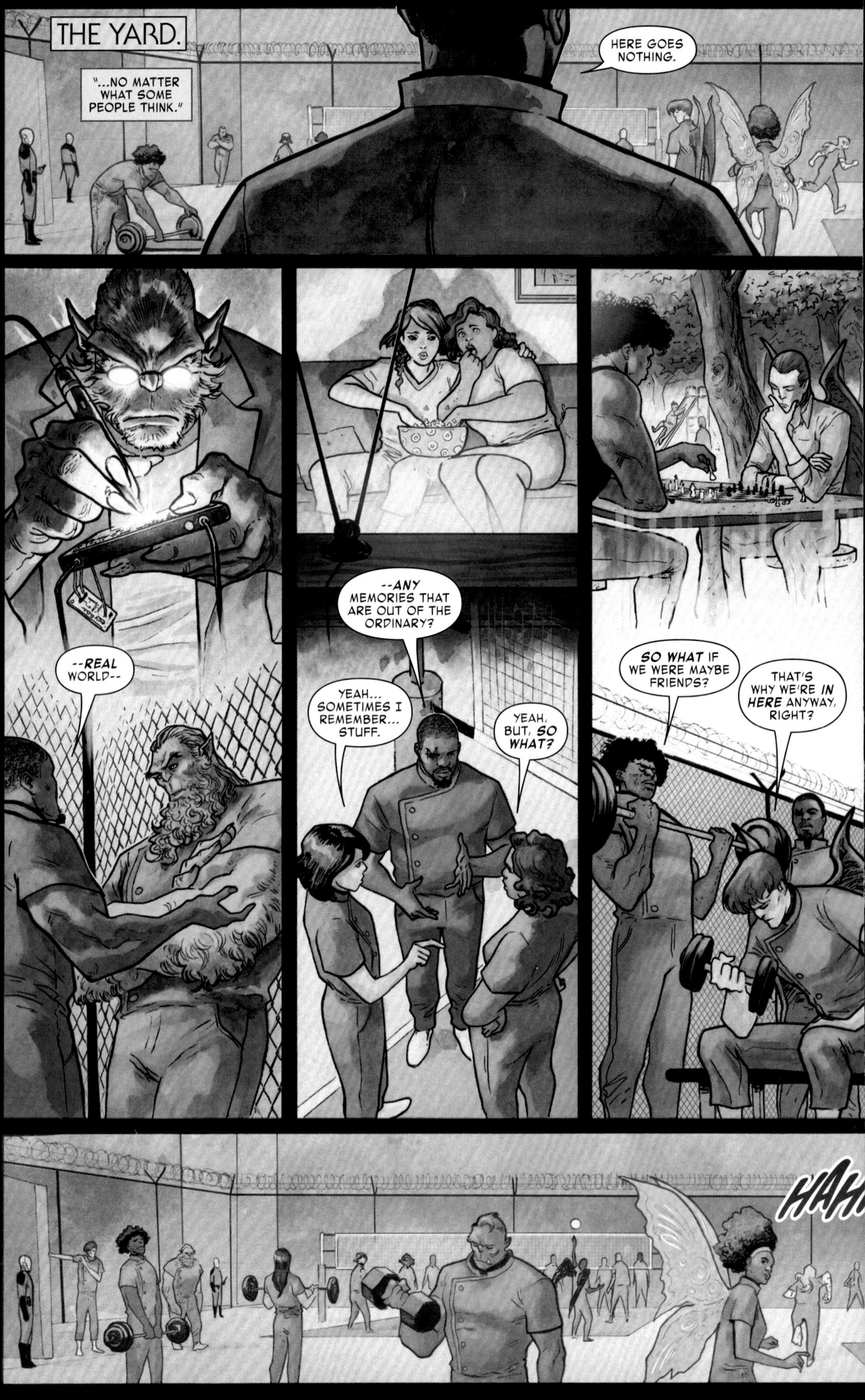
THE YARD.
"...NO MATTER WHAT SOME PEOPLE THINK."
HERE GOES NOTHING.
--ANY MEMORIES THAT ARE OUT OF THE ORDINARY?
--REAL WORLD--
YEAH... SOMETIMES I REMEMBER... STUFF.
YEAH, BUT, SO WHAT?
SO WHAT IF WE WERE MAYBE FRIENDS?
THAT'S WHY WE'RE IN HERE ANYWAY, RIGHT?

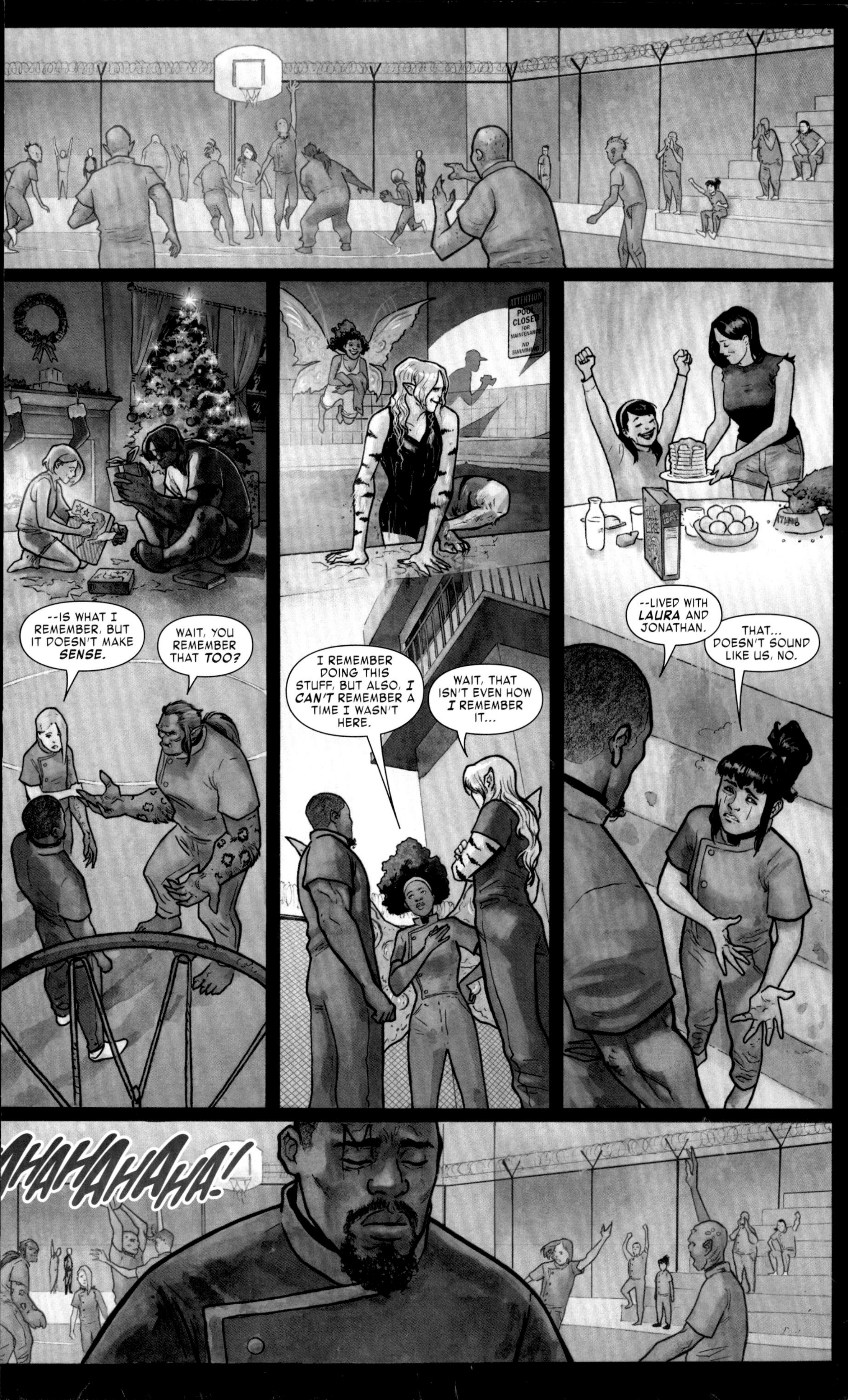
--IS WHAT I REMEMBER, BUT IT DOESN'T MAKE SENSE.
WAIT, YOU REMEMBER THAT TOO?
I REMEMBER DOING THIS STUFF, BUT ALSO, I CAN'T REMEMBER A TIME I WASN'T HERE.
WAIT, THAT ISN'T EVEN HOW I REMEMBER IT...
ATTENTION POOL CLOSED FOR MAINTENANCE NO SWIMMING
--LIVED WITH LAURA AND JONATHAN.
THAT... DOESN'T SOUND LIKE US, NO.
AHAHAHAHA!

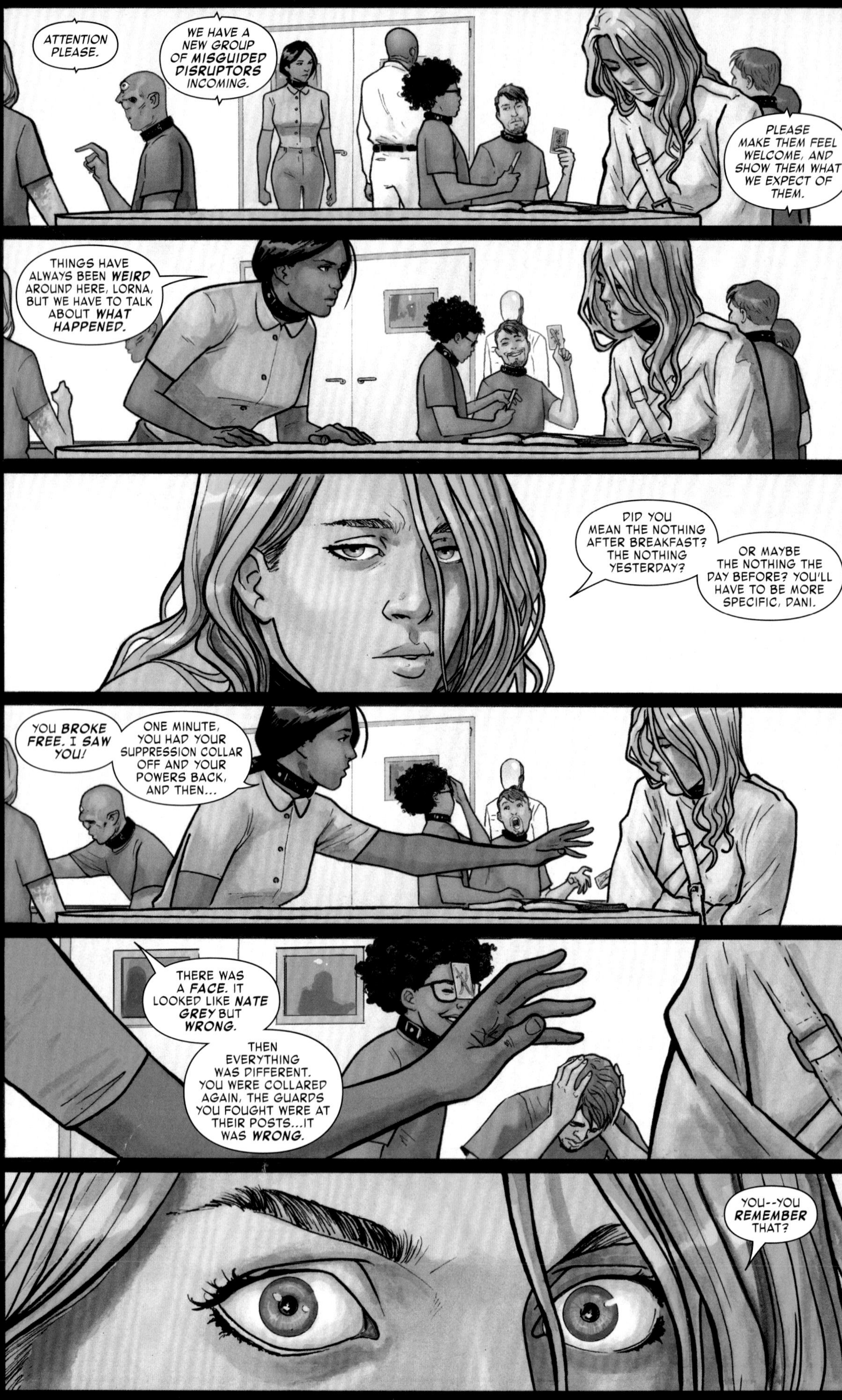
ATTENTION PLEASE.
WE HAVE A NEW GROUP OF MISGUIDED DISRUPTORS INCOMING.
PLEASE MAKE THEM FEEL WELCOME, AND SHOW THEM WHAT WE EXPECT OF THEM.
THINGS HAVE ALWAYS BEEN WEIRD AROUND HERE, LORNA, BUT WE HAVE TO TALK ABOUT WHAT HAPPENED.
DID YOU MEAN THE NOTHING AFTER BREAKFAST? THE NOTHING YESTERDAY?
OR MAYBE THE NOTHING THE DAY BEFORE? YOU'LL HAVE TO BE MORE SPECIFIC, DANI.
YOU BROKE FREE. I SAW YOU!
ONE MINUTE, YOU HAD YOUR SUPPRESSION COLLAR OFF AND YOUR POWERS BACK, AND THEN...
THERE WAS A FACE. IT LOOKED LIKE NATE GREY BUT WRONG.
THEN EVERYTHING WAS DIFFERENT. YOU WERE COLLARED AGAIN, THE GUARDS YOU FOUGHT WERE AT THEIR POSTS...IT WAS WRONG.
YOU--YOU REMEMBER THAT?

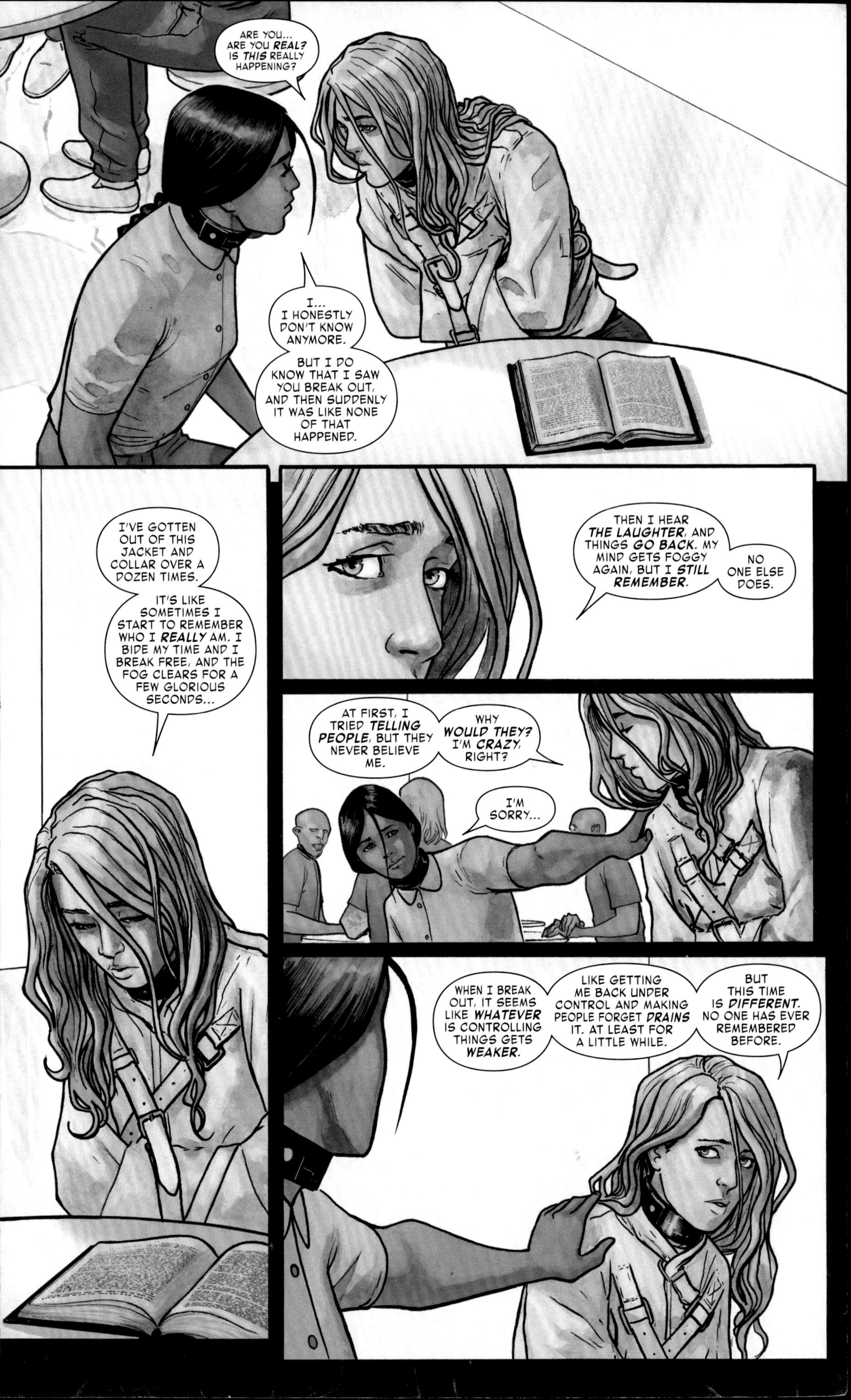
ARE YOU... ARE YOU REAL? IS THIS REALLY HAPPENING?
I... I HONESTLY DON'T KNOW ANYMORE.
BUT I DO KNOW THAT I SAW YOU BREAK OUT, AND THEN SUDDENLY IT WAS LIKE NONE OF THAT HAPPENED.
I'VE GOTTEN OUT OF THIS JACKET AND COLLAR OVER A DOZEN TIMES.
IT'S LIKE SOMETIMES I START TO REMEMBER WHO I REALLY AM. I BIDE MY TIME AND I BREAK FREE, AND THE FOG CLEARS FOR A FEW GLORIOUS SECONDS...
THEN I HEAR THE LAUGHTER, AND THINGS GO BACK. MY MIND GETS FOGGY AGAIN, BUT I STILL REMEMBER.
NO ONE ELSE DOES.
AT FIRST, I TRIED TELLING PEOPLE, BUT THEY NEVER BELIEVE ME.
WHY WOULD THEY? I'M CRAZY, RIGHT?
I'M SORRY...
WHEN I BREAK OUT, IT SEEMS LIKE WHATEVER IS CONTROLLING THINGS GETS WEAKER.
LIKE GETTING ME BACK UNDER CONTROL AND MAKING PEOPLE FORGET DRAINS IT. AT LEAST FOR A LITTLE WHILE.
BUT THIS TIME IS DIFFERENT. NO ONE HAS EVER REMEMBERED BEFORE.

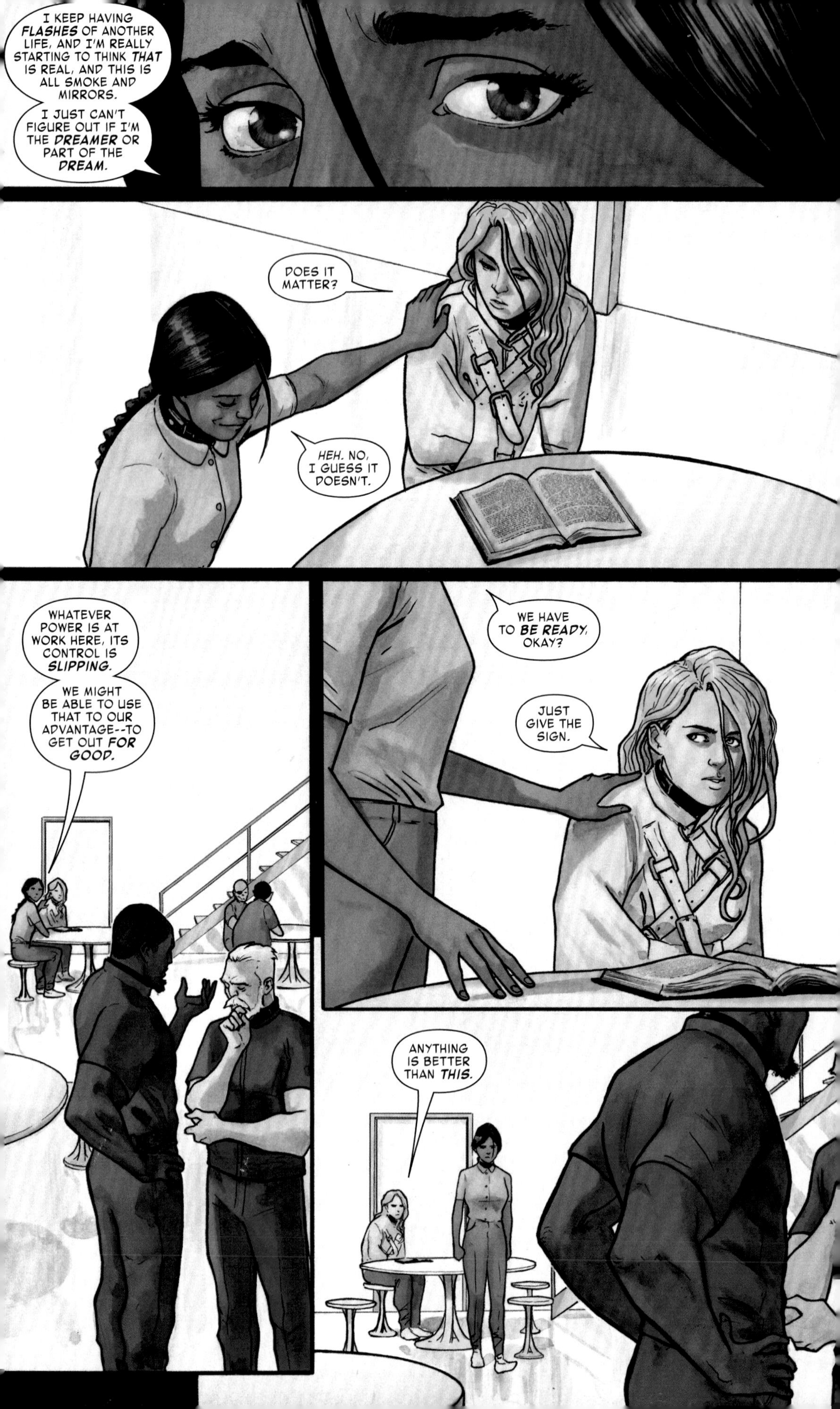
I KEEP HAVING FLASHES OF ANOTHER LIFE, AND I'M REALLY STARTING TO THINK THAT IS REAL, AND THIS IS ALL SMOKE AND MIRRORS.
I JUST CAN'T FIGURE OUT IF I'M THE DREAMER OR PART OF THE DREAM.
DOES IT MATTER?
HEH. NO, I GUESS IT DOESN'T.
WHATEVER POWER IS AT WORK HERE, ITS CONTROL IS SLIPPING.
WE MIGHT BE ABLE TO USE THAT TO OUR ADVANTAGE--TO GET OUT FOR GOOD.
WE HAVE TO BE READY, OKAY?
JUST GIVE THE SIGN.
ANYTHING IS BETTER THAN THIS.

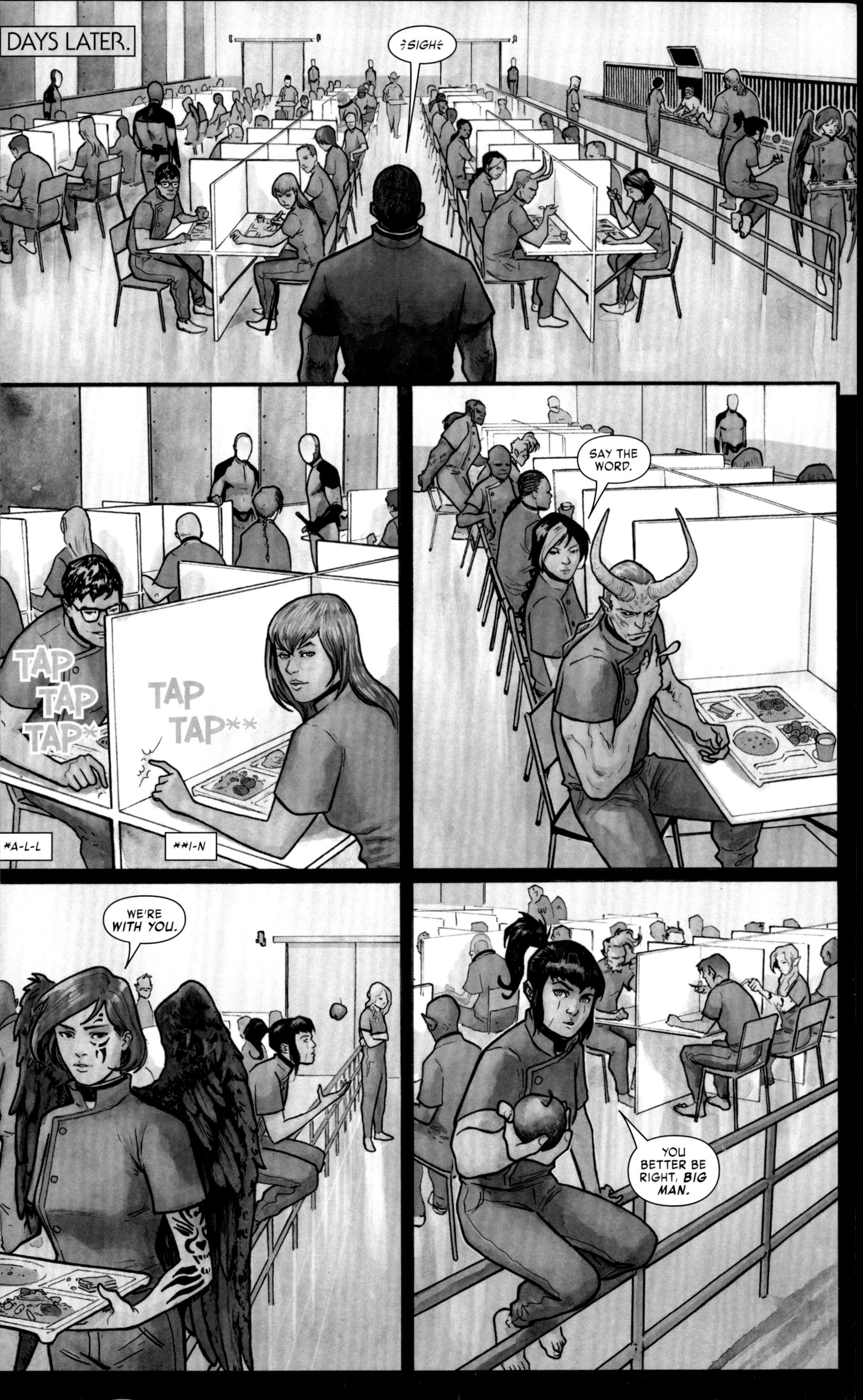
DAYS LATER.
SIGH
TAP TAP TAP*
TAP TAP**
*A-L-L
**I-N
SAY THE WORD.
WE'RE WITH YOU.
YOU BETTER BE RIGHT, BIG MAN.

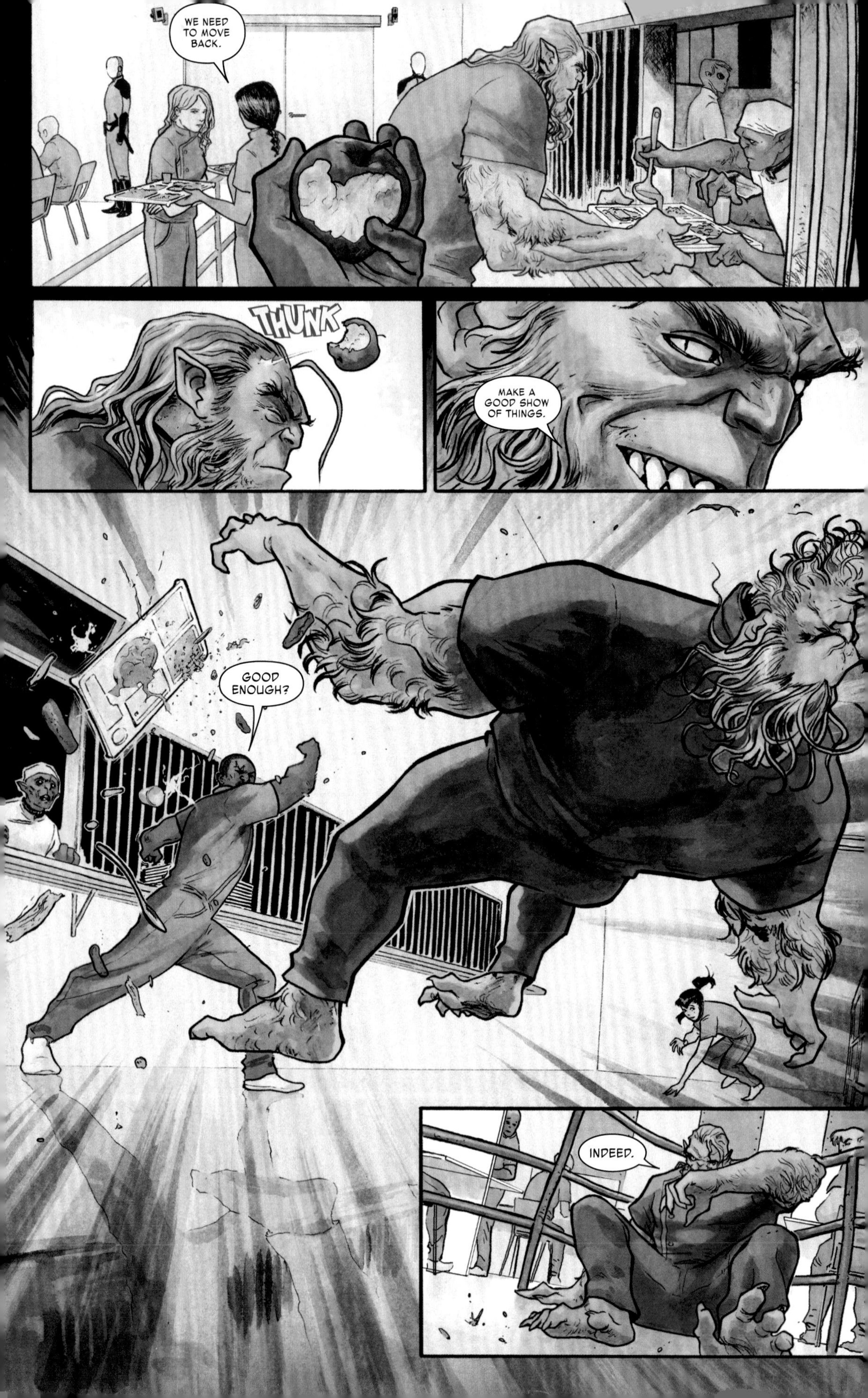
WE NEED TO MOVE BACK.
THUNK
MAKE A GOOD SHOW OF THINGS.
GOOD ENOUGH?
INDEED.

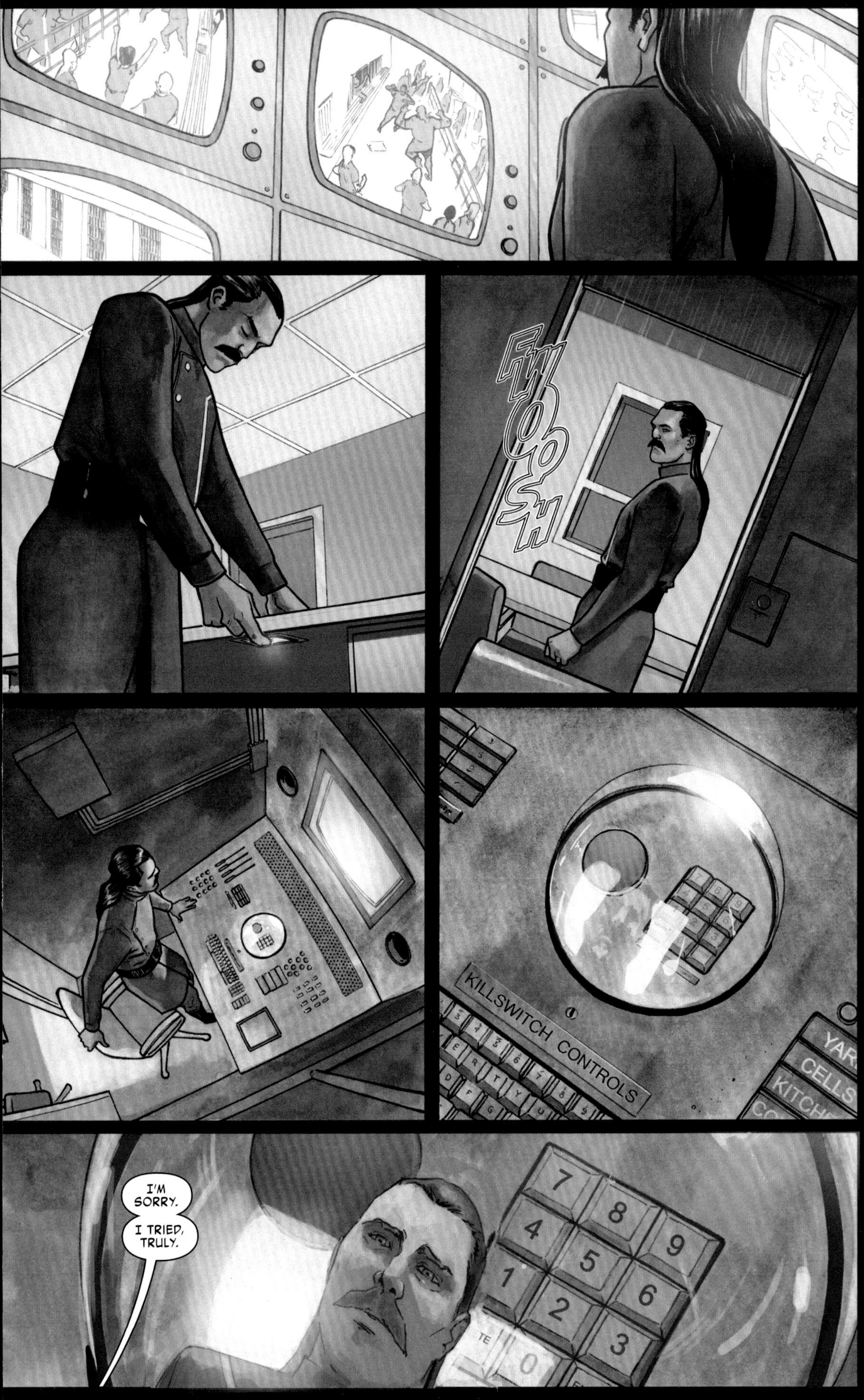
FWOOOSH
KILLSWITCH CONTROLS
YAR
CELLS
KITCHE
7 8 9
4 5 6
1 2 3
0
I'M SORRY.
I TRIED, TRULY.

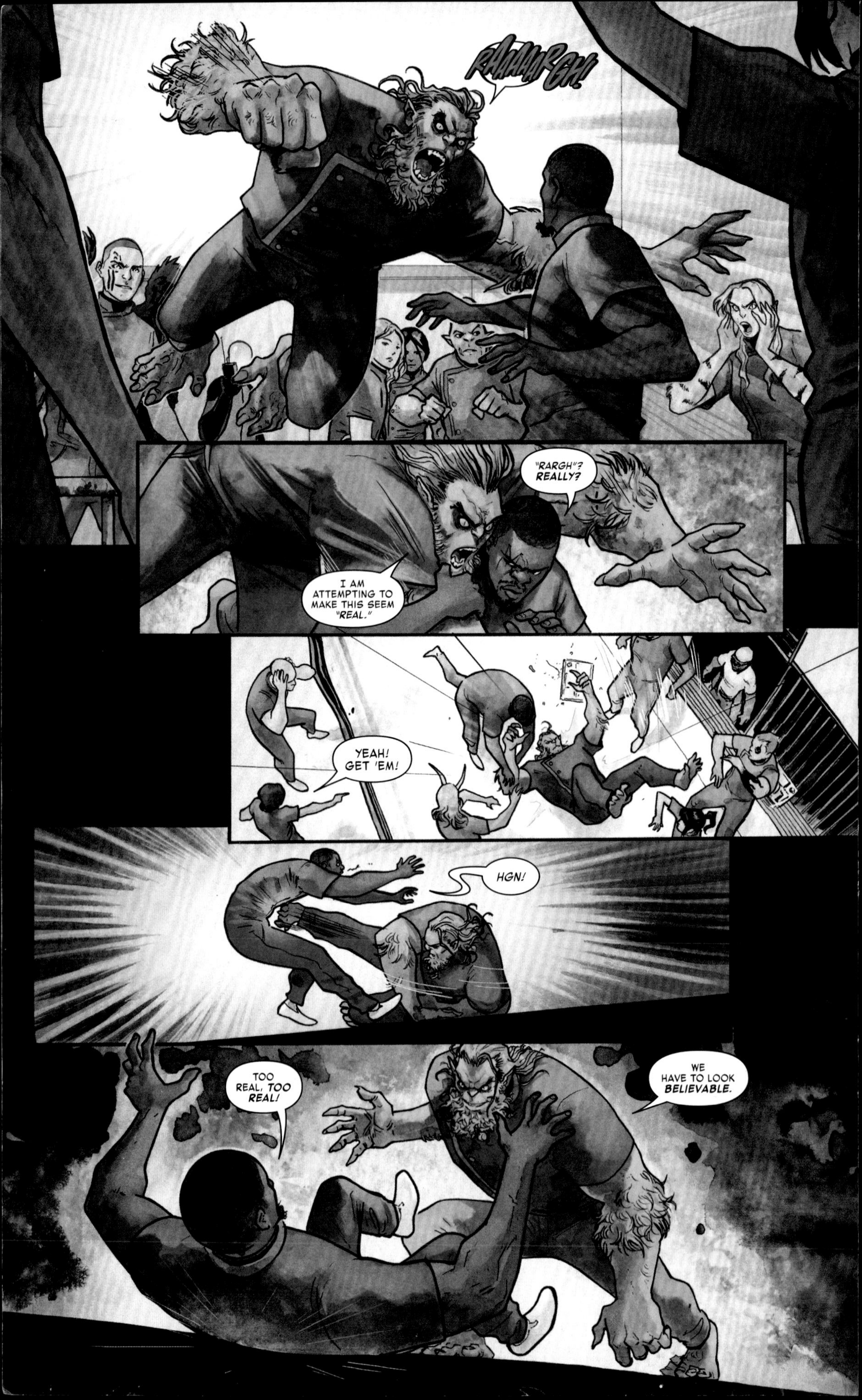
RAAAAARGH!
"RARGH"? REALLY?
I AM ATTEMPTING TO MAKE THIS SEEM "REAL."
YEAH! GET 'EM!
HGN!
TOO REAL, TOO REAL!
WE HAVE TO LOOK BELIEVABLE.

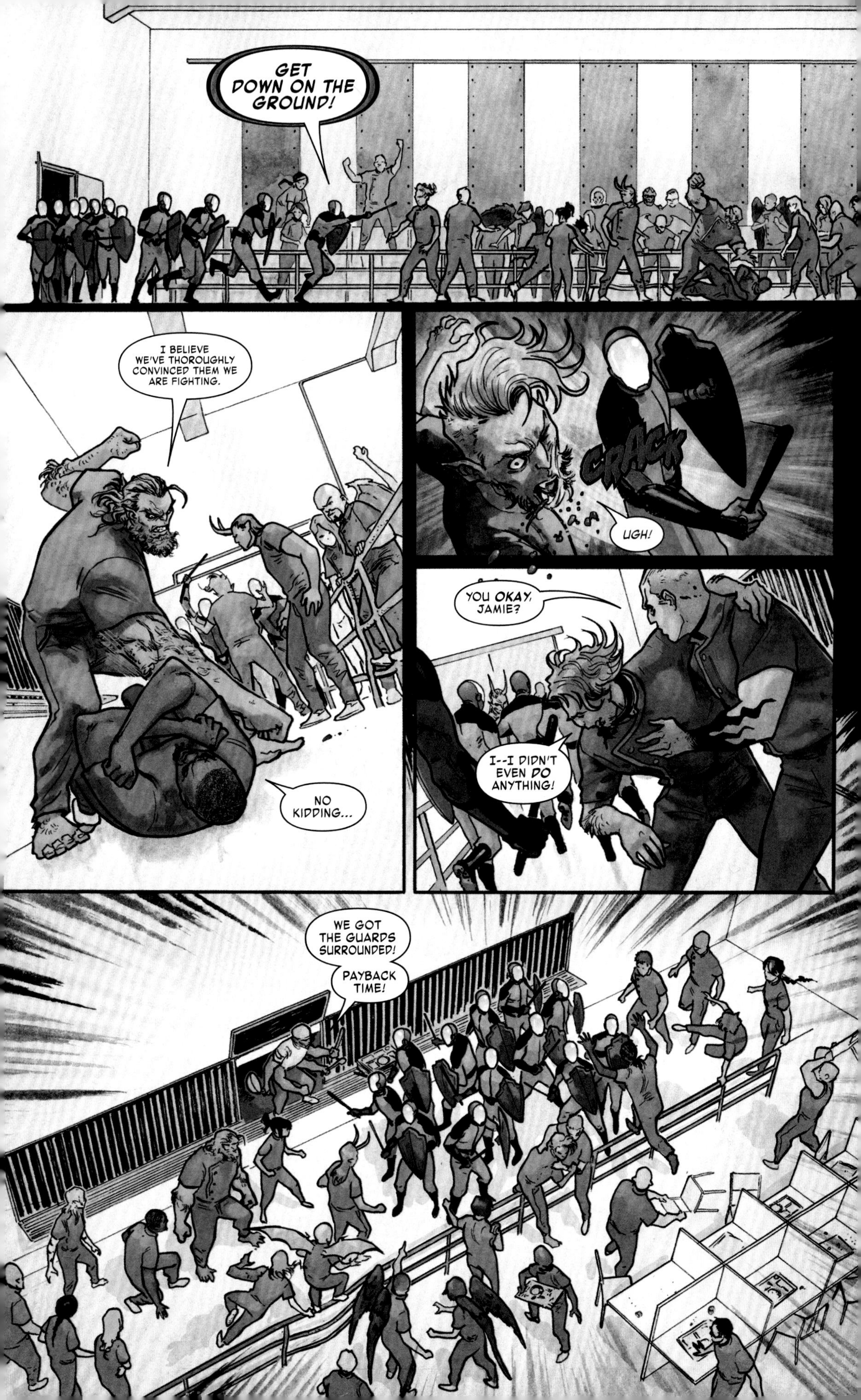
GET DOWN ON THE GROUND!
I BELIEVE WE'VE THOROUGHLY CONVINCED THEM WE ARE FIGHTING.
NO KIDDING...
CRACK
UGH!
YOU OKAY, JAMIE?
I--I DIDN'T EVEN DO ANYTHING!
WE GOT THE GUARDS SURROUNDED!
PAYBACK TIME!

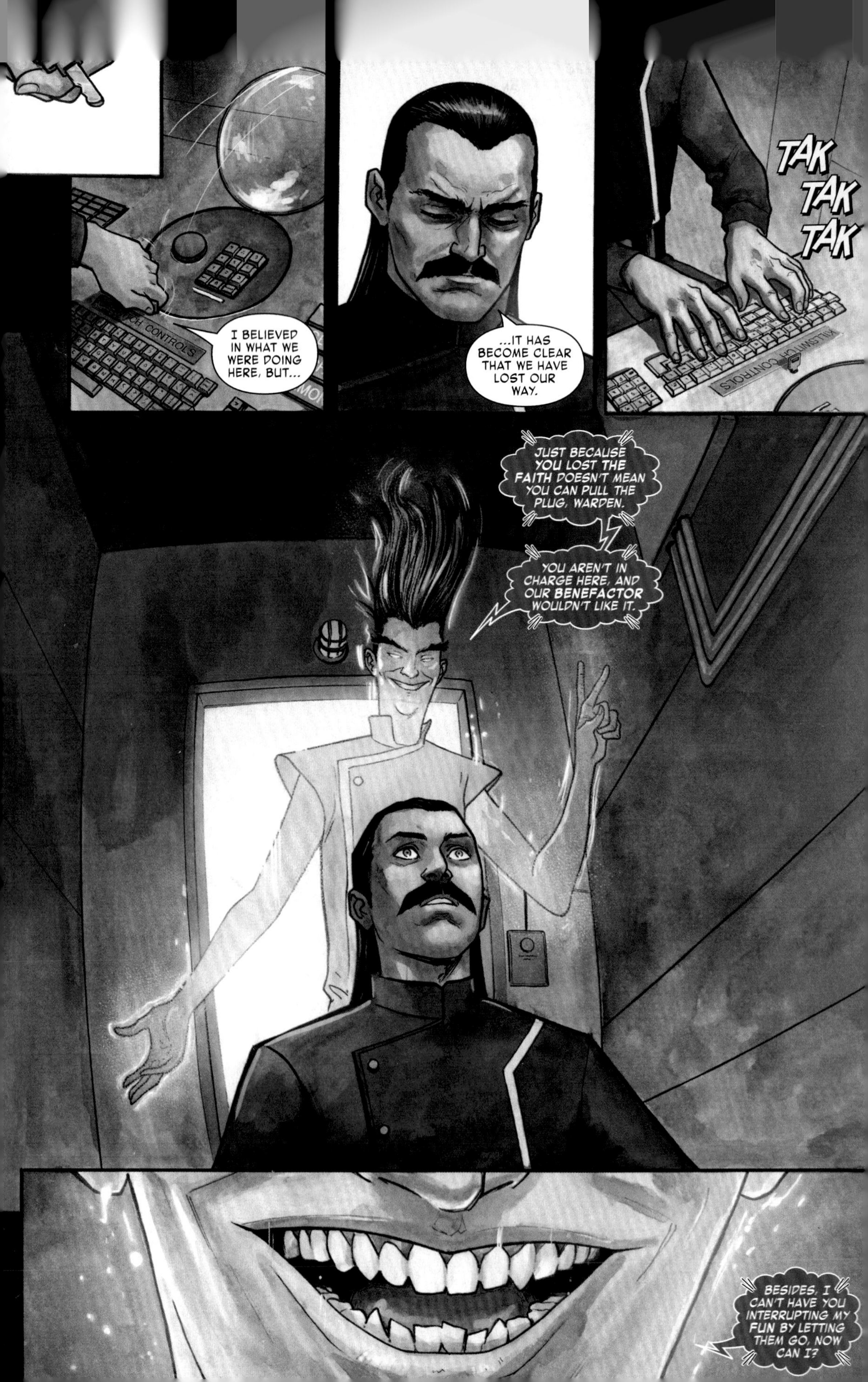
I BELIEVED IN WHAT WE WERE DOING HERE, BUT...
...IT HAS BECOME CLEAR THAT WE HAVE LOST OUR WAY.
TAK TAK TAK
JUST BECAUSE YOU LOST THE FAITH DOESN'T MEAN YOU CAN PULL THE PLUG, WARDEN.
YOU AREN'T IN CHARGE HERE, AND OUR BENEFACTOR WOULDN'T LIKE IT.
BESIDES, I CAN'T HAVE YOU INTERRUPTING MY FUN BY LETTING THEM GO, NOW CAN I?

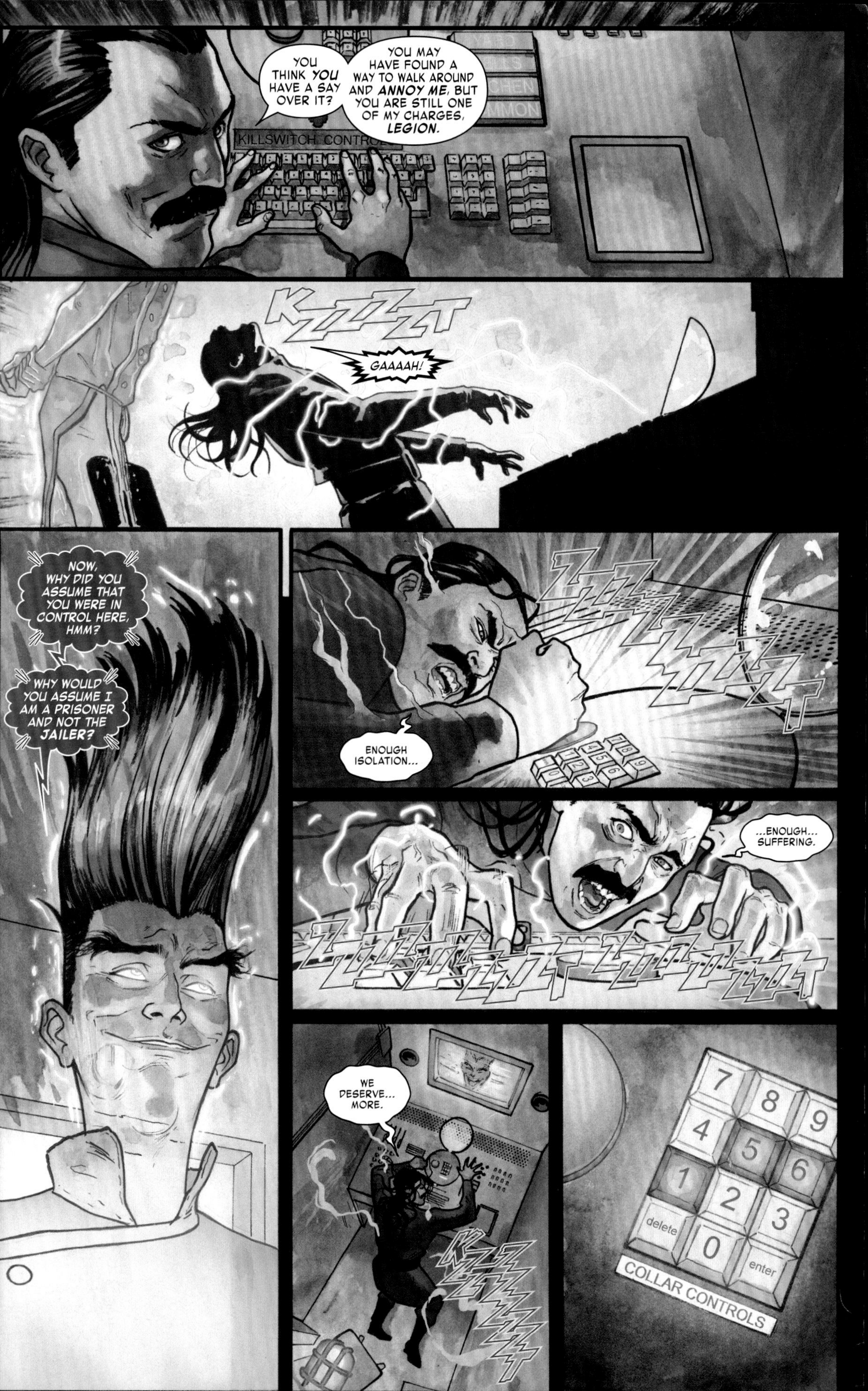
KILLSWITCH CONTROL
YOU THINK YOU HAVE A SAY OVER IT?
YOU MAY HAVE FOUND A WAY TO WALK AROUND AND ANNOY ME, BUT YOU ARE STILL ONE OF MY CHARGES, LEGION.
KZZZZZT
GAAAAH!
NOW, WHY DID YOU ASSUME THAT YOU WERE IN CONTROL HERE, HMM?
WHY WOULD YOU ASSUME I AM A PRISONER AND NOT THE JAILER?
ENOUGH ISOLATION...
...ENOUGH... SUFFERING.
WE DESERVE... MORE.
COLLAR CONTROLS

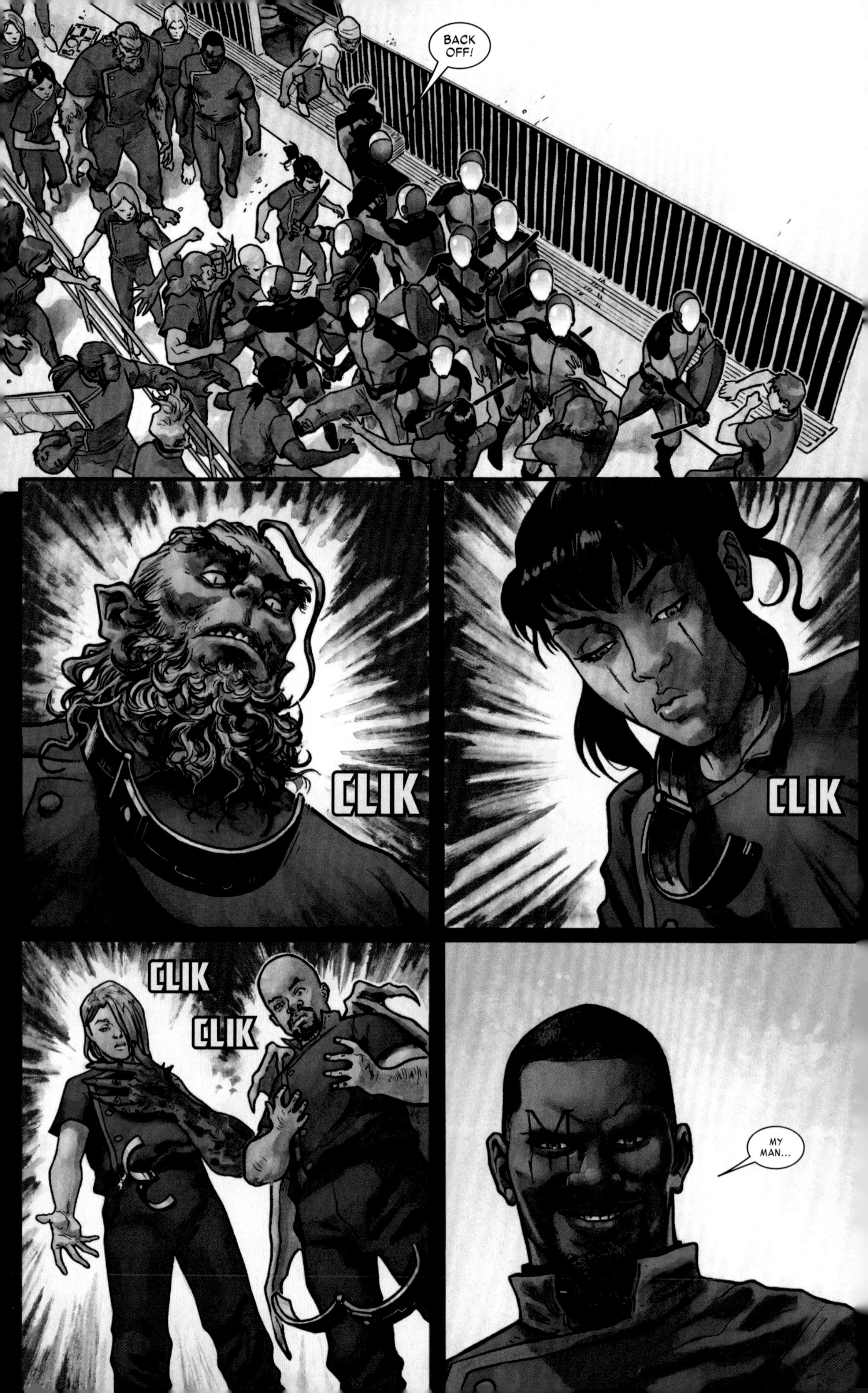
BACK OFF!
CLIK
CLIK
CLIK
CLIK
MY MAN...

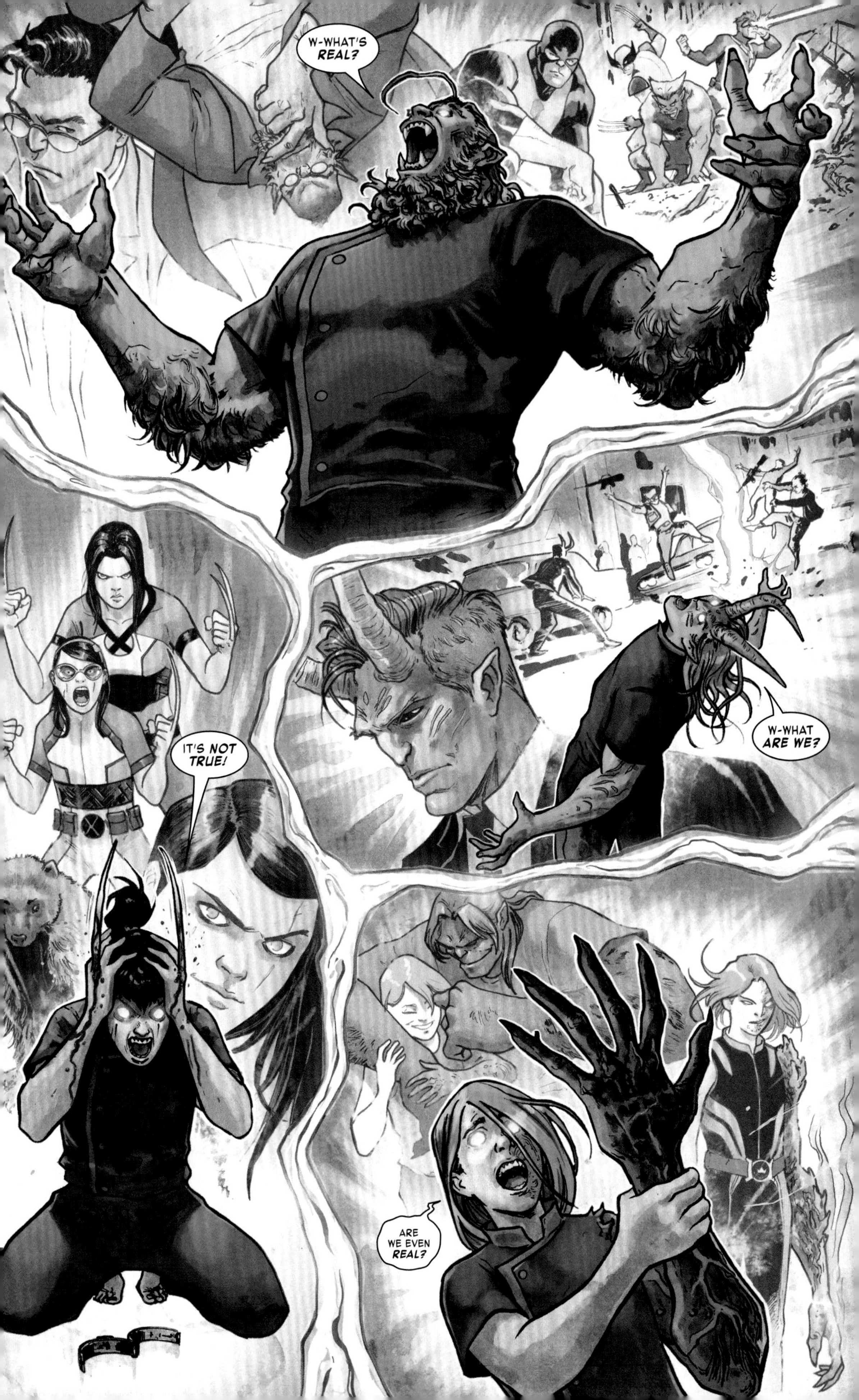
W-WHAT'S REAL?
IT'S NOT TRUE!
W-WHAT ARE WE?
ARE WE EVEN REAL?

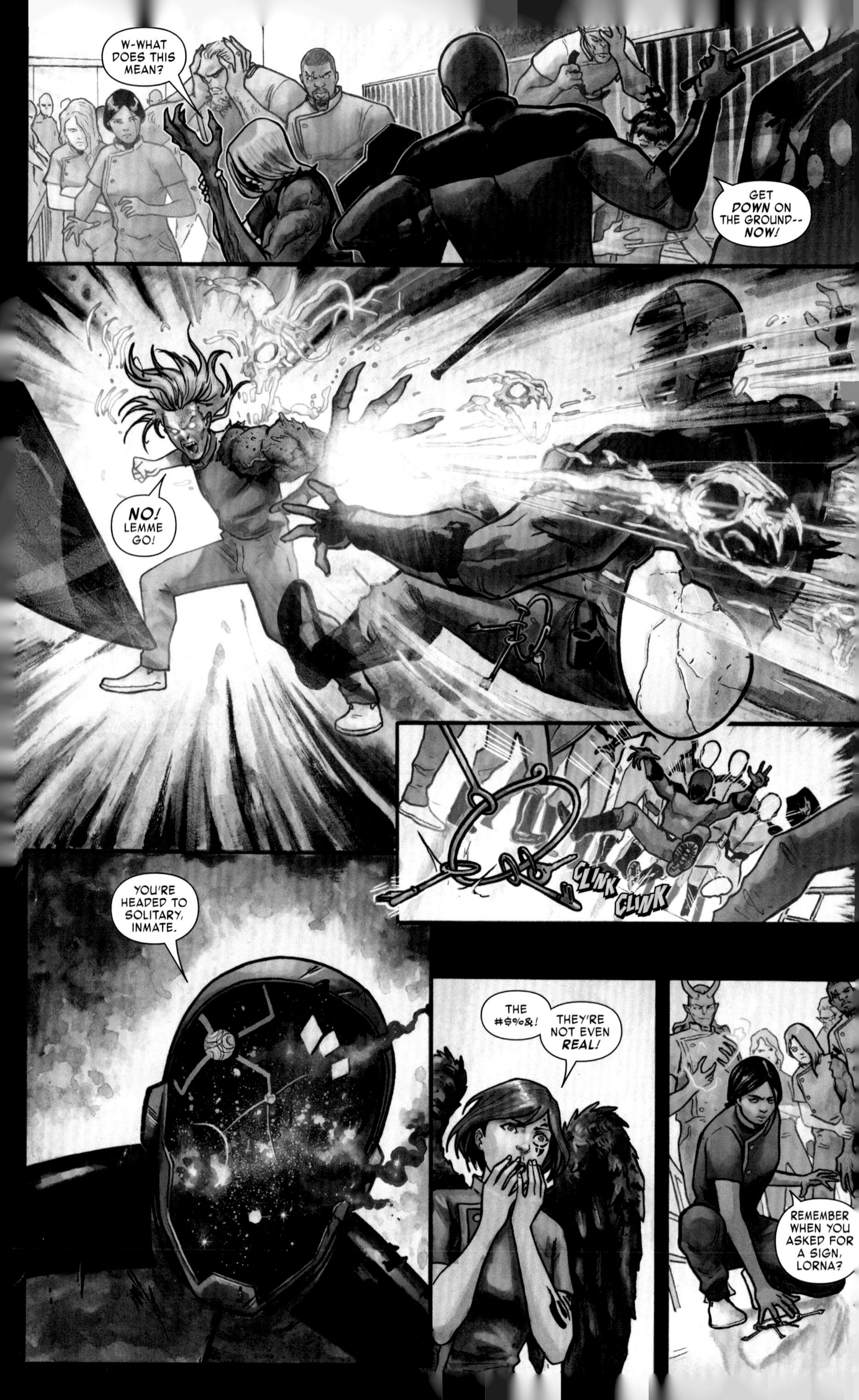
W-WHAT DOES THIS MEAN?
GET DOWN ON THE GROUND-- NOW!
NO! LEMME GO!
CLINK
CLINK
YOU'RE HEADED TO SOLITARY, INMATE.
THE #$%&!
THEY'RE NOT EVEN REAL!
REMEMBER WHEN YOU ASKED FOR A SIGN, LORNA?

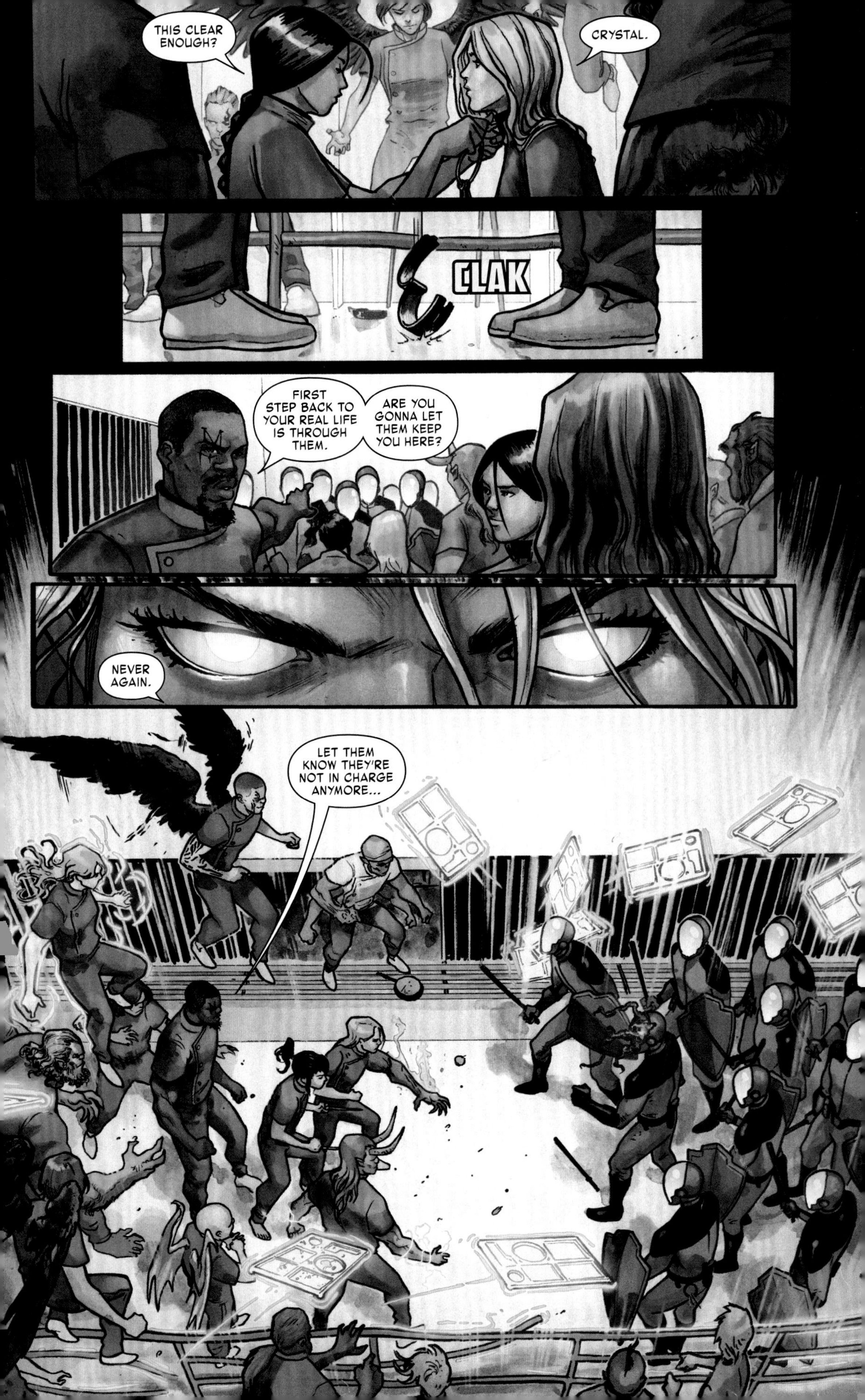
THIS CLEAR ENOUGH?
CRYSTAL.
CLAK
FIRST STEP BACK TO YOUR REAL LIFE IS THROUGH THEM.
ARE YOU GONNA LET THEM KEEP YOU HERE?
NEVER AGAIN.
LET THEM KNOW THEY'RE NOT IN CHARGE ANYMORE...

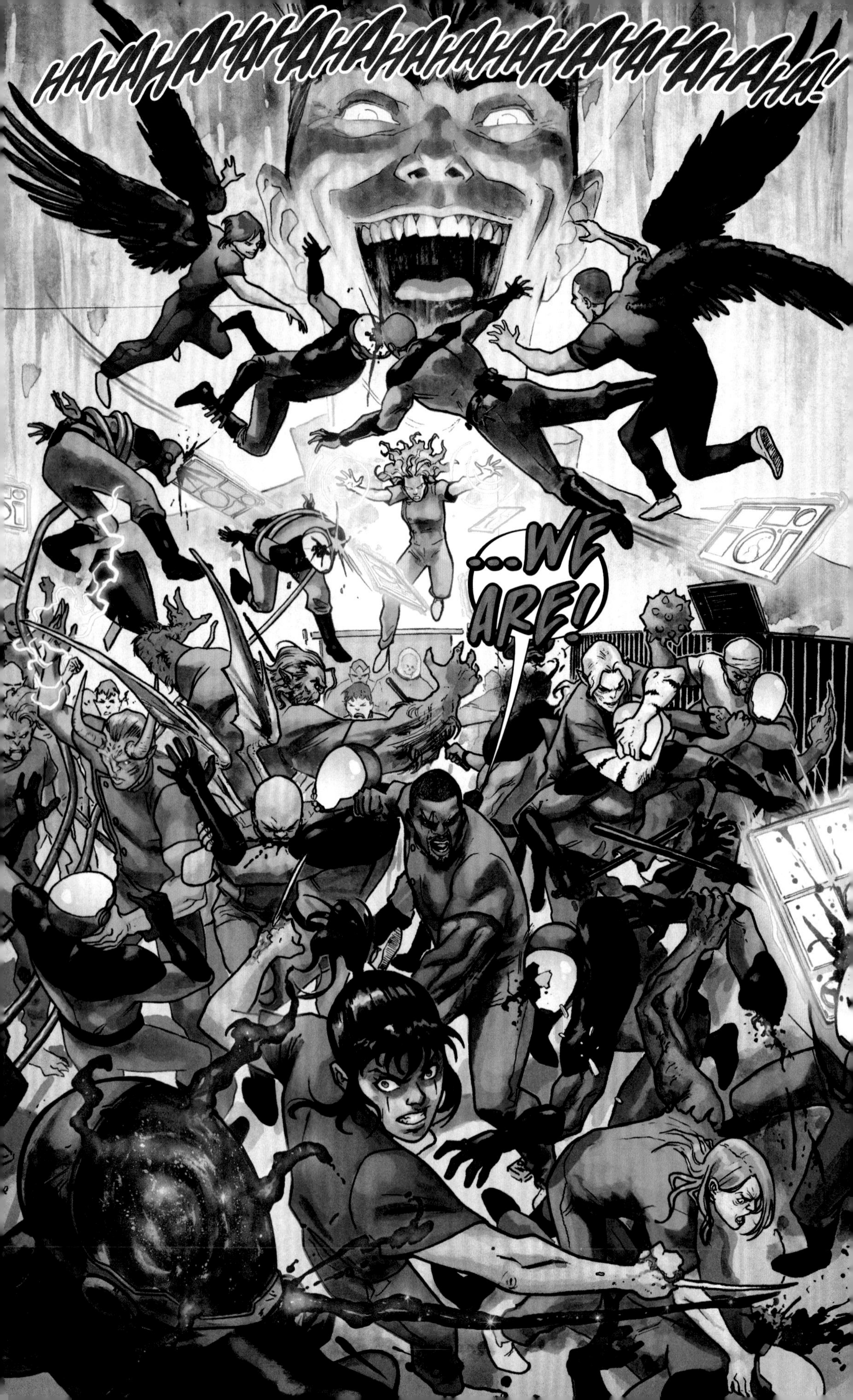
HAHAHAHAHAHAHAHAHAHAHAHAHAHAHAHAHAHAHAHA!
...WE ARE!

5

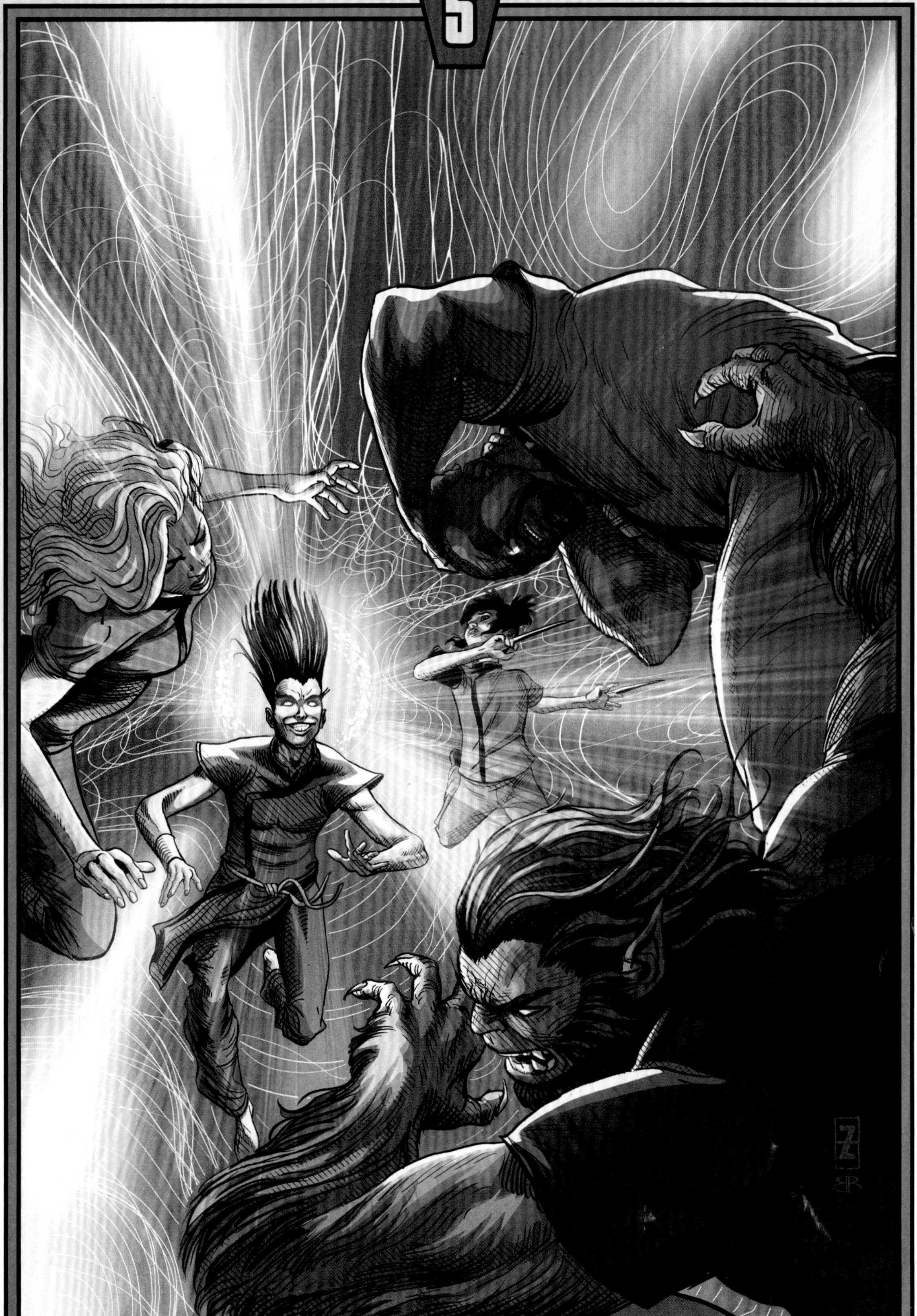

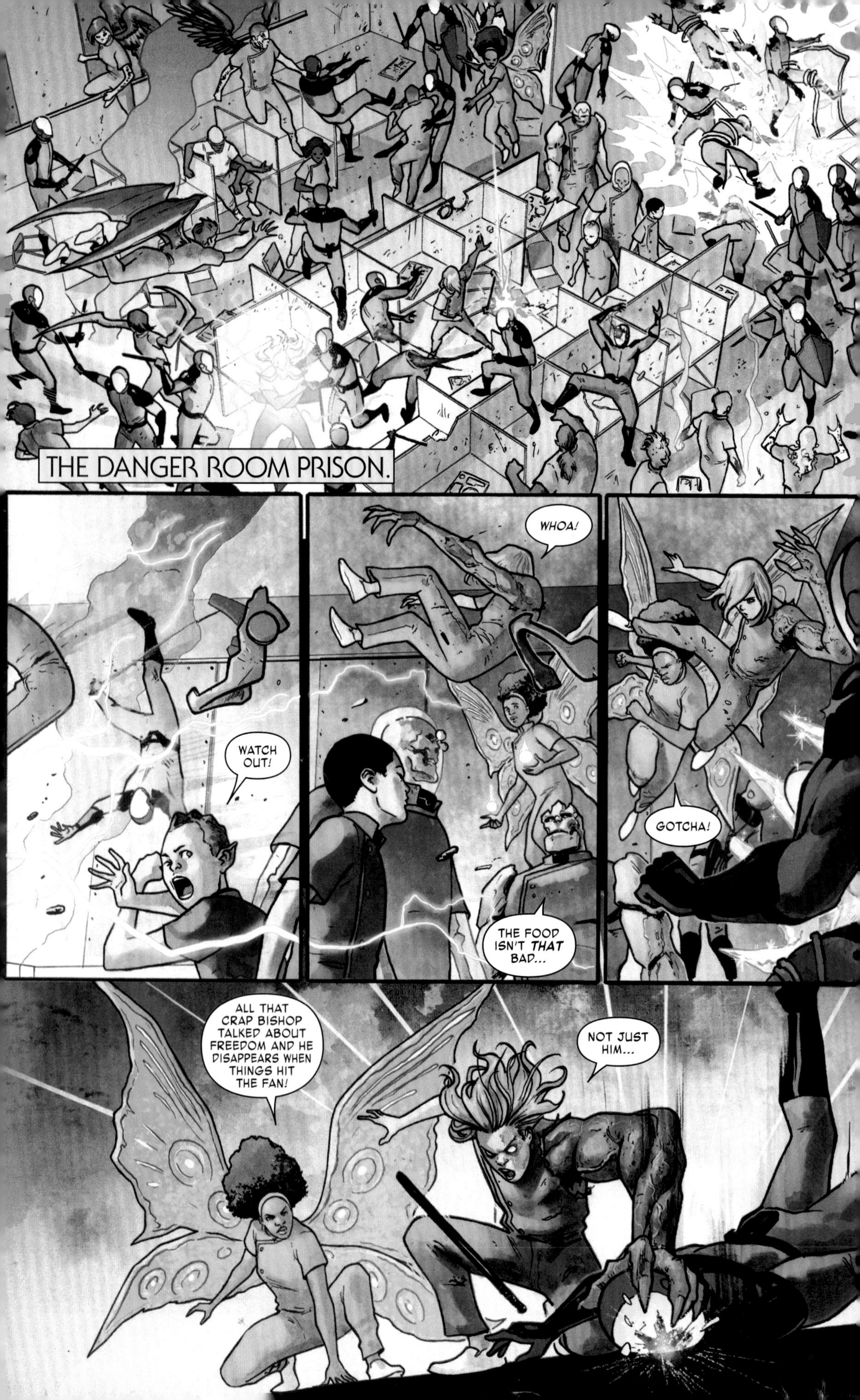
THE DANGER ROOM PRISON.
WATCH OUT!
WHOA!
THE FOOD ISN'T *THAT* BAD...
GOTCHA!
ALL THAT CRAP BISHOP TALKED ABOUT FREEDOM AND HE DISAPPEARS WHEN THINGS HIT THE FAN!
NOT JUST HIM...

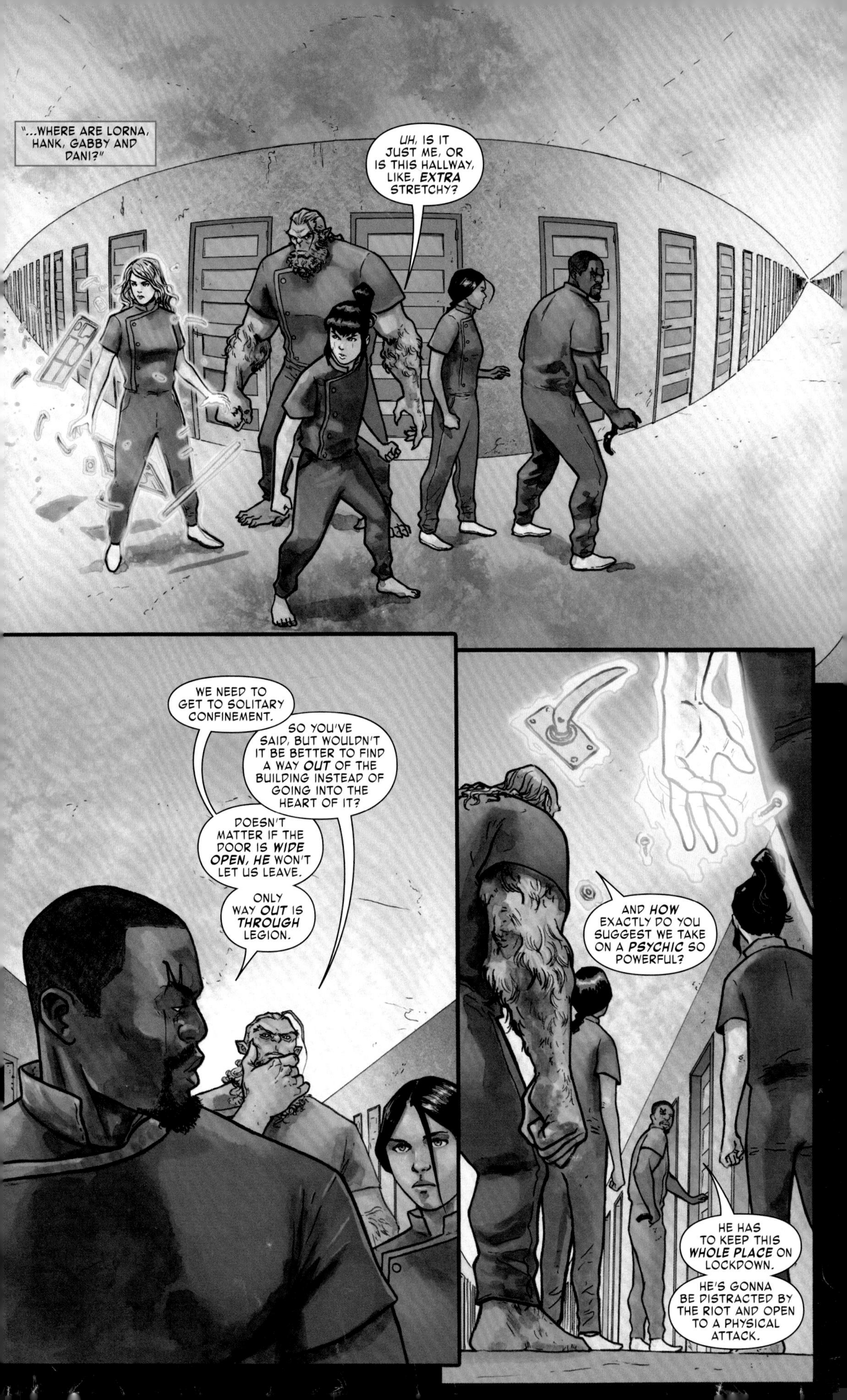
"...WHERE ARE LORNA, HANK, GABBY AND DANI?"
UH, IS IT JUST ME, OR IS THIS HALLWAY, LIKE, EXTRA STRETCHY?
WE NEED TO GET TO SOLITARY CONFINEMENT.
SO YOU'VE SAID, BUT WOULDN'T IT BE BETTER TO FIND A WAY OUT OF THE BUILDING INSTEAD OF GOING INTO THE HEART OF IT?
DOESN'T MATTER IF THE DOOR IS WIDE OPEN, HE WON'T LET US LEAVE.
ONLY WAY OUT IS THROUGH LEGION.
AND HOW EXACTLY DO YOU SUGGEST WE TAKE ON A PSYCHIC SO POWERFUL?
HE HAS TO KEEP THIS WHOLE PLACE ON LOCKDOWN.
HE'S GONNA BE DISTRACTED BY THE RIOT AND OPEN TO A PHYSICAL ATTACK.

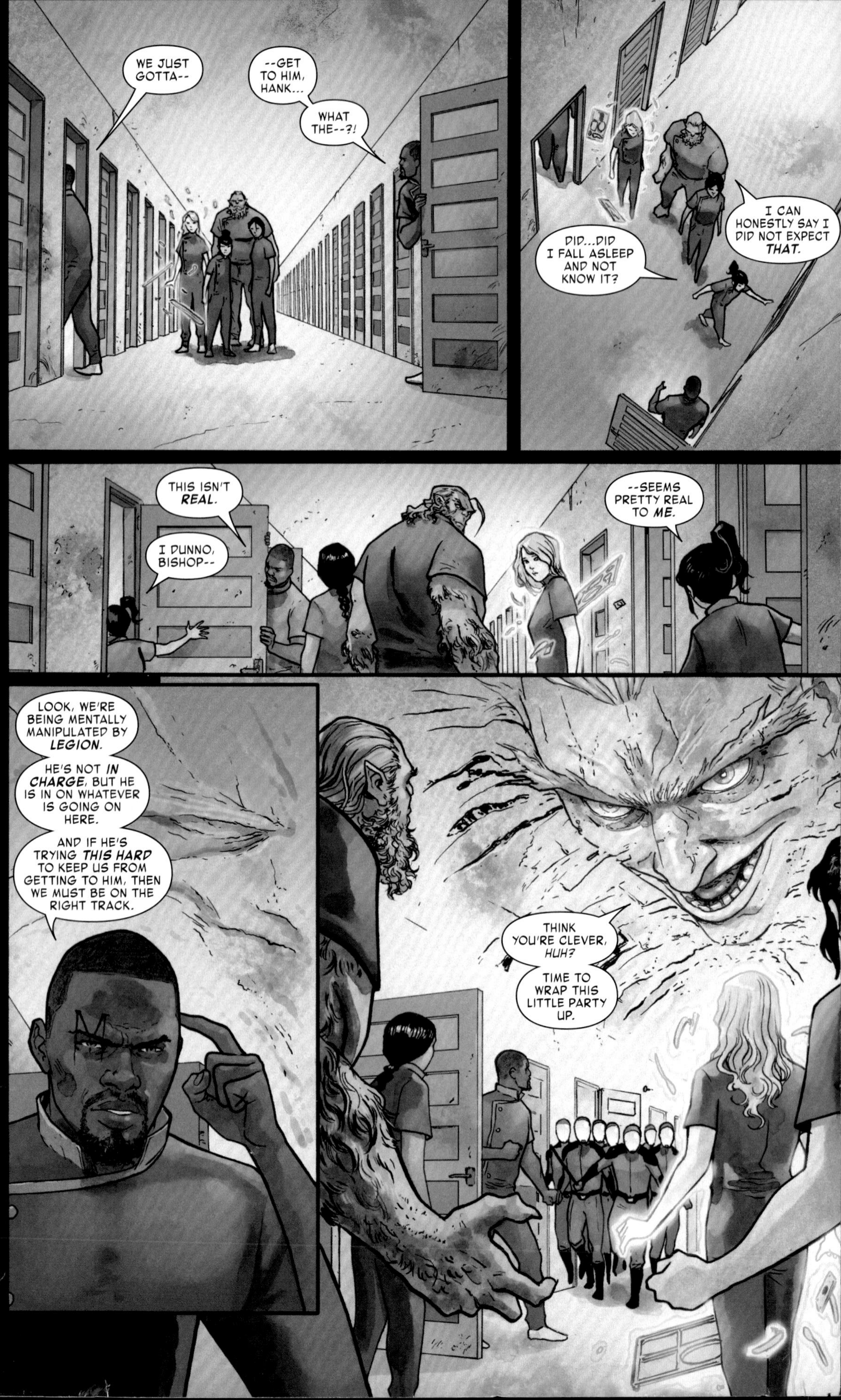
WE JUST GOTTA--
--GET TO HIM, HANK...
WHAT THE--?!
DID...DID I FALL ASLEEP AND NOT KNOW IT?
I CAN HONESTLY SAY I DID NOT EXPECT THAT.
THIS ISN'T REAL.
I DUNNO, BISHOP--
--SEEMS PRETTY REAL TO ME.
LOOK, WE'RE BEING MENTALLY MANIPULATED BY LEGION.
HE'S NOT IN CHARGE, BUT HE IS IN ON WHATEVER IS GOING ON HERE.
AND IF HE'S TRYING THIS HARD TO KEEP US FROM GETTING TO HIM, THEN WE MUST BE ON THE RIGHT TRACK.
THINK YOU'RE CLEVER, HUH?
TIME TO WRAP THIS LITTLE PARTY UP.

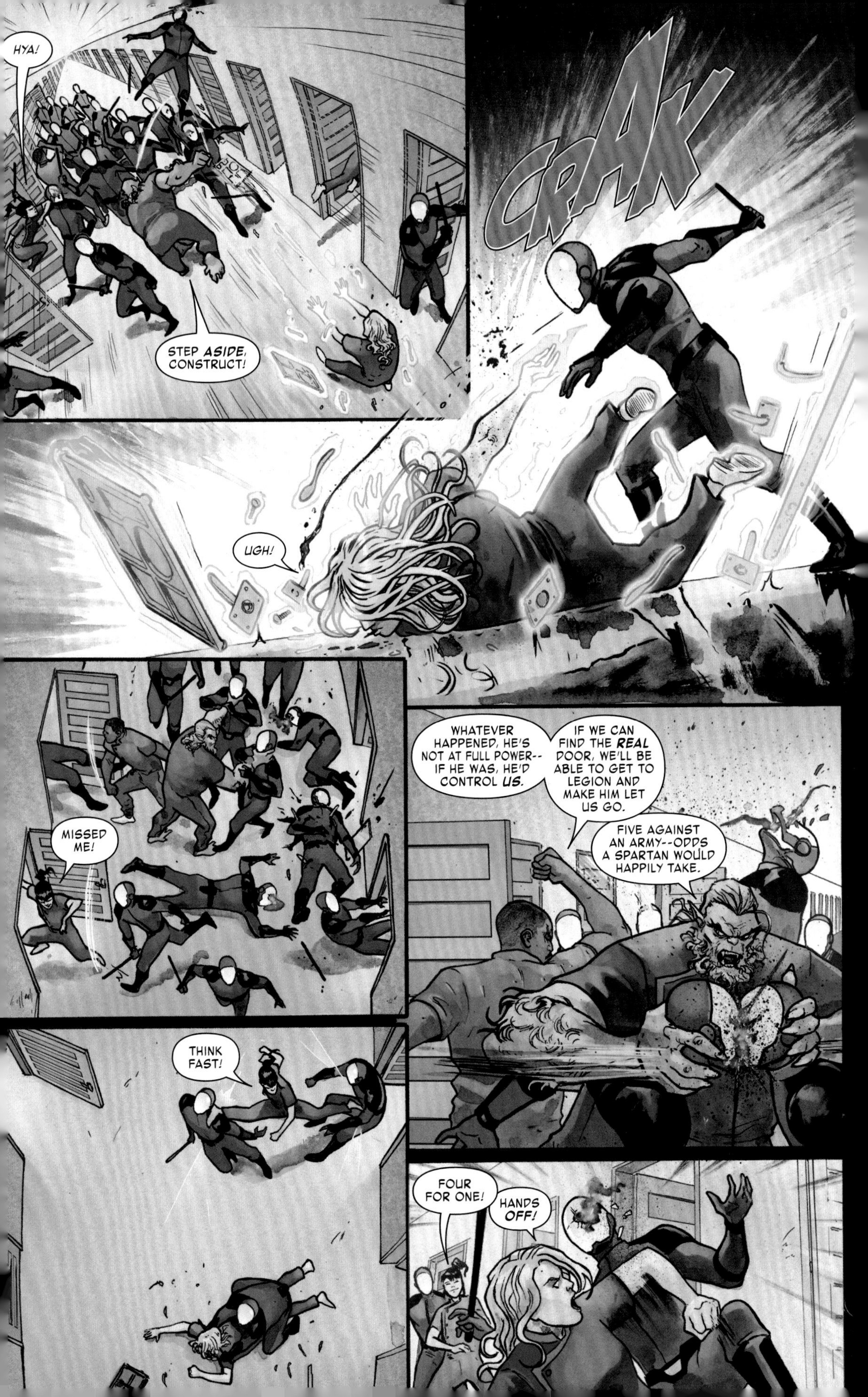
HYA!
CRAK
STEP ASIDE, CONSTRUCT!
UGH!
MISSED ME!
WHATEVER HAPPENED, HE'S NOT AT FULL POWER-- IF HE WAS, HE'D CONTROL US.
IF WE CAN FIND THE REAL DOOR, WE'LL BE ABLE TO GET TO LEGION AND MAKE HIM LET US GO.
FIVE AGAINST AN ARMY--ODDS A SPARTAN WOULD HAPPILY TAKE.
THINK FAST!
FOUR FOR ONE!
HANDS OFF!

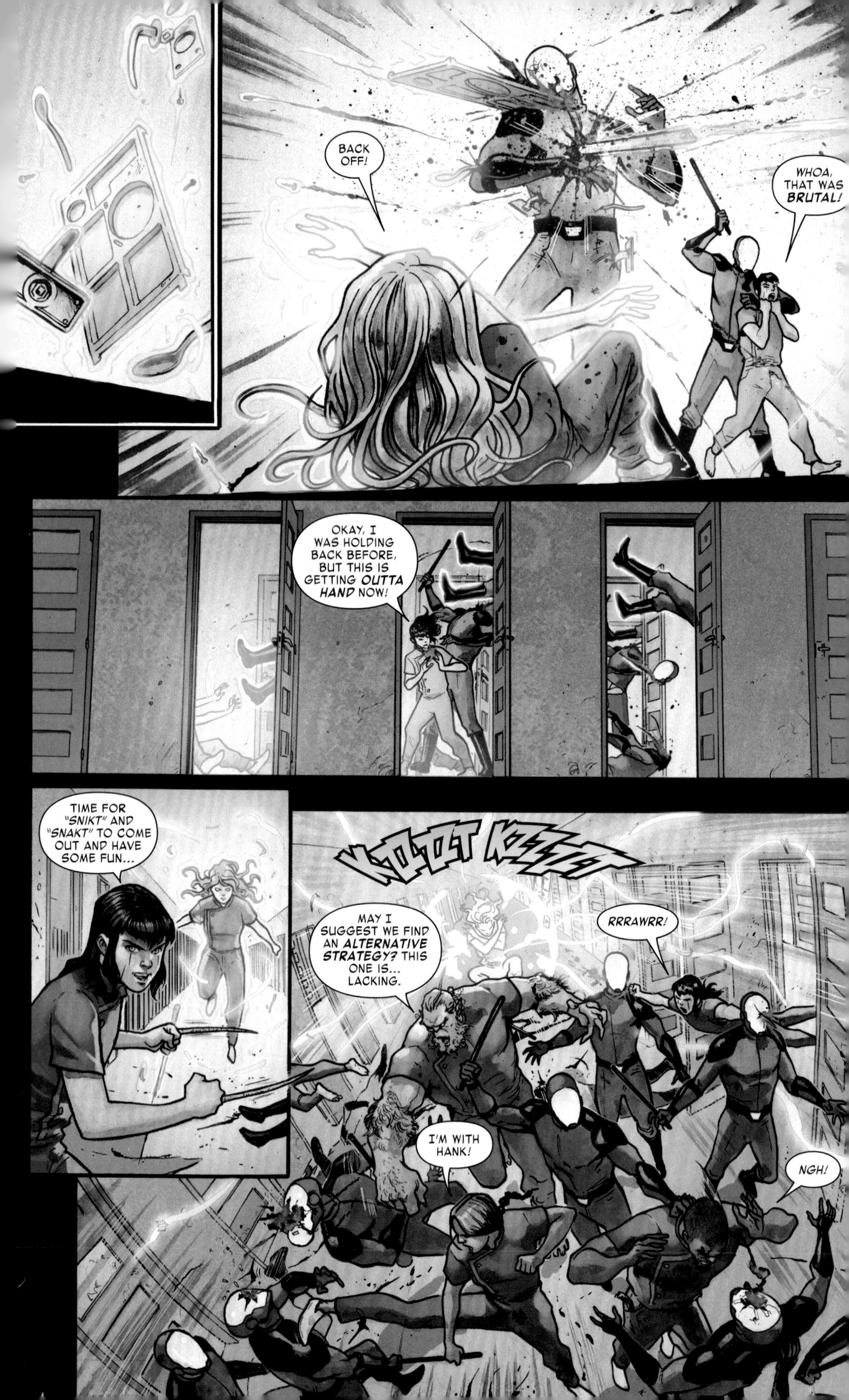
BACK OFF!
WHOA, THAT WAS BRUTAL!
OKAY, I WAS HOLDING BACK BEFORE, BUT THIS IS GETTING OUTTA HAND NOW!
TIME FOR "SNIKT" AND "SNAKT" TO COME OUT AND HAVE SOME FUN...
MAY I SUGGEST WE FIND AN ALTERNATIVE STRATEGY? THIS ONE IS... LACKING.
RRRAWRR!
I'M WITH HANK!
NGH!

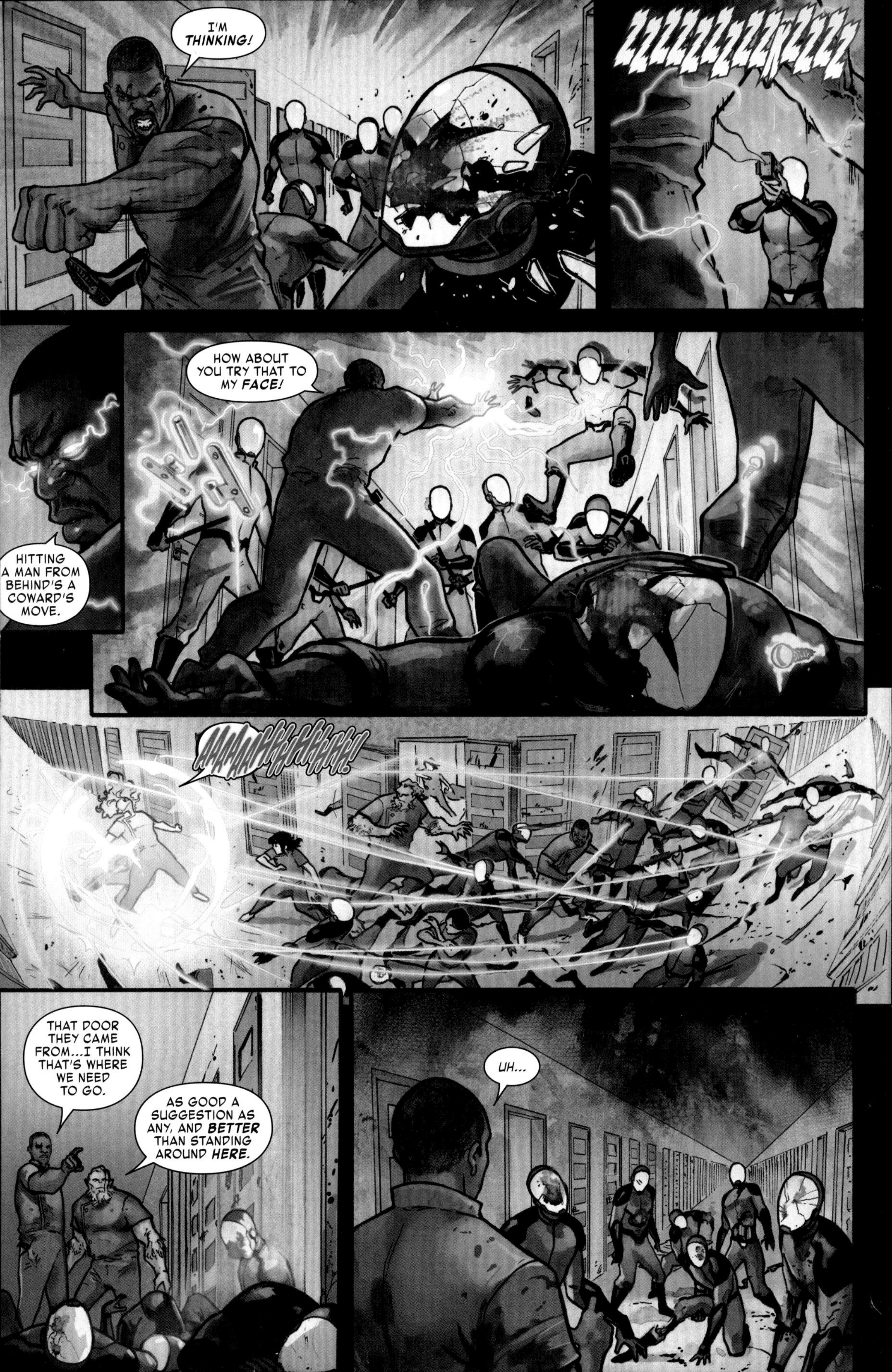
I'M THINKING!
ZZZZZZZZZRZZZZ
HOW ABOUT YOU TRY THAT TO MY FACE!
HITTING A MAN FROM BEHIND'S A COWARD'S MOVE.
THAT DOOR THEY CAME FROM...I THINK THAT'S WHERE WE NEED TO GO.
AS GOOD A SUGGESTION AS ANY, AND BETTER THAN STANDING AROUND HERE.
UH...

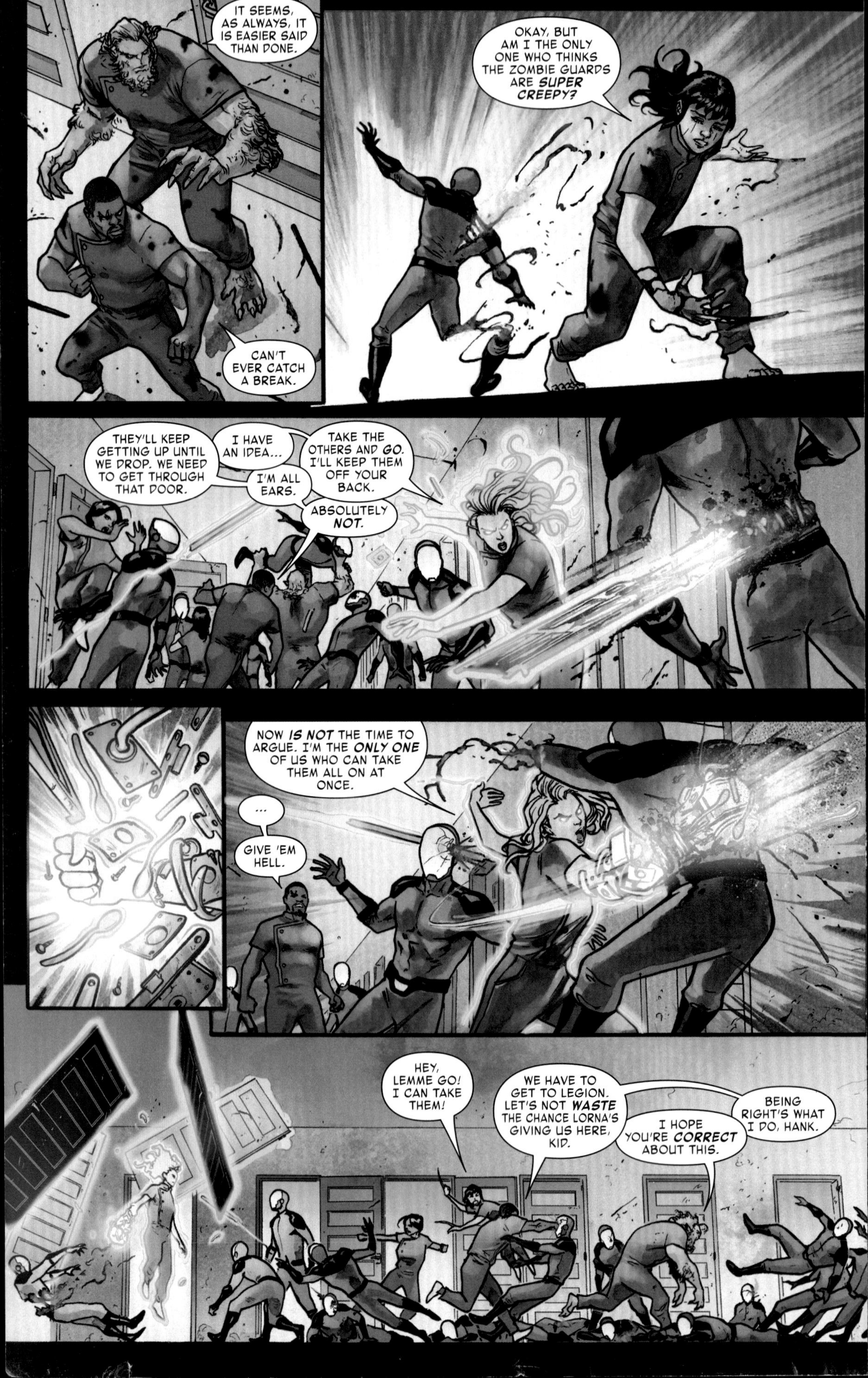
IT SEEMS, AS ALWAYS, IT IS EASIER SAID THAN DONE.
CAN'T EVER CATCH A BREAK.
OKAY, BUT AM I THE ONLY ONE WHO THINKS THE ZOMBIE GUARDS ARE SUPER CREEPY?
THEY'LL KEEP GETTING UP UNTIL WE DROP. WE NEED TO GET THROUGH THAT DOOR.
I HAVE AN IDEA...
I'M ALL EARS.
TAKE THE OTHERS AND GO. I'LL KEEP THEM OFF YOUR BACK.
ABSOLUTELY NOT.
NOW IS NOT THE TIME TO ARGUE. I'M THE ONLY ONE OF US WHO CAN TAKE THEM ALL ON AT ONCE.
...
GIVE 'EM HELL.
HEY, LEMME GO! I CAN TAKE THEM!
WE HAVE TO GET TO LEGION. LET'S NOT WASTE THE CHANCE LORNA'S GIVING US HERE, KID.
I HOPE YOU'RE CORRECT ABOUT THIS.
BEING RIGHT'S WHAT I DO, HANK.

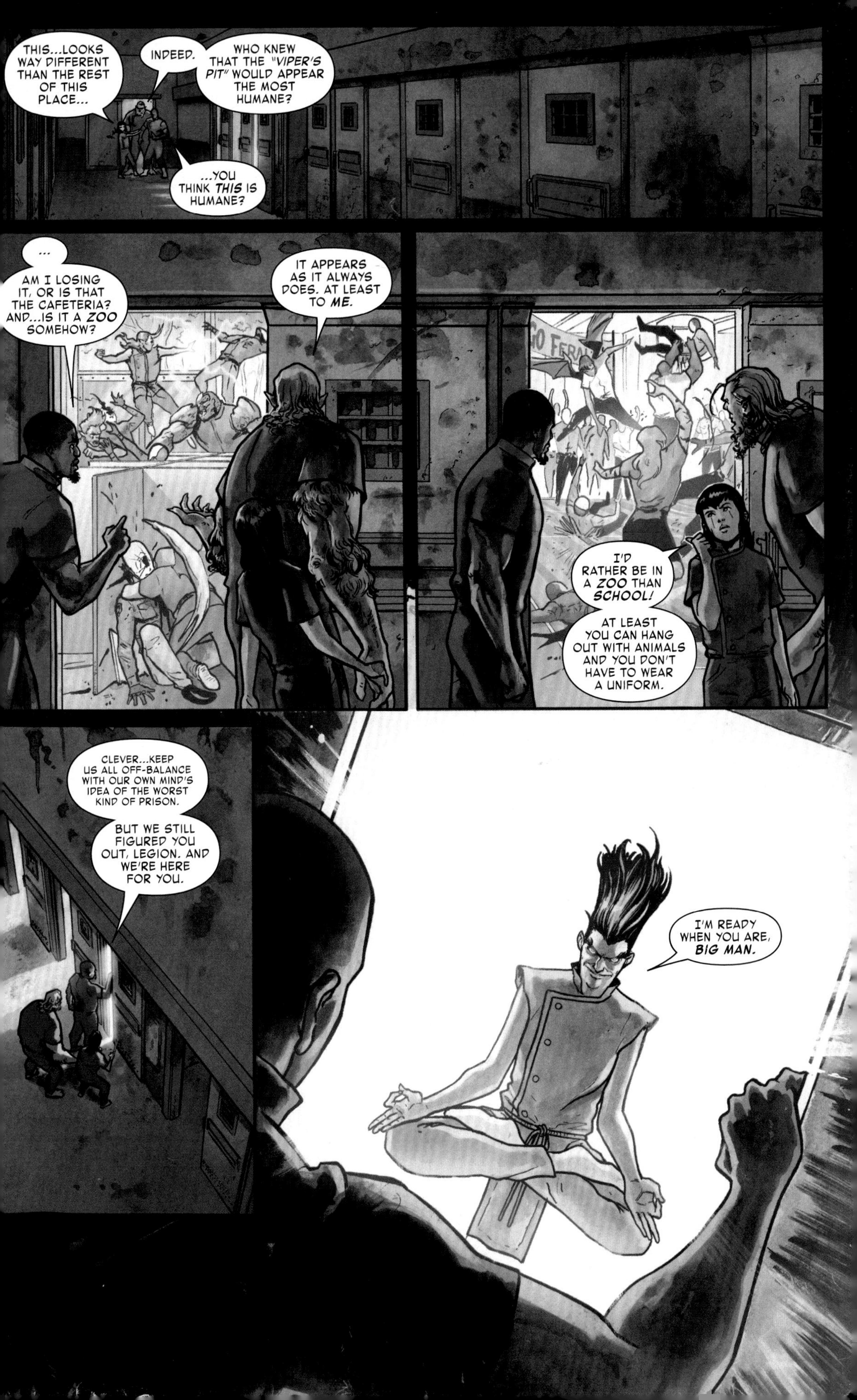
THIS...LOOKS WAY DIFFERENT THAN THE REST OF THIS PLACE...
INDEED.
WHO KNEW THAT THE "VIPER'S PIT" WOULD APPEAR THE MOST HUMANE?
...YOU THINK THIS IS HUMANE?
...
AM I LOSING IT, OR IS THAT THE CAFETERIA? AND...IS IT A ZOO SOMEHOW?
IT APPEARS AS IT ALWAYS DOES. AT LEAST TO ME.
GO FERA
I'D RATHER BE IN A ZOO THAN SCHOOL!
AT LEAST YOU CAN HANG OUT WITH ANIMALS AND YOU DON'T HAVE TO WEAR A UNIFORM.
CLEVER...KEEP US ALL OFF-BALANCE WITH OUR OWN MIND'S IDEA OF THE WORST KIND OF PRISON.
BUT WE STILL FIGURED YOU OUT, LEGION. AND WE'RE HERE FOR YOU.
I'M READY WHEN YOU ARE, BIG MAN.

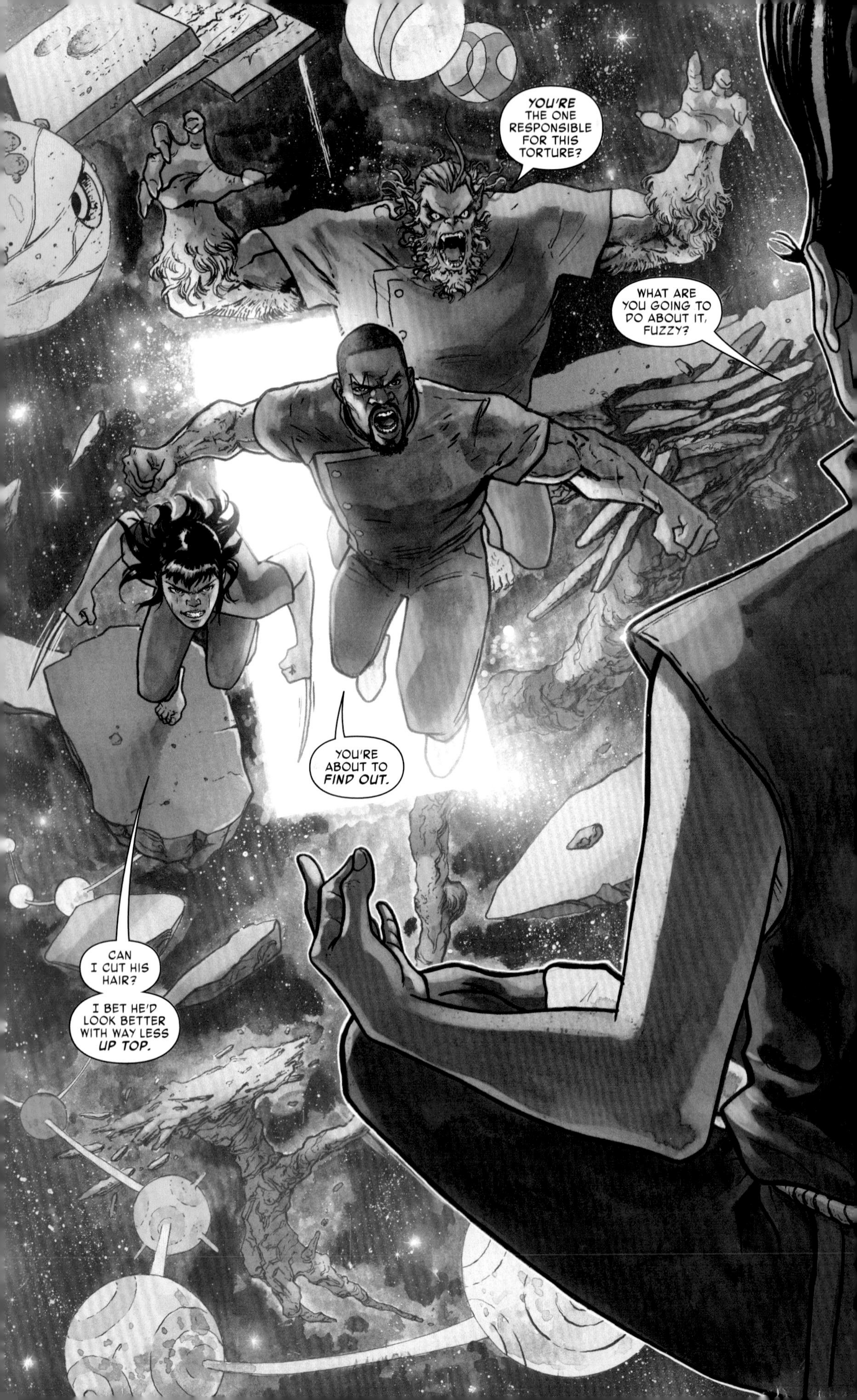
YOU'RE THE ONE RESPONSIBLE FOR THIS TORTURE?
WHAT ARE YOU GOING TO DO ABOUT IT, FUZZY?
YOU'RE ABOUT TO FIND OUT.
CAN I CUT HIS HAIR?
I BET HE'D LOOK BETTER WITH WAY LESS UP TOP.

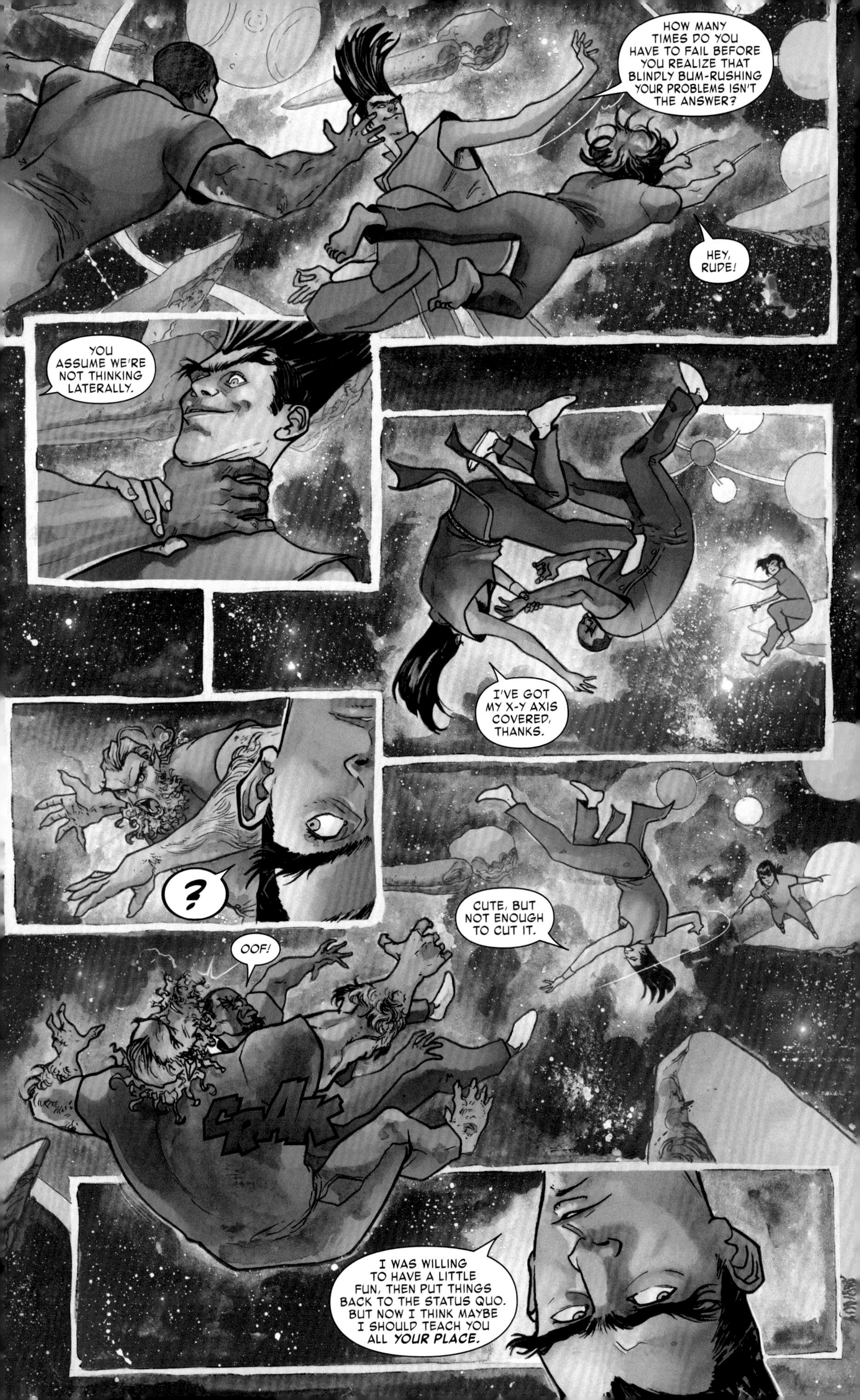
HOW MANY TIMES DO YOU HAVE TO FAIL BEFORE YOU REALIZE THAT BLINDLY BUM-RUSHING YOUR PROBLEMS ISN'T THE ANSWER?
HEY, RUDE!
YOU ASSUME WE'RE NOT THINKING LATERALLY.
I'VE GOT MY X-Y AXIS COVERED, THANKS.
?
CUTE, BUT NOT ENOUGH TO CUT IT.
OOF!
CRAK
I WAS WILLING TO HAVE A LITTLE FUN, THEN PUT THINGS BACK TO THE STATUS QUO. BUT NOW I THINK MAYBE I SHOULD TEACH YOU ALL *YOUR PLACE.*

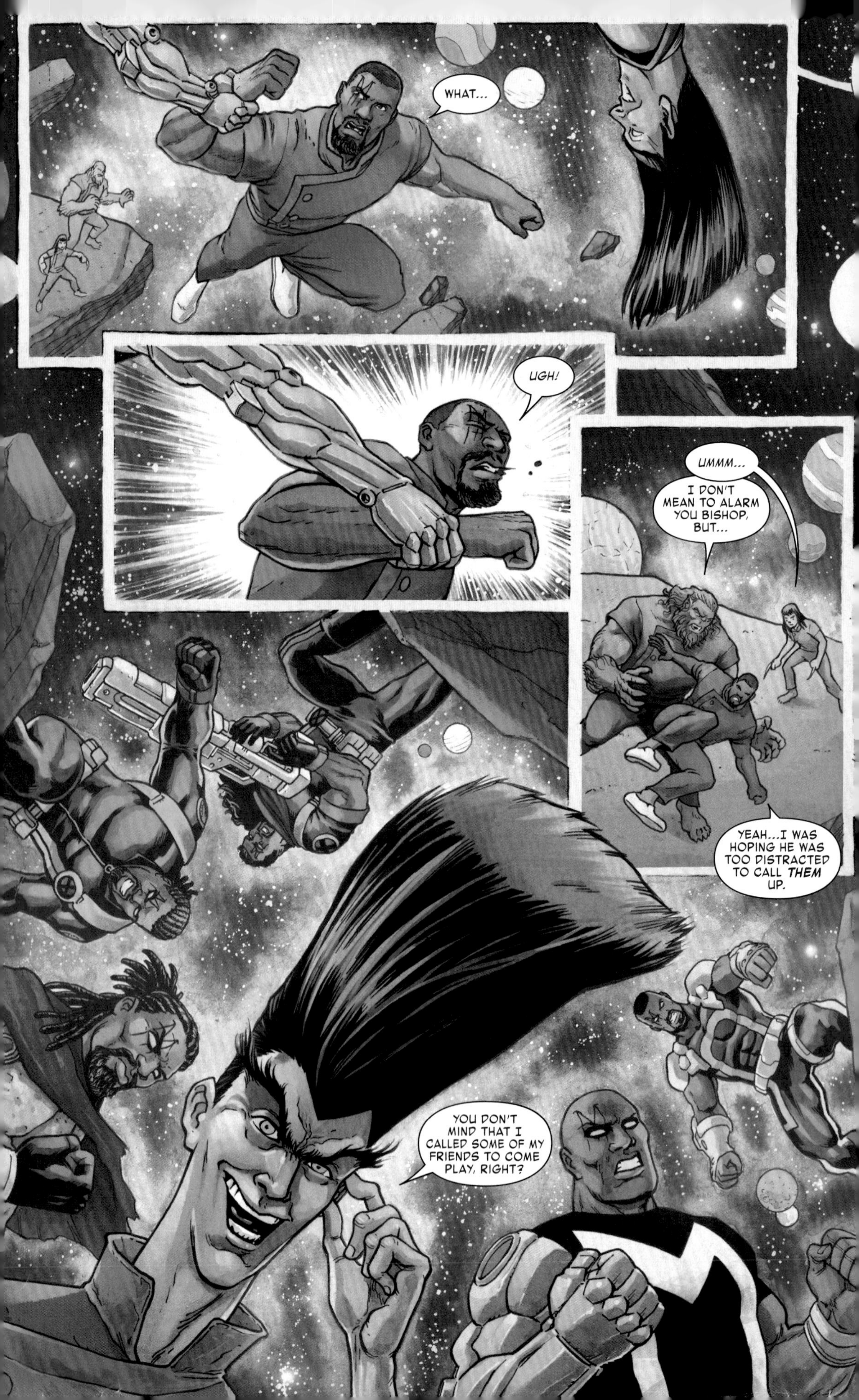
WHAT...
UGH!
UMMM...
I DON'T MEAN TO ALARM YOU BISHOP, BUT...
YEAH...I WAS HOPING HE WAS TOO DISTRACTED TO CALL THEM UP.
YOU DON'T MIND THAT I CALLED SOME OF MY FRIENDS TO COME PLAY, RIGHT?

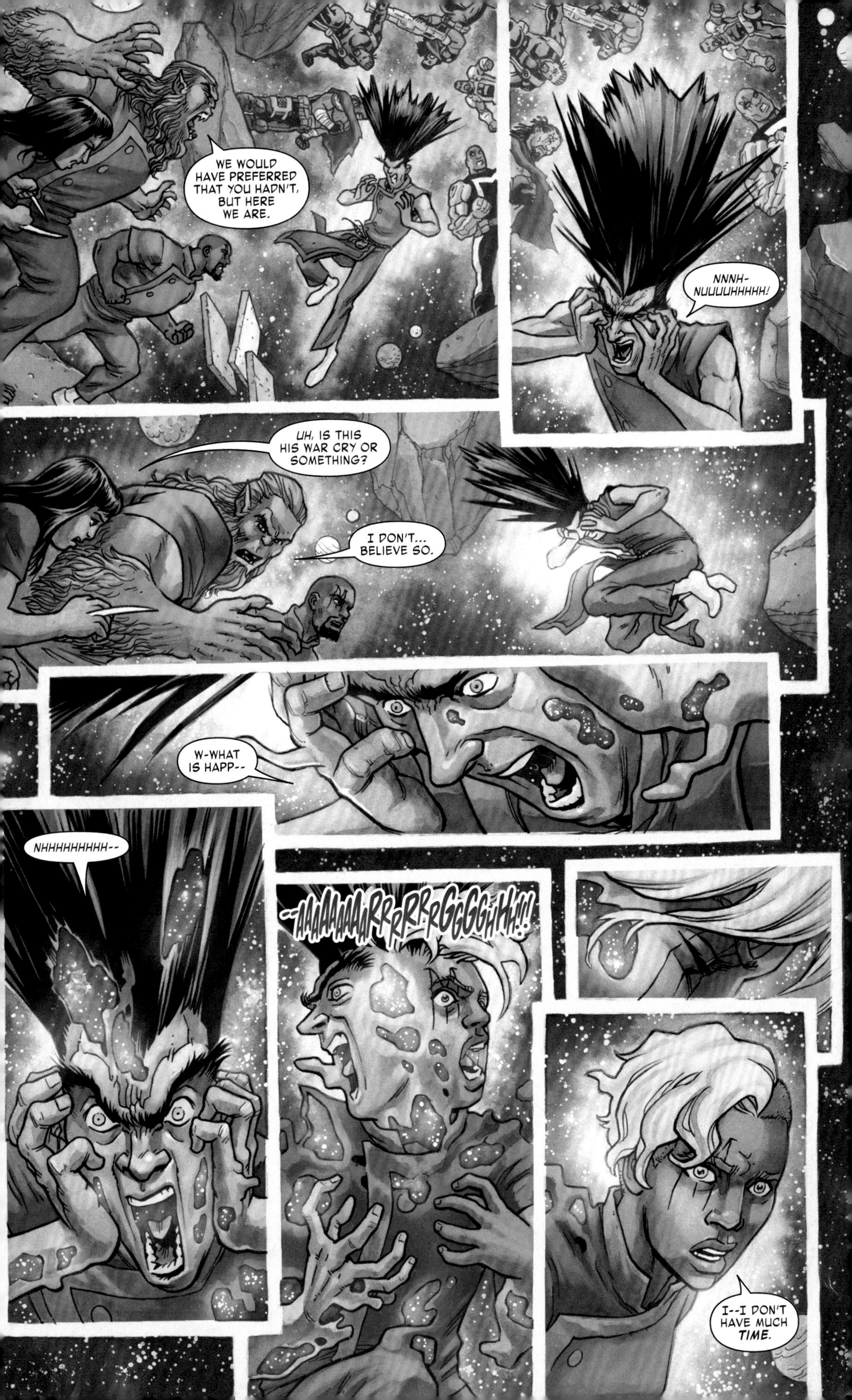
WE WOULD HAVE PREFERRED THAT YOU HADN'T, BUT HERE WE ARE.
NNNH-NUUUUHHHHH!
UH, IS THIS HIS WAR CRY OR SOMETHING?
I DON'T... BELIEVE SO.
W-WHAT IS HAPP--
NHHHHHHHHHH--
--AAAAAAAAARRRRRRGGGGHHH!!!
I--I DON'T HAVE MUCH TIME.

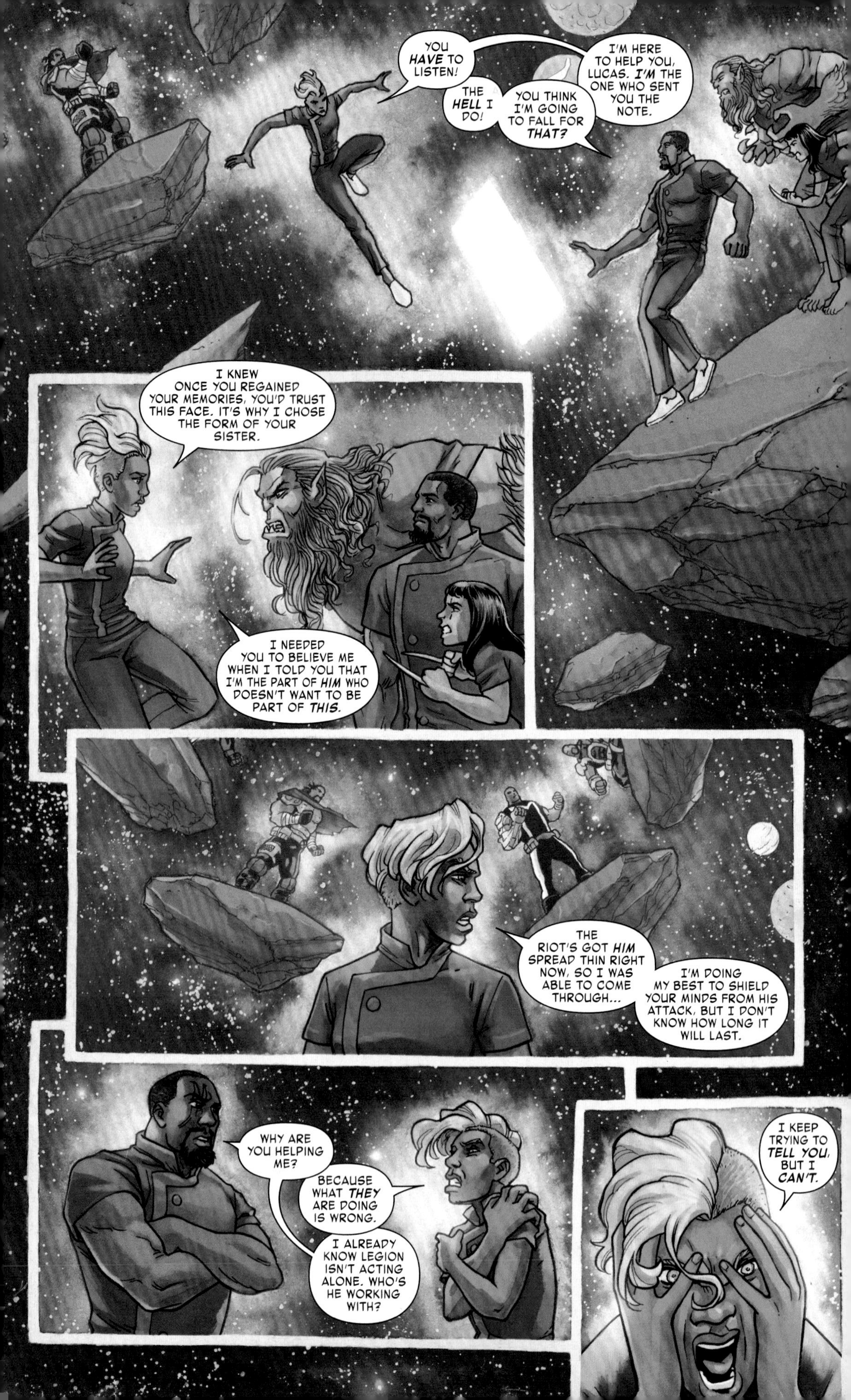
YOU HAVE TO LISTEN!
THE HELL I DO!
YOU THINK I'M GOING TO FALL FOR THAT?
I'M HERE TO HELP YOU, LUCAS. I'M THE ONE WHO SENT YOU THE NOTE.
I KNEW ONCE YOU REGAINED YOUR MEMORIES, YOU'D TRUST THIS FACE. IT'S WHY I CHOSE THE FORM OF YOUR SISTER.
I NEEDED YOU TO BELIEVE ME WHEN I TOLD YOU THAT I'M THE PART OF HIM WHO DOESN'T WANT TO BE PART OF THIS.
THE RIOT'S GOT HIM SPREAD THIN RIGHT NOW, SO I WAS ABLE TO COME THROUGH...
I'M DOING MY BEST TO SHIELD YOUR MINDS FROM HIS ATTACK, BUT I DON'T KNOW HOW LONG IT WILL LAST.
WHY ARE YOU HELPING ME?
BECAUSE WHAT THEY ARE DOING IS WRONG.
I ALREADY KNOW LEGION ISN'T ACTING ALONE. WHO'S HE WORKING WITH?
I KEEP TRYING TO TELL YOU, BUT I CAN'T.

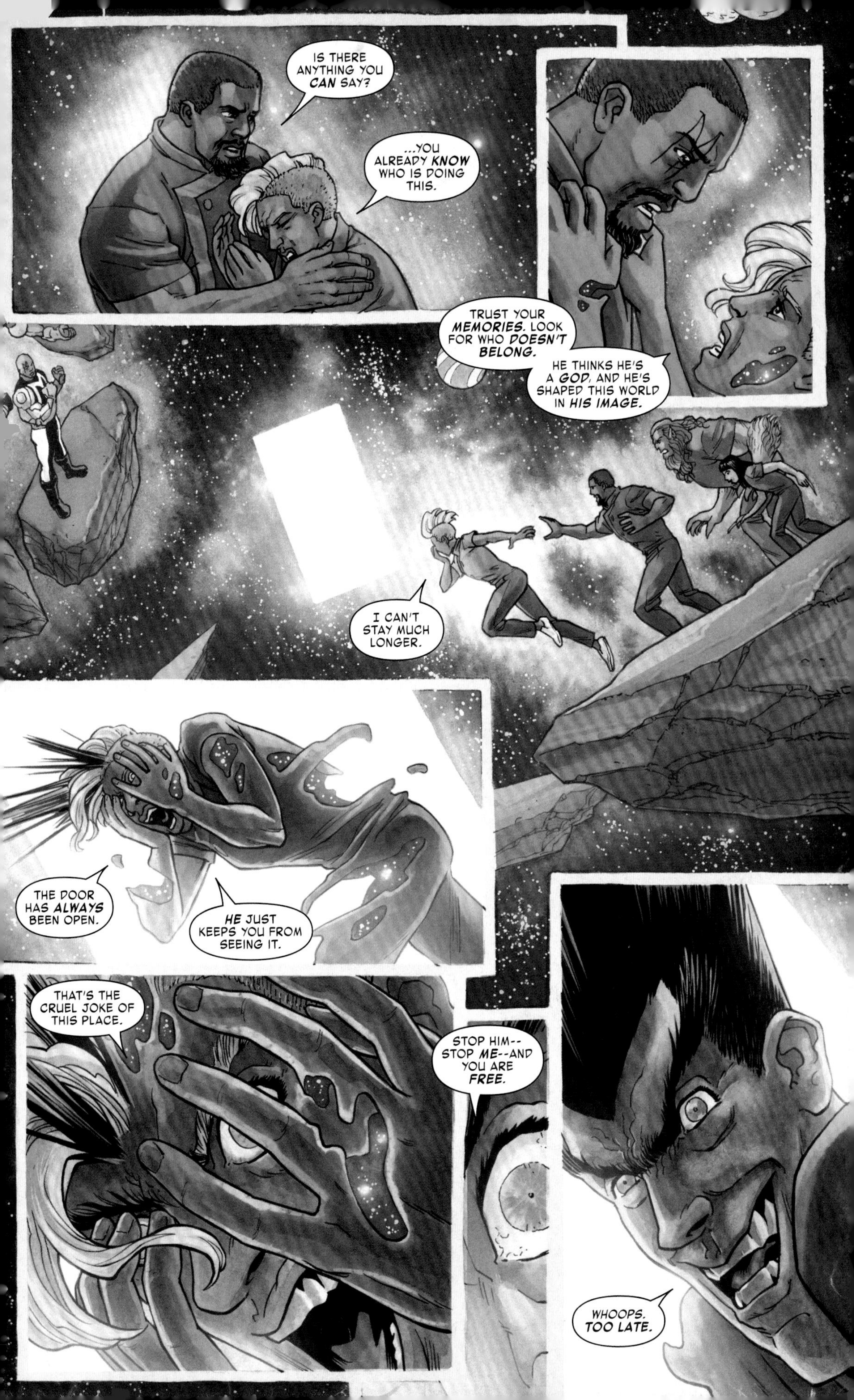
IS THERE ANYTHING YOU CAN SAY?
...YOU ALREADY KNOW WHO IS DOING THIS.
TRUST YOUR MEMORIES. LOOK FOR WHO DOESN'T BELONG.
HE THINKS HE'S A GOD, AND HE'S SHAPED THIS WORLD IN HIS IMAGE.
I CAN'T STAY MUCH LONGER.
THE DOOR HAS ALWAYS BEEN OPEN.
HE JUST KEEPS YOU FROM SEEING IT.
THAT'S THE CRUEL JOKE OF THIS PLACE.
STOP HIM-- STOP ME--AND YOU ARE FREE.
WHOOPS. TOO LATE.

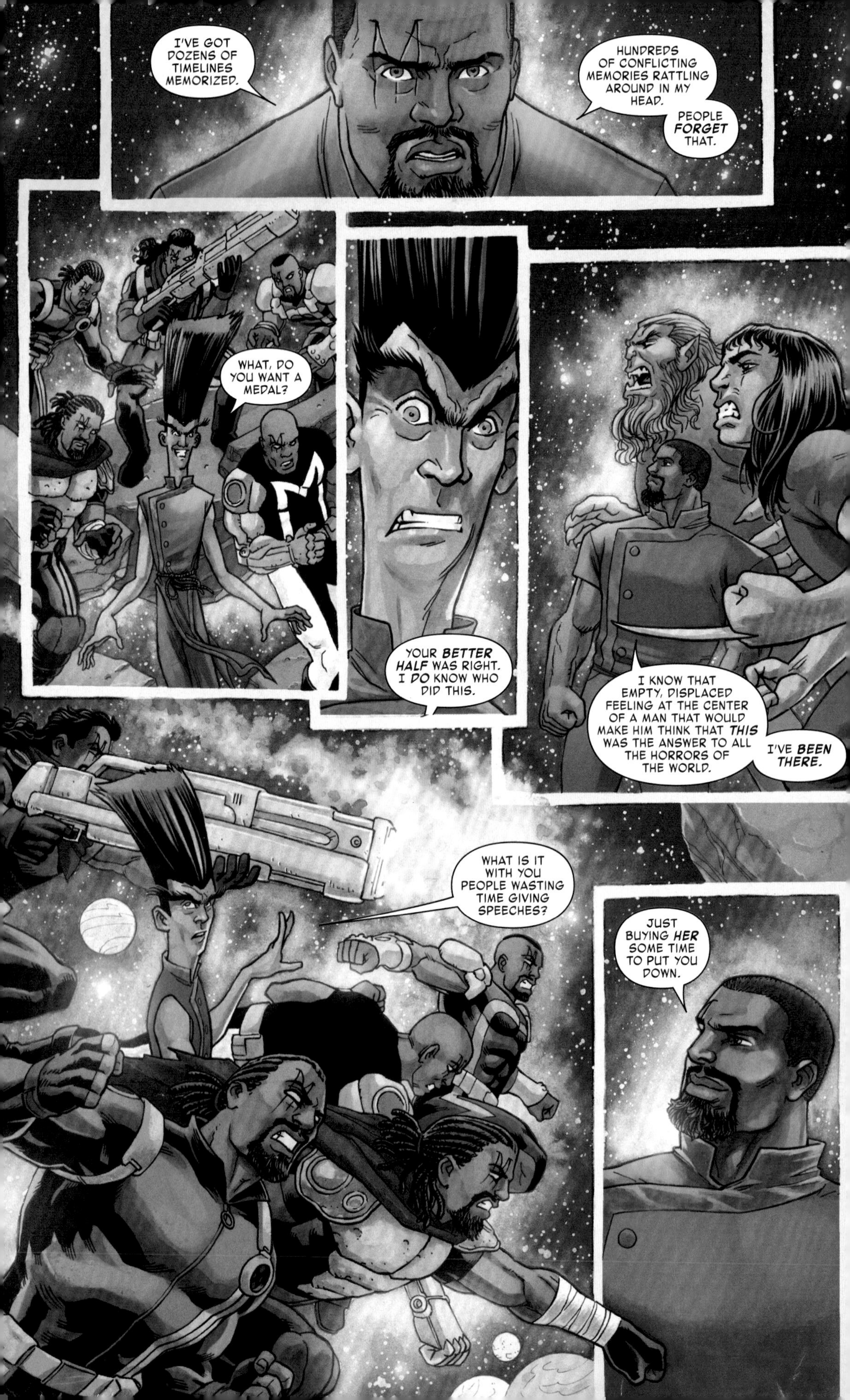
I'VE GOT DOZENS OF TIMELINES MEMORIZED.
HUNDREDS OF CONFLICTING MEMORIES RATTLING AROUND IN MY HEAD.
PEOPLE FORGET THAT.
WHAT, DO YOU WANT A MEDAL?
YOUR BETTER HALF WAS RIGHT. I DO KNOW WHO DID THIS.
I KNOW THAT EMPTY, DISPLACED FEELING AT THE CENTER OF A MAN THAT WOULD MAKE HIM THINK THAT THIS WAS THE ANSWER TO ALL THE HORRORS OF THE WORLD.
I'VE BEEN THERE.
WHAT IS IT WITH YOU PEOPLE WASTING TIME GIVING SPEECHES?
JUST BUYING HER SOME TIME TO PUT YOU DOWN.

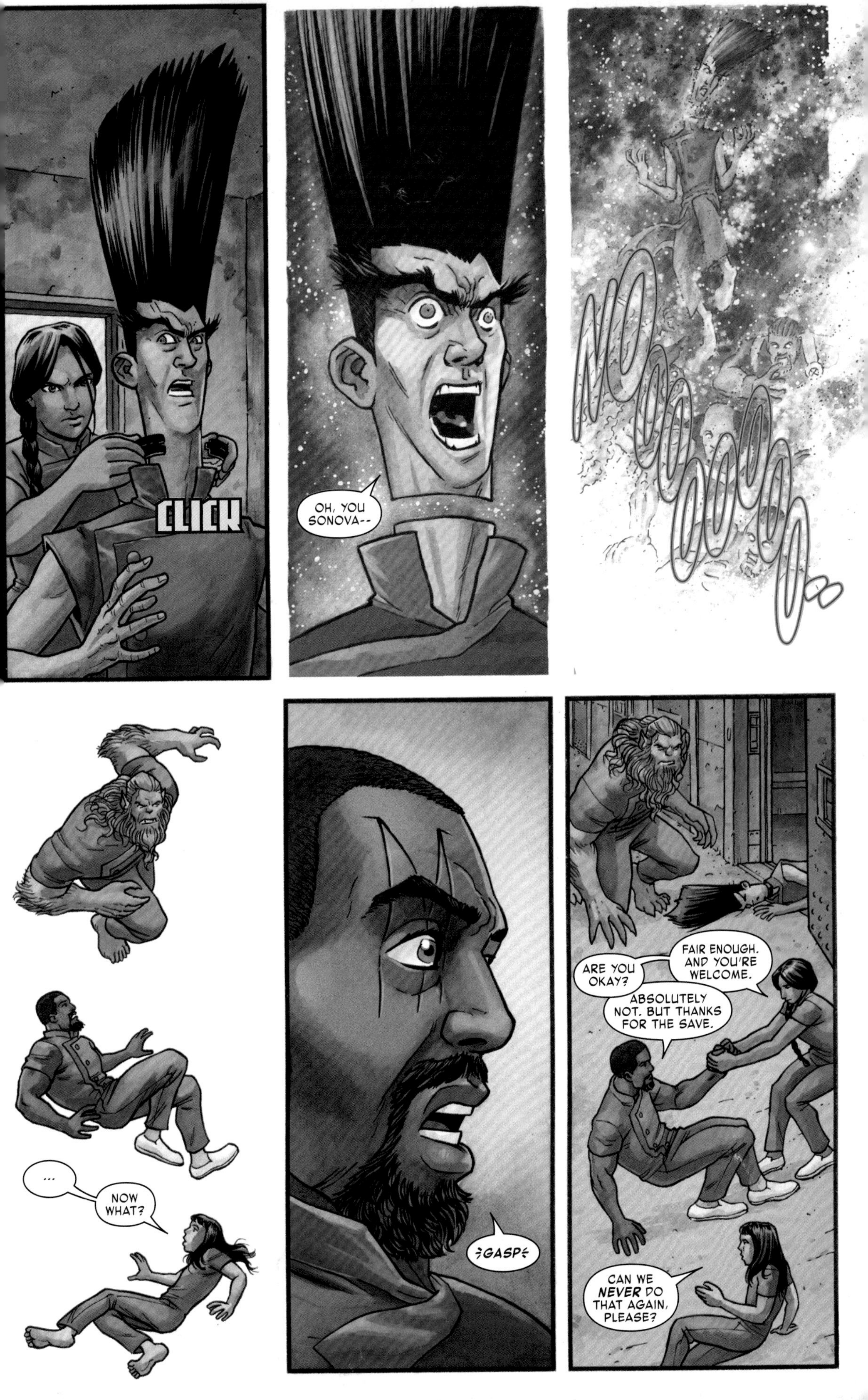

CLICK
OH, YOU SONOVA--
NOOOOOOOOOO
...
NOW WHAT?
GASP
ARE YOU OKAY?
ABSOLUTELY NOT. BUT THANKS FOR THE SAVE.
FAIR ENOUGH. AND YOU'RE WELCOME.
CAN WE NEVER DO THAT AGAIN, PLEASE?

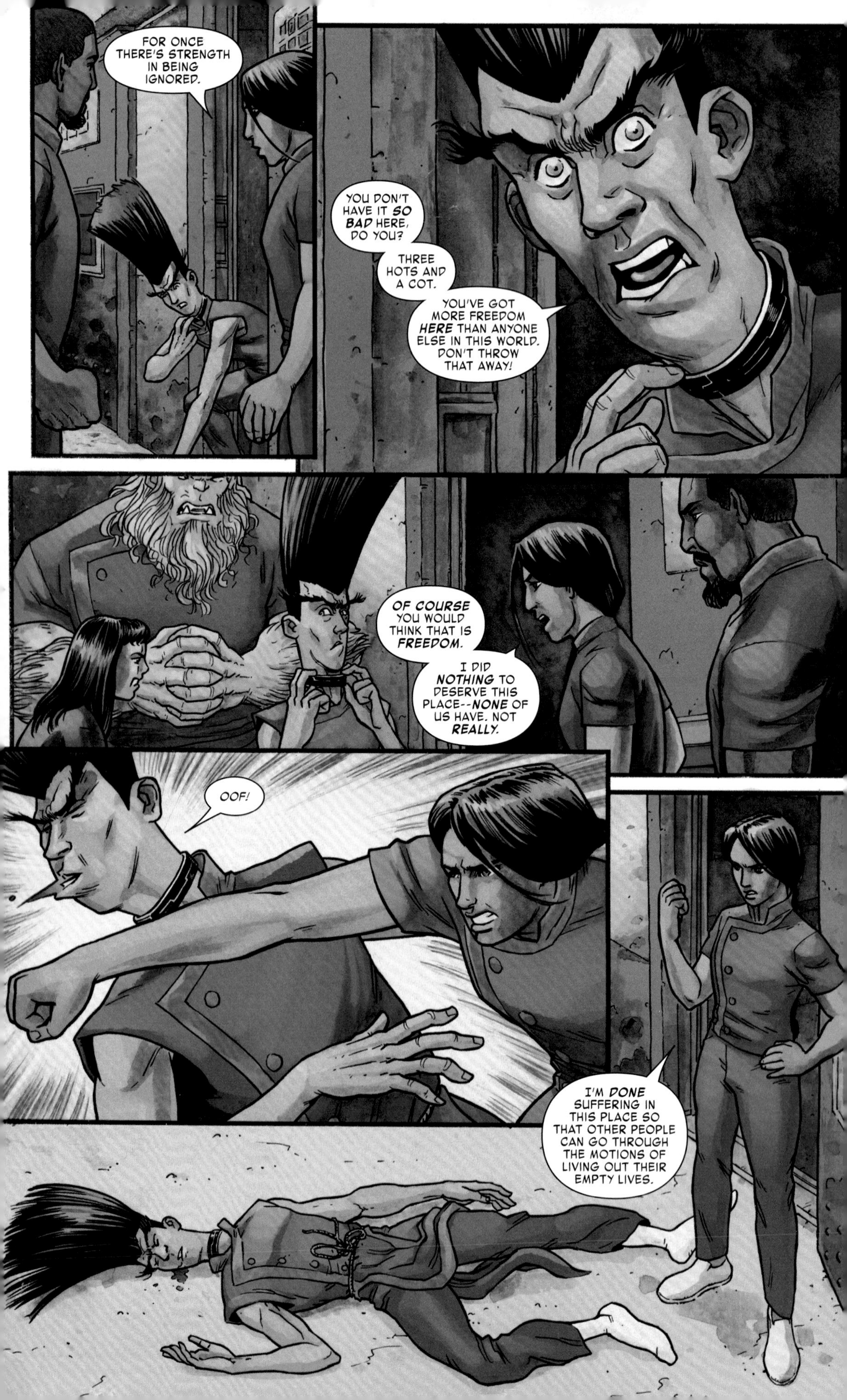
FOR ONCE THERE'S STRENGTH IN BEING IGNORED.
YOU DON'T HAVE IT SO BAD HERE, DO YOU?
THREE HOTS AND A COT.
YOU'VE GOT MORE FREEDOM HERE THAN ANYONE ELSE IN THIS WORLD. DON'T THROW THAT AWAY!
OF COURSE YOU WOULD THINK THAT IS FREEDOM.
I DID NOTHING TO DESERVE THIS PLACE--NONE OF US HAVE. NOT REALLY.
OOF!
I'M DONE SUFFERING IN THIS PLACE SO THAT OTHER PEOPLE CAN GO THROUGH THE MOTIONS OF LIVING OUT THEIR EMPTY LIVES.

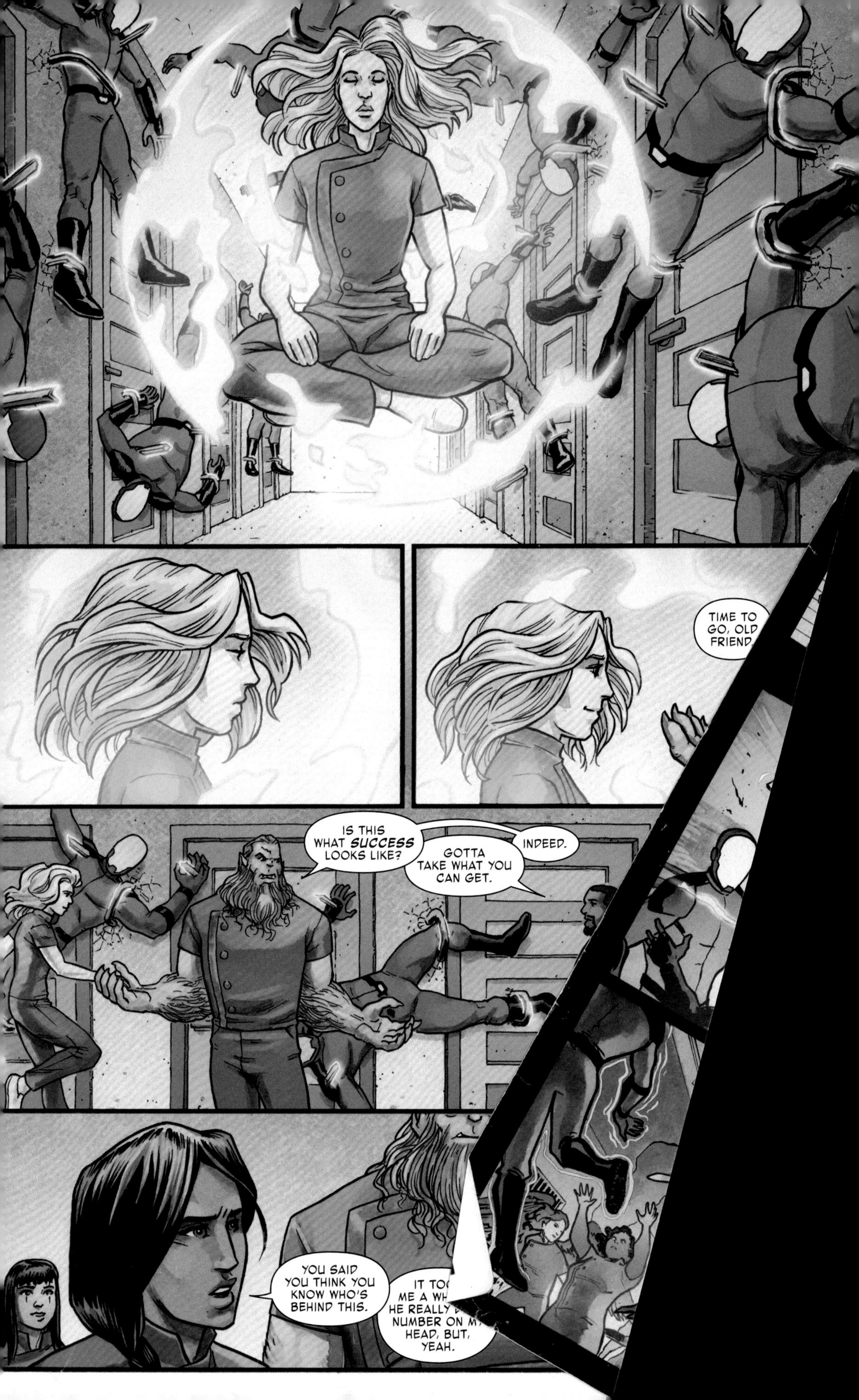
TIME TO GO, OLD FRIEND.
IS THIS WHAT SUCCESS LOOKS LIKE?
INDEED.
GOTTA TAKE WHAT YOU CAN GET.
YOU SAID YOU THINK YOU KNOW WHO'S BEHIND THIS.
ME A HE REALLY NUMBER ON HEAD, BUT, YEAH.

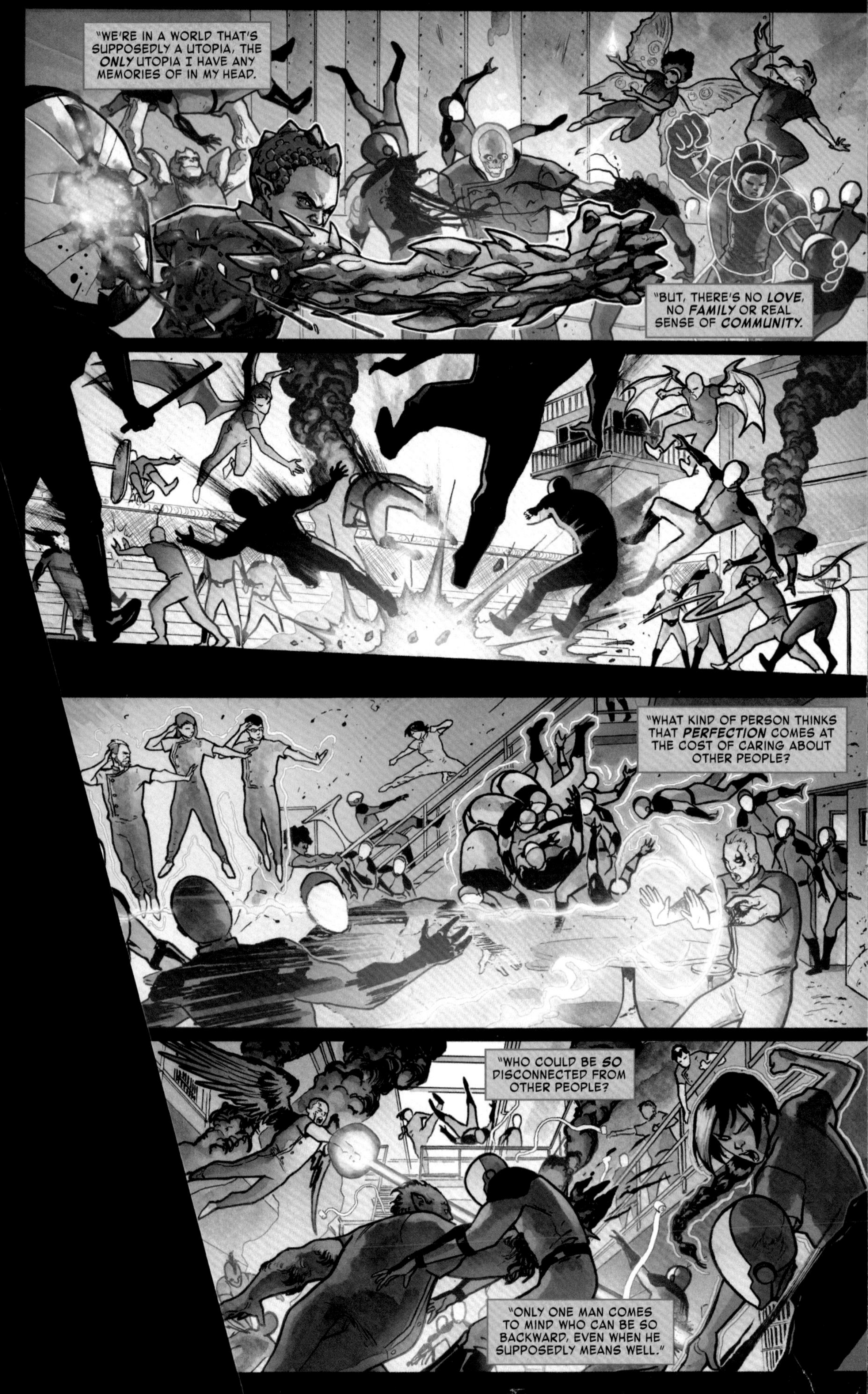
"WE'RE IN A WORLD THAT'S SUPPOSEDLY A UTOPIA, THE ONLY UTOPIA I HAVE ANY MEMORIES OF IN MY HEAD.
"BUT, THERE'S NO LOVE, NO FAMILY OR REAL SENSE OF COMMUNITY.
"WHAT KIND OF PERSON THINKS THAT PERFECTION COMES AT THE COST OF CARING ABOUT OTHER PEOPLE?
"WHO COULD BE SO DISCONNECTED FROM OTHER PEOPLE?
"ONLY ONE MAN COMES TO MIND WHO CAN BE SO BACKWARD, EVEN WHEN HE SUPPOSEDLY MEANS WELL."

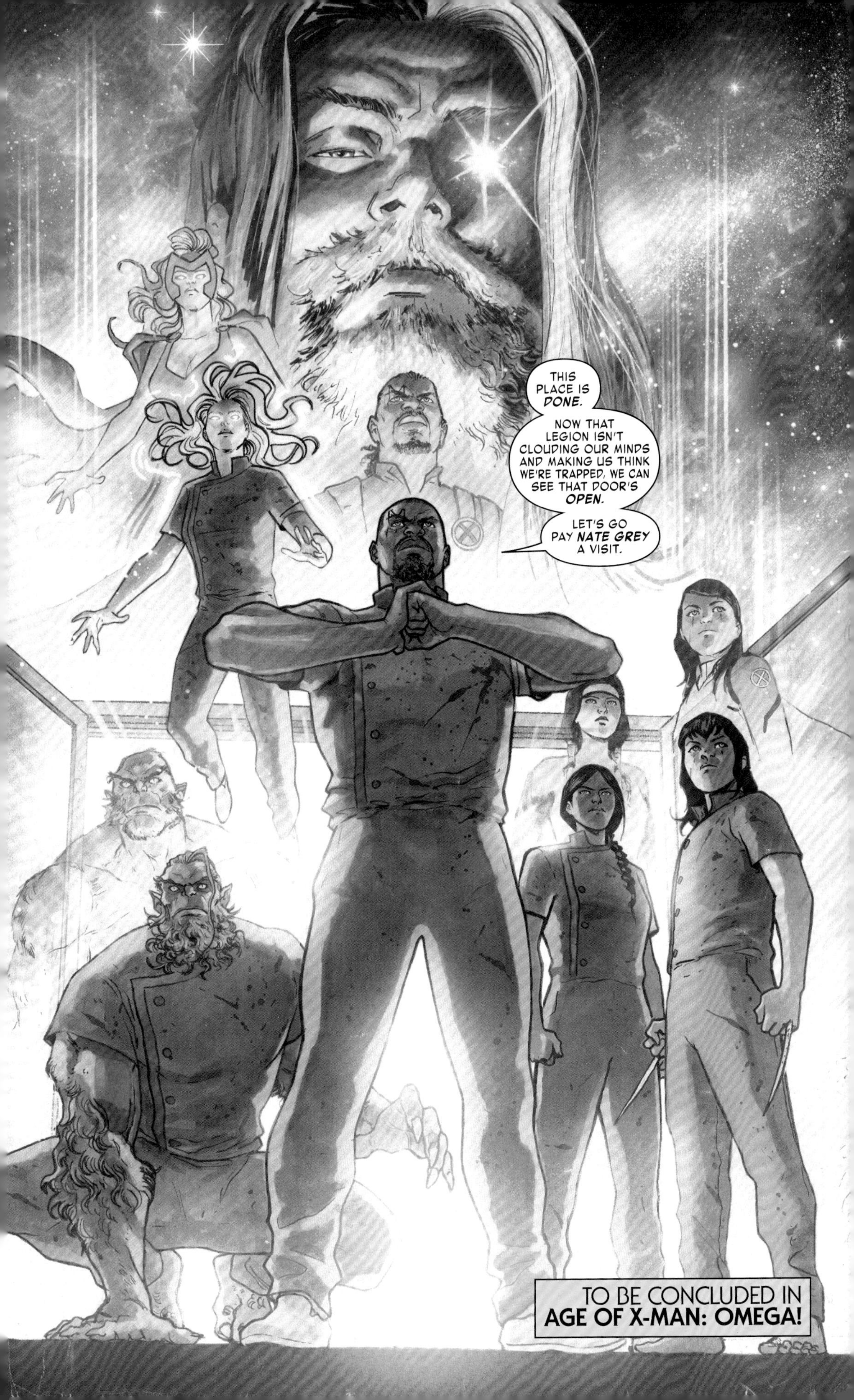
THIS PLACE IS DONE.
NOW THAT LEGION ISN'T CLOUDING OUR MINDS AND MAKING US THINK WE'RE TRAPPED, WE CAN SEE THAT DOOR'S OPEN.
LET'S GO PAY NATE GREY A VISIT.
TO BE CONCLUDED IN AGE OF X-MAN: OMEGA!

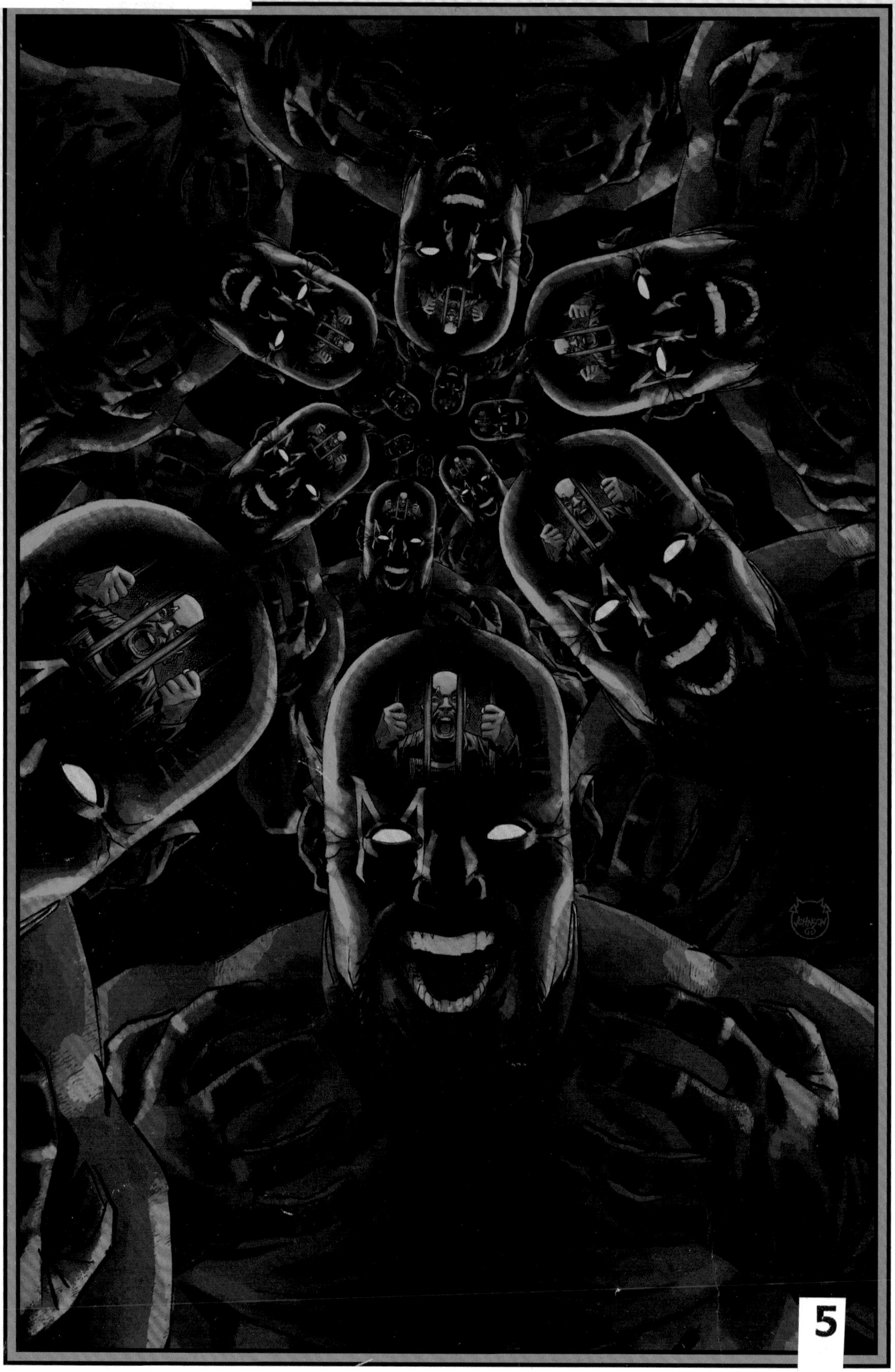
5

#2 VARIANT BY **DAVE JOHNSON**